Millennials, News, and Social Media

This book is part of the Peter Lang Media and Communication list.
Every volume is peer reviewed and meets
the highest quality standards for content and production.

PETER LANG
New York • Washington, D.C./Baltimore • Bern
Frankfurt • Berlin • Brussels • Vienna • Oxford

PAULA M. POINDEXTER

Millennials, News, and Social Media

Is News Engagement a Thing of the Past?

PETER LANG
New York • Washington, D.C./Baltimore • Bern
Frankfurt • Berlin • Brussels • Vienna • Oxford

Library of Congress Cataloging-in-Publication Data
Poindexter, Paula Maurie.
Millennials, news, and social media: is news engagement a thing of the past? /
Paula M. Poindexter.
p. cm.
Includes bibliographical references and index.
1. Journalism—United States—History. 2. Electronic news gathering—
United States—History. 3. Social media—United States—History.
4. Generation Y. I. Title.
PN4888.N48P65   071'.3—dc23   2012005914
ISBN 978-1-4331-1498-4 (hardcover)
ISBN 978-1-4331-1497-7 (paperback)
ISBN 978-1-4539-0815-0 (e-book)

Bibliographic information published by **Die Deutsche Nationalbibliothek**.
Die Deutsche Nationalbibliothek lists this publication in the "Deutsche
Nationalbibliografie"; detailed bibliographic data is available
on the Internet at http://dnb.d-nb.de/.

The paper in this book meets the guidelines for permanence and durability
of the Committee on Production Guidelines for Book Longevity
of the Council of Library Resources.

© 2012 Peter Lang Publishing, Inc., New York
29 Broadway, 18th floor, New York, NY 10006
www.peterlang.com

Printed in the United States of America

To Rachael Elizabeth Tillmon Poindexter,
my first role model for reading newspapers.

CONTENTS

LIST OF ILLUSTRATIONS

Figures

Tables

PREFACE

My interest in news engagement by young people began long before the Millennial Generation was born. I was at Syracuse University in graduate school searching through the academic journals when I found a study published in 1964 that showed, despite the authors' assertion that newspaper reading was "one of the most thoroughly institutionalized behaviors of Americans" (Westley & Severin, 1964, p. 45), everyone did not read a newspaper. Having grown up in a home in which my parents subscribed to two newspapers, I was shocked, troubled, and yes, inspired by this study. It became the inspiration for my master's thesis, my Ph.D. dissertation, my first published study, my subsequent publications, and even for my teaching and public service.

Though my interest in news engagement began with young non-newspaper readers, that interest has grown to include the diverse factors that facilitate and impede news consumption regardless of type or age of audience. Before the Internet and social media upended the news media landscape and made assumptions about news consumption obsolete, parents were instrumental in developing news consumers because as their child's first role model, they determined whether news was present in the home and whether, or how, it was engaged with. In homes where news was not present, teachers were invaluable in getting kids to engage with news.

The news industry could have been a leader in developing news consumers, but it "did nothing to help create a new generation interested in news" (Kovach & Rosenstiel, 2007, p. 211). Even worse, according to the authors of *The Elements of Journalism*, the industry had "a business strategy that helped create non-news consumers."

With the news industry more responsible for creating non-news consumers than news consumers, fewer role models for news consumption in homes, and fewer teachers devoting class time to cultivating an interest in news because of the demands of standardized test preparation, news consumption has declined. And despite today's vast array of digital news outlets and mobile devices that can access news anytime and anywhere, the Millennial Generation has not embraced news in the same way in which its grandparents' generation did.

Who or what is responsible for the rejection of news by the Millennial Generation? Is Millennial enthusiasm for social media related to a lack of affection for news? Is it too late to transform Millennials into consumers of news? *Millennials, News, and Social Media: Is News Engagement a Thing of the Past?* answers these questions and more.

Using never-before reported data from the National Survey of News Engagement, *Millennials, News, and Social Media* helps us understand the generation that has come of age as the importance of news has waned and social media has emerged. It provides a detailed portrait of the Millennial Generation's engagement with news and social media. It reveals the grades Millennials have assigned to news that is about their generation, and it proposes "Best Practices" for news coverage relevant to them. Additionally, *Millennials, News, and Social Media* offers insight into which factors will determine whether we will be a society of news consumers who believe being informed is important or a nation in which news illiteracy is the norm. Finally, this first-of-its-kind book discloses the devastating consequences that await the news media, journalism schools, our democracy, and the everyday lives of individuals if we become a nation in which news consumers are extinct, and being informed of news is no longer valued.

Millennials, News, and Social Media concludes with a plan and an urgent call to parents, teachers, the news and social media, journalism schools, business, foundation and civic leaders, and Millennials to share responsibility for resurrecting the importance of being informed in society and developing young people into informed and civically engaged citizens.

ACKNOWLEDGMENTS

Just as I grew up in a home in which my parents subscribed to two newspapers, my daughter grew up in a home in which her parents subscribed to two newspapers. Because reading the news, watching the news, and listening to the news have been central to our home life, I expected or at least hoped that my daughter would love newspapers as I do. But despite my best efforts, it didn't take long for me to realize that getting a young person to engage with news was not that easy. Because my daughter made it possible for me to learn up close how complicated it can be to get a young person to engage with news is why my first acknowledgment is to my Millennial daughter Alexandra Wilson. Alexandra is the inspiration behind *Millennials, News, and Social Media: Is News Engagement a Thing of the Past?*

My daughter has not exactly been a guinea pig in this grand experiment to understand the Millennial Generation and its relationship with news, but she has come pretty close. I have observed her like an ethnographer. I have asked focus group type questions of her. I have had her complete questionnaires and fill out diaries to track her Internet behavior. She pre-tested my questionnaire for the National Survey of News Engagement and gave me her Millennial feedback. She was the first one to tell me about Facebook. She introduced me to the Collegiate Readership program at her university where she could pick up a free newspaper with a swipe of her student ID. And she gave me insight into how Twitter can be a gateway to news for Millennials. Because of her vision, enthusiasm, and commitment, Alexandra has worked side by side with me to create *Millennials and News* as a one-stop digital source to engage Millennials with news.

While my daughter made it possible for me to observe Millennial news behavior and attitudes up close, my Millennial undergraduate journalism and liberal arts students enrolled in my course Journalism, Society, and the Citizen Journalist, which was created as part of the Carnegie-Knight Initiative on the Future of Journalism Education, provided additional insight into this generation. That's why I'm acknowledging my undergraduate students. On the first day of class, I would always ask them about accessing news. Over the past six years, I observed the transformation taking place in the wider media landscape, emerging in my own classroom. Six years ago, the majority of my students said they got their news from hard copy newspapers. Today, virtually none of them read a hard copy newspaper; they are just as likely to access news through smartphones and tablet computers. Facebook is a must-have and Twitter, unlike four years ago, is a go-to place for news.

I also want to thank my graduate students for both helping pre-test my questionnaire for the National Survey of News Engagement and helping me code some of the open-ended responses on the questionnaire. A very special thank you is given to Ph.D. student Barbara Audet for designing Figure 2.1.

Mary Savigar, my editor at Peter Lang, deserves a very special thank you. When I proposed the idea of the book to her at our national AEJMC conference in Denver, she was immediately intrigued. Every author should have an editor like Mary. She is wonderful to work with. Mary as well as the reviewers and copy editor made the manuscript better. Thanks to Sarah Stack, whose attention to detail and diplomatic emails made for a smooth book production process. I also give a special thank you to my husband Dr. Terry A. Wilson who read every word and gave constructive and thoughtful feedback that improved the manuscript. He even cross-checked every reference with the in-text citations, a task that requires patience and perseverance. But it's not just his reading every word of the manuscript; it's the news-filled home environment that we created together that I want to thank him for. Reading, watching, discussing, and debating news together has been a joy.

Since *Millennials, News, and Social Media* would not have been the same without the National Survey of News Engagement that I commissioned specifically for the book, I want to give a very special thank you to Veronica

Inchauste, the director of the Office of Survey Research at the University of Texas at Austin, and her staff for overseeing the fieldwork, collecting the survey data, and delivering it to me in an SPSS file.

Support from the Carnegie Corporation of New York enabled me to create the course Journalism, Society, and the Citizen Journalist in which I could explore the Millennial Generation and news literacy. The grant also enabled me to bring in national speakers for two summits that explored news coverage and the Millennial Generation. It is for that reason that I thank the Carnegie Corporation as well as former School of Journalism directors Lorraine Branham and Tracy Dahlby for involving me in the initial and expanded grants for the Carnegie-Knight Initiative on the Future of Journalism Education. Fellowships from the Dean's office enabled me to conduct the National Survey of NIE managers and start and expand the mynews@school program discussed in Chapter 6, so appreciation is expressed to Dean Rod Hart. Appreciation is also expressed to Sandy Woodcock, director of the NAA Foundation, and her staff who gave me feedback on the questionnaire as well as the NIE managers around the country who completed the survey. Additionally, Debra Joiner of the *Austin American-Statesman* is acknowledged for recruiting teachers to participate in the mynews@school program and making sure the newspapers and e-editions of the newspapers were delivered on time to participating classrooms. The weekly classroom activities provide the foundation for understanding the purpose, principles, and process of journalism, so special appreciation is also expressed to Fred Zipp, Bill Minutaglio, Corrie MacLaggan, and Carolyn Yaschur for sharing their journalism knowledge and experience so that I could develop weekly activities for mynews@school classrooms. When mynews@school was launched, Fred Zipp, then editor of the *Austin American-Statesman*, also approved participation by newsroom staff, so an additional acknowledgment is extended to him. A very special thank you is also given to mynews@school teachers and students whose program participation over the past four years has enabled me to test my ideas about engaging Wave II Millennials with news. Just as Wave II Millennials are thanked, I want to acknowledge this year's class of Wave I Millennials who are reading, discussing, sharing, and answering questions about news posted on *Millennials and News*. Their feedback has confirmed for me that by aggregating news stories of interest to the Millennial Generation, it is possible to get their attention and engage them.

A very special thanks is also given to my friend, colleague, and mentor Dr. Maxwell McCombs. The first lessons I learned about researching the audience for news were from Max. It was because of a research project that he assigned to me when I was a graduate student at Syracuse University that I discovered the 1964 *Journalism Quarterly* article on non-readers with that marvelous quote about newspaper reading that sadly is no longer true: "Reading the daily newspaper is doubtless one of the most thoroughly institutionalized behaviors of Americans" (Westley & Severin, 1964, p. 45).

Finally, I want to thank my mother Rachael Elizabeth Tillmon Poindexter and my father Dr. Alfred N. Poindexter Jr. who taught their five children, through example, that whether news arrives through a newspaper thrown on the driveway, a TV, radio, computer, smartphone or iPad, it's important to have news present in one's home and one's life.

· 1 ·

SOCIETY WITHOUT
NEWS CONSUMERS?

...we did nothing to help create a new generation interested in news.
—BILL KOVACH AND TOM ROSENSTIEL, AUTHORS OF
THE ELEMENTS OF JOURNALISM

In 1986, when Alex was born in Cedars-Sinai Hospital in Los Angeles, no one owned laptops or smartphones because they hadn't been invented yet. No one updated their status on Facebook or announced what they were doing on Twitter because these social media hadn't been created. Two years before Alex was born, when a desktop computer was delivered to the desk of her mother's secretary, it was considered a novelty. At least another year would pass before her mother and other managers who worked at the Fortune 500 company would adopt desktop computers like their secretaries.

Seventeen years before Alex was born, when computer scientists at UCLA sent a message on what eventually would be called the Internet, few people outside of an elite group had ever heard of this communication medium. Alex would be almost six years old before word of the Internet was even mentioned by anyone other than academics and Department of Defense techies. Five years later at age 11, Alex first ventured onto the Internet. Alex, like many in America, was introduced to the Internet through America Online (AOL).

With America Online, you didn't have to be an academic or a Department of Defense techie to get on the Internet. You could be a kid.

While American Online made it easy to connect to and explore the Internet, the Internet had yet to be developed for exploration. America Online, though, was not just a gateway to the Internet; it was a provider of easily accessible family-friendly activities, information, and entertainment. Plus, America Online offered methods of communication that did not require a stamp or a phone. While news headlines were visible when Alex dialed up America Online on her mother's computer, news wasn't Alex's destination. In fact, if Alex had wanted news, she could have read one of the two newspapers her parents subscribed to. Or she could have watched the network and local news that her parents turned on every day in the morning and around the dinner hour. But when Alex first ventured onto the Internet, she wasn't trying to find out the latest news; her interest was in looking things up for school.

It wasn't unusual that Alex was disinterested in news; that's pretty typical of kids her age. What was unusual was that Alex's generation was the first to grow up with a wealth of information and entertainment choices that diverted them away from news.

By the time Alex was 17, she was spending three to five hours a day on the Internet, and none of that time was spent reading news. Mostly, she used the Internet for instant messaging, e-mail, and school work, but some of this time on the Internet was spent visiting chatrooms, browsing the Web, shopping, and playing games.

Alex also had her own cell phone which her parents had bought her two years before. At the time of the purchase there was no Internet connection, but Alex quickly discovered she could communicate with her friends by texting. Alex's parents were unaware of texting, until the first bill arrived, that is. Despite its mobility, Alex's cell phone was strictly a portable communication device. At the time, neither Alex nor her parents envisioned that in seven years, with the introduction of the iPhone and apps, a cell phone would never again be just a portable communication device.

When older generations had been in their teenage years like Alex, there was no Internet to consume their time and distract them from acquiring the habit of getting news. Although Baby Boomers and Generation X may not have picked up the news consumption habit like their parents and grandparents, it wasn't because the Internet consumed their time and attention. In the early 1960s when Baby Boomers were teens, TV was king and newspaper reading was considered "one of the most thoroughly institutionalized behaviors of

Americans" (Westley & Severin, 1964, p. 45). But even though King TV was in virtually every living room in America, there were only three channels to watch. Cable as a source of original news, sports, and entertainment programming was still in the distant future; another two decades would pass before CNN, ESPN, and MTV would emerge on the media scene. In addition to TV, media for Baby Boomer teens meant radio, movies, magazines, comics, books, and newspapers; for Generation X teens, the same media were available, but the popularity of movies and comic books had declined.

By the early 1980s, when Generation X was beginning to enter the teenage years, cable was offering a new kind of programming: CNN, ESPN, HBO, and MTV. Though few people probably realized it at the time, these cable channels dedicated exclusively to news, sports, movies, and even youth programming were the first hint that the future of media would look nothing like the past. While there were different offerings, and some media company visionaries in the U.S., Europe, and Asia were beginning to imagine a communication medium that would transform the delivery of news, information, entertainment, and consumer services, the Internet as a consumer-oriented medium was still 15 years into the future. What couldn't be foreseen in this vision of the future was the impact that the Internet would have on youth, and how this would affect this generation's news consumption.

A systematic comparison of media use by teens of three generations found Millennial teens were nothing like Baby Boomers and Generation X in their use of media (Poindexter, 2008). This pronounced media use difference was why in 2008 I predicted that future news consumption of Millennials would be unlike anything in the past (Poindexter, 2008). What I didn't say in 2008, but now believe, is that the difference in media use will have far-reaching consequences for society and future generations.

It's not surprising that the Internet captured the attention of Alex and other Millennial teens. There were so many things to do with the Internet; plus, it was easy and convenient. For the first Millennials to enter the teenage years, communicating and networking through e-mail and instant messaging were the most popular activities, and getting informed by visiting online news Web sites was the least popular (Poindexter, 2008). The Internet also made it easy, and presumably fun, to pursue pastimes and hobbies, research rites of passage information, and to do school, or job-related, work. And Millennial teens could do all of these things at the same time; they elevated multi-tasking to an art form.

News on the Internet was least popular with Alex, too, but after she started college in 2004, news began to attract her attention. It's not clear why, after so many years of purposely ignoring news, Alex became interested in news. Maybe the newspaper industry's assumption was actually true: The newspaper industry believed that once young people established roots and started investing in their communities and caring about the world around them, they would start reading the paper. This automatic adoption of the newspaper habit may have lured the newspaper industry into at best, complacency, and at worst, a reckless disregard for their future.

In fact, authors of *The Elements of Journalism* Bill Kovach and Tom Rosenstiel (2007) acknowledged profits trumped the future when it came to cultivating the next generation of news consumers:

> In the name of efficiency and profit margins, we did nothing to help create a new generation interested in news. Today, audience data from the Internet show that young people are interested in news but not in any of the old forms of presentation in older technologies. While the news business cannot take all the blame, it had in fact a business strategy that helped create non-news consumers. (p. 211)

Alex had no knowledge of the newspaper industry's assumption about becoming an adult and picking up the newspaper reading habit. As a college student, Alex thought her sudden interest in news might have been related to the free newspapers available on her college campus. With just a swipe of her student ID, she could pick up a free copy of *The New York Times*, *USA Today*, the nearest big city paper, and the local paper. The rival university, located an hour and a half down the freeway, also provided a free *Wall Street Journal* for its students. The free newspapers were courtesy of the Collegiate Readership Program that Alex's university and many universities around the country participated in to encourage the development of informed adults.

Since Alex had ignored the free newspapers around her home while she was growing up, it's unlikely that the free newspapers on her campus mattered that much. Perhaps the years that her parents had encouraged her to read newspapers were finally taking hold. Or it may have been news discussions around her in college and in class. Or maybe it was because she observed other students picking up the free papers and reading them. Or, maybe it was the 2004 presidential election.

Alex had become a registered voter a month before leaving for college, and with the 2004 presidential election only a few months away, she was excited to cast her first vote. Alex took her civic responsibility seriously. She wanted to learn about the candidates and the issues, and what better place to do that than the newspaper?

For someone who had been a borderline news avoider, Alex might have morphed into a news enthusiast except there was, perhaps, the next new thing getting her attention and the attention of Millennials around the country. This new thing would not only transform how Alex and other Millennials spent time on the Internet, it's possible that it may have hampered their acquisition of the news consumption habit.

Three days before George W. Bush was inaugurated to begin his second term as president of the United States, Alex first ventured onto Facebook. It was 2005, the beginning of the spring semester of Alex's freshman year in college. Facebook was so new that Alex's Baby Boomer parents, like most Boomers, had never heard of it. Facebook was so new that the Pew Research Center had yet to ask questions about it in its biennial news consumption survey. In fact, it would be four more years before Pew would even include Facebook (as well as MySpace) in its national survey questionnaire that asked about news consumption. When the Pew Research Center finally asked about Facebook and other social media, they found that for Millennials, online news had taken a "back seat" to social media (Key News Audiences, 2008, p. 27). Not only were an overwhelming majority of Millennials on Facebook in 2008, almost half visited a social networking site at least daily, but less than a third of Millennials got news online at least daily. Millennials, though, were not necessarily purposely searching for news; encountering news may have been accidental.

One can only wonder, if there had been an Internet but no Facebook, would the Millennial Generation have become news enthusiasts or at least news betweeners, "news consumers who are connected to the news one to six days weekly?" (Poindexter, 2008, p. 9). It's impossible to know. But there is something to be said for the idea that at the very moment that the first Millennials who were enrolled in college may have been ready to adopt the news consumption habit, they were invited to become members of an exclusive club initially called The Facebook (Kirkpatrick, 2010). This club was not only respectful of and attentive to this young generation; it was everything newspapers were not.

By the time Alex graduated in 2008 with a degree in psychology, she had become disillusioned with Facebook because the social networking site was no longer the exclusive domain of college students. Now anyone and everyone could be on Facebook—middle and high school kids, old people, advertisers, politicians, the news media, even her parents if they chose to. Plus, while in college, Alex had primarily used Facebook for communicating; after graduating and starting her first real job, she had replaced leaving messages and updating her Facebook status with texting on her smartphone.

Alex's smartphone not only opened new venues for communicating with her friends, it also offered a convenient and easy way to keep up with the news if she chose to use it that way. With her second opportunity to vote since turning 18 and a candidate who reached out to young voters, the 2008 presidential election promised to be as engaging for Alex and other young voters as a cable reality show that had them texting back and forth: lol.

Since presidential elections are usually the times when the public is in a news-seeking-and-monitoring mode as they try to fill in the blanks about candidates and their stand on issues, it's an opportune, but rarely used, time for the news media to cultivate news consumers. The news media could have learned a lot from then-Democratic presidential candidate Barack Obama, who demonstrated that if you court young voters, they will respond. More young voters turned out in the 2008 presidential election than at any other time except for the first presidential election following the Twenty-Sixth Amendment to the U.S. Constitution that gave 18-year-olds the right to vote. Unfortunately, the news media failed to use the 2008 presidential election to nurture the next generation of news consumers. Covering the 2008 presidential election was not only business as usual; it may also have been the last chance to court Millennials before they turned away from news for good.

The idea that Millennials might be on a path that leads to the endangered species list is not unthinkable—that is, if the news industry doesn't make it its business to create a new generation interested in news. Of course, if news consumers become endangered, the news industry will not be the only ones responsible—blame can be shared by virtually every generation and institution, beginning with the home that Millennials grew up in.

If on September 25, 1690, at least one person read the first newspaper published in the U.S., it would be fair to say that news consumers have been present in the U.S. for more than three centuries. In 1965, more than two-and-a-half centuries after the first newspaper was read, "71%" of the adult population read a newspaper (Pew Research Center—Online Papers Modestly Boost, 2006, p. 19). Forty-five years later, the percent of adults reading a newspaper had dropped 40 percentage points, with less than one-third of adults reading a paper (Pew Research Center—Americans Spending More Time, 2010).

The drop-off in newspaper reading does not necessarily mean all news consumption has declined, because thanks to cable and the Internet, news can be found anytime, day or night. Still, with less than half of the population saying getting news is not enjoyable, consuming news is not overwhelmingly endorsed (Pew Research Center, 2010). Among Millennials, only 27% enjoy keeping up with news a lot and even fewer (23%) read a newspaper regularly (Pew Research Center, 2010).

If the youngest generation does not replace older generations who are dropping out and dying as they reach their 70s, 80s, and 90s, news consumers will become endangered. Furthermore, it is possible that newspaper readers, TV news viewers, radio news listeners, news magazine readers, and online news consumers will cease to exist. If the very existence of news consumers is threatened, the effects could reach far beyond the news media landscape.

News consumers did not become candidates for the endangered species list overnight. In fact, with so many opportunities today to get news everywhere, anyplace, anytime, whether one is sedentary or on the move, one would think that consuming news would be an established custom. But consuming news is anything but the norm, and for many, being informed of the news isn't even important.

While outside forces such as the Internet, and each generation's young adults, have been blamed for the decline in newspaper reading, inside forces endemic to newspaper industry culture must share responsibility for the decline. But regardless of who or what the culprit is, the fact remains that if the trend of declining newspaper reading continues at the current pace, by 2030, less than 10% of all adults, not just Millennials, will be regular newspaper readers. And the complementary relationship of the past between media may be replaced by a kind of domino effect where dropping out of one news medium precipitates dropping out of another until there are no news media left to drop out of. The result of this domino effect could lead to the unthinkable becoming reality: living in a society in which news consumers are not just endangered but extinct—like dinosaurs.

What would a society in which news consumers are extinct be like? First and foremost, without newspaper readers, there would be no need for a newspaper business model, old or new. Without news consumers to buy their products, advertisers would have no reason to place ads in newspapers, whether the print or online edition. Advertisers would also have no need for newspapers to print and deliver their four-color ad inserts featuring their products and announcing their latest specials. With no newspaper readers, what's left of classified advertising would vanish. If no one picked up a newspaper or read it online, on a smartphone, or on an iPad, there would be no one to sell a car to, rent an apartment to, or sell a house to, so the remaining classified advertisers would move on to Craigslist or eBay. Basically, without newspaper readers, there would be no revenue from display advertising, classified advertising, advertising inserts, subscriptions, or single-copy sales.

If there were no newspaper readers, there would also be no need for pre-dawn deliveries to homes, apartments, stores, coffee houses, airports, news-stands, or news racks. With the disappearance of advertising and circulation, these newspaper departments would shut down, and thousands of workers would be laid off. While, perhaps, the pressrooms could be re-purposed, there would be no need for gigantic printing presses or colossal spools of newsprint, since readers of newspapers would have disappeared.

Since there would be no advertising or circulation revenue without news-paper readers, newsroom employees would no longer receive paychecks, health insurance, or 401k-company matches. But, of course, without income, journal-ists would have no 401ks to match. Journalists could still report and edit the news as a public service but with mortgages and rent to pay, food and health insurance to buy, and kids to send to college, journalists wouldn't be able to be full-time volunteers for long.

With the eventual disappearance of print, broadcast, and digital journal-ists, the effects would extend to prestigious journalism awards and affiliated organizations and institutions as well as to select industries and occupations. Pulitzer Prizes and Peabody Awards would no longer be given, because there would be no journalism to award the highest journalism honors to. There would be no need for the alphabet soup of journalism associations such as SPJ, ASNE, NABJ, NAHJ, AAJA, NAJA (Society of Professional Journalists, American Society of Newspaper Editors, National Association of Black Journalists, National Association of Hispanic Journalists, Asian American Journalists Association, Native American Journalists Association).

Journalism schools and programs would also shut down. Why train future journalists if journalism jobs no longer exist? College newspapers and magazines, TV programs, and news Web sites would also close their doors. There would be no need for journalism Ph.D. programs since there would be no journalism schools or programs to teach in. There would also be nothing new to research or theories to propose if there were no journalists, news, or news consumers. The Indiana University professors who have surveyed journalists every decade since the 1980s could close up shop since there would be no journalists to survey. The premiere scholarly journal *Journalism & Mass Communication Quarterly* would shut down, and the editor would be out of a job. *Newspaper Research Journal, Journalism & Communication Monographs,* and *Journalism & Mass Communication Educator* likewise would shut down. Academic and textbook publishers that focus on journalism would downsize or shut down altogether. Journalism edu-cation associations such as AEJMC (Association for Education in Journalism

& Mass Communication) and BEA (Broadcast Education Association) would disappear and so would the Accrediting Council on Education in Journalism and Mass Communications, ACEJMC.

Once newspapers shut down, TV and cable news programs and bloggers would also go out of business. Where would they get their story ideas if newspapers, their primary source of material, no longer existed? What would cable talking heads and bloggers opine about? And the Sunday morning gotcha moments on NBC's *Meet the Press*, CBS's *Face the Nation*, and ABC's *This Week* would become a thing of the past. There would be no *New York Times* or *Washington Post* quote to display on the screen to contradict the guest newsmaker's most recent assertion. With even less news of substance on TV and cable newscasts, TV news viewers would also disappear.

Satirical news programs such as Comedy Central's *The Daily Show* and *The Colbert Report*, and monologues and skits on late night and *SNL* that lampoon newsmakers would disappear if there were no news to poke fun at. The annual State of the Media and the Pew Research Center People & the Press surveys would also shut down since there would be no data on the news media or news consumers to sift through or questions to ask.

The Newseum, the magnificent 250,000-square-foot museum of journalism and news located in Washington DC, where Pennsylvania Avenue and Sixth Street N.W. intersect, would be needed more than ever to safeguard the history of something that once was. Since newspapers would be no more, the virtual display of the day's newspaper front pages from around the country would disappear, and the engraving on the top floor of the Newseum would be puzzling:

> The Free Press is a Cornerstone of Democracy. People have a need to know. Journalists have a right to tell. Finding the facts can be difficult. Reporting the story can be dangerous. Freedom includes the right to be outrageous. Responsibility includes the duty to be fair. News is history in the making. Journalists provide the first draft of history. A Free Press, at its best, Reveals the Truth. (The Newseum, Washington DC)

So much of the world of digital news that we now take for granted would also vanish: Web sites of news organizations, updated online news, the most e-mailed news stories. Google would also take a hit. Its news aggregator service would shut down because without the news that newspapers update online, there would be no news to aggregate. Ad revenue from searches would decline because without news stories, advertisers would be less inclined to place ads on Google. Apple's Safari browser would delete the news tabs since news organizations would no longer exist.

There would also be no need for RSS feeds. And what would there be to tweet about? And *The New York Times* app, CNN's app, and all of the news apps that directly link news consumers to their digitized news could be deleted from the iPhone and iPad. Even Wikipedia would be affected. Without news, how would Wikipedia contributors know to update an entry? If the American press ceased to exist, Wikipedia would lose a major source of information for its entries. For example, a glance through the references used for the entry on the 2011 revolution in Egypt found a cornucopia of American news sources, including the Legacy Big Four (*The New York Times, Washington Post, Los Angeles Times, Wall Street Journal*), Associated Press, the wire service, network TV news, including ABC News and CBS News, cable news' CNN, MSNBC, and Fox, public broadcasting's NPR Radio and Web-only news sites such as the Huffington Post (Egyptian Revolution, 2011).

Without news, network, syndicated, and cable topical talk shows would also suffer. What would talk show hosts chat about if they didn't have newspaper headlines to spark the conversation? Syndicated game shows such as *Jeopardy!* and *Who Wants to Be a Millionaire* would also be big losers. Questions based on the most recent newspaper headlines could no longer be written.

And WikiLeaks would have more than the U.S. federal government to worry about. If news organizations vanished, who would publish stories from their leaked documents?

Without news, information managers and programmers would lose their jobs, and there would be no need for news-based databases such as LexisNexis. The jobs of journalism librarians and archivists would be downsized because there would be no new material to purchase, research, catalogue, or archive.

And what would historians do if they no longer had access to the first draft of history that once was published in newspapers? Even documentary film makers would be affected. What would *Eyes on the Prize: America's Civil Rights, Years 1954–1965, Enron: The Smartest Guys in the Room, Waiting for Superman,* or *Inside Job* have been like if they hadn't had news as source material?

Without news, PR jobs would also disappear. Where would they pitch publicity about their clients?

Without news, presidential candidates would get a free pass. They could say whatever and there would be no one to hold them to account. Actually, no one would know what presidential candidates were saying because there would be no journalists to inform the public. If voters didn't know what candidates stood for, they would skip the election, and presidents would be elected with the tiniest number of votes. In fact, without newspapers to remind voters about an upcoming election, voters wouldn't put the election on their digital calendars and wouldn't show up at the polls. There could still be presidential and gubernatorial debates, but who would moderate and ask questions if journalists no longer existed? Candidates could exaggerate and make untrue statements but without journalists, who would know the assertions were overstated or false?

Without journalists and news, being president of the United States would be a piece of cake; there would be no White House Press Corps to cover the president's every move and analyze every speech or parsed phrase. The president could start an unnecessary war, raise taxes, gut the social safety net, or nominate divisive or incompetent justices to the Supreme Court, and the people wouldn't complain because the Fourth Estate would no longer exist to be a check on government. The State of the Union address would become a non-news event and the tradition of the president having the State of the Union report hand-delivered to Congress would return. Without news coverage of the State of the Union, the president could put forth a rosy or bleak state of the nation, but who would know the difference because there would be no journalists to cover it?

Without the press, what would stop Wall Street investment firms and big banks from running amuck? Banks might once again offer subprime mortgage loans to people who couldn't afford them. Who would know, if the watchdog press weren't there to tell? Who would even know how or why the Great Recession of 2008 happened if the press hadn't been there to explain it all? Though the press has at times been asleep, or acted more like a lapdog than a watchdog, eventually a free press discovered and reported the truth, even if the truth arrived late. But when there is no press, holding public officials and businesses accountable would be an impossible feat.

Without newspapers, who would inform the public about new laws, policy changes, or Supreme Court rulings? Without the news media, how would people with pre-existing illnesses know, courtesy of the healthcare bill signed into law, that insurance companies could no longer refuse to insure them? Who would tell Millennials and their parents they could breathe a sigh of relief, thanks to the healthcare bill? How else would they have known that the maximum age to remain on a parents' health insurance had been increased to age 26? Or how, without the news, would the flying public know of a potentially traumatizing encounter with a body scanner at the airport?

Without the local news, who would tell the public which are the best and worst schools or that school districts are laying off teachers and increasing class sizes? How would the public know about the most dangerous roads and intersections? Who would inform the public about recalls of unsafe products or tainted meats, canned goods, or even fresh produce? Without the news, who would tell the public about corruption, abuse, or crime? And how would the public know about devastating earthquakes and tsunamis and how to help victims?

Without the news, good news would be a best-kept secret. If journalism disappears, who would tell about convicted felons who had been exonerated after being wrongly incarcerated for decades? Who would shine a light on the public good and people who are making a difference? Who would inform the public about the noble work of non-profits and small businesses that are filling unique niches? How would the public know about innovation, and scientific and medical advances? Who would keep the public posted on competitiveness in the global economy? How would the public know if the U.S. is winning the future, to use President Obama's phrasing in his 2011 State of the Union address, or losing?

Without the news, how would the public know about the results of a presidential primary, general, or mid-term election? Who would inform us of the latest public opinion polls, presidential approval ratings, or of how communities may have changed based on the most recent U.S. census? Without news to read, watch, or listen to, everyone would be ignorant of events, both important and not so important.

The loss of news would not just take a societal and cultural toll; if news disappeared, individuals would be affected because, for some, the process of reading, watching, listening to, and talking about news is integral to the lives they lead. Without news, people would feel less sure, less secure, and a little lost.

It's comforting to know that journalists are monitoring the environment to inform us if something is amiss, or if there's nothing to worry about. While the latest goings-on inside the Beltway may dominate the network evening news, the front page of *The New York Times*, and the cable talking heads, news is so much more than the nation's capital, and that's why there would be a void in our collective daily lives if news was no longer available.

The news warns of dangerous weather patterns on the horizon; it informs us of school and office closings due to blizzards, ice storms, and wildfires. The news tells us when to carry an umbrella or if it's going to be a bad hair day because of high humidity. News alerts allergy sufferers when to expect to be miserable. The news also advises us when to take an alternate route because of a mile-long traffic tie-up on the main freeway. News also highlights what's happening around town; it helps us decide whether or not to spend money on a new film that's opening on the weekend. The news also tells football and basketball fans if their team won or lost and the reasons why. Because of the news, we know the Grammy and Oscar winners and the upsets, too.

Just as a good neighbor keeps a watchful eye on your home or apartment when you're away, news reports where bank robberies, assaults, murders, and even arsons occurred while you were sleeping. Danger can come in all forms—it might be a boating accident, a drowning at the city pool, a death at a day-care center, a financial scam, predators on the Internet—the news keeps us updated and on guard.

Newspapers not only deliver the news; they are there for us in times of grief. Newspapers both help us get the word out and keep us informed of death. With a cherished photo and carefully crafted prose, newspaper obituaries recognize the life and legacy of a loved one. And with its online counterpart, friends far beyond the circulation area can read the obituary and leave a comment that recalls a memory or expresses sympathy. With dignity and discretion, newspaper obituaries can also communicate family preferences for donations to charities in lieu of flowers.

For TV news to observe a passing, some level of fame must have been achieved, even if it's less than 15 minutes. When TV notes the death of some-one famous or infamous, the news might get a few seconds of the newscast or a crawl on the bottom line. If it's a major figure such as a former president, TV will break in with the news. In fact, if news disappears, so will breaking news. We'll never again know about news that was so important it couldn't wait to be told.

If news disappears, we will no longer have the benefit of expert and some-times humorous commentary and context that we find on newspapers' editorial and opinion pages. Even the editorial cartoon would disappear, and we'll miss out on that visual zinger that through its simplicity and sophistication evokes a raised eyebrow, head nod, or knowing smile.

Without news, how would we connect to, and make sense of, the world beyond our door? Without news to commemorate history, provide context, and mark events seared in our mind's eye, how would we pass on what we stand for to the next generation?

Without news, citizens would be unable to fulfill their civic responsibility of being informed. Without news, professionals would not just feel out of touch; they would be disadvantaged in the marketplace. Without news, the sense of empowerment that accompanies being informed would be in short sup-ply. Without news, what would Malcolm Gladwell's mavens and connectors talk about? Without news, what would any of us talk and tweet about? There would be less to post on Facebook and life would be boring.

Without news our society would no longer have an informed public, making it harder to hold businesses, public officials, institutions, and the news media accountable. The educational system would decline at an even faster rate, diminishing our ability to be the world leader in a global economic competition. Our freedoms would be at risk, threatening our democracy and the symbol of hope that America stands for around the world. Without news, we wouldn't be able to heed the advice and warning of Pulitzer Prize-winning reporter Bob Woodward when he was a guest on *Oprah* during its final season. "You have to be informed," he said. "You get into trouble when you don't pay attention" (Woodward, 2011).

When news is doing its job, it can get you out of trouble and much more. When news is at its best, it doesn't just inform, it establishes common ground; it surprises and inspires us. At its best, news is educator, tour guide, and magician. News magically takes us places we've never been. News motivates us and introduces us to people to care about. News can awaken empathy. News can also evoke disbelief and dismay. News can outrage us: Think Columbine, 9/11, Katrina, the BP Gulf Coast oil spill, Wall Street bonuses, and the U.S. debt ceiling crisis that had Americans and citizens around the world wondering if Washington was capable of putting the public good ahead of self interests. At its best, news fascinates. When news is doing its job, it enables us to vicariously experience the past and present and to imagine a future that has yet to arrive. When news is doing its job, it looks after the public good. When news is at its best, it not only provides information that people need to be "free and self-governing," (Kovach & Rosenstiel, 2007, p. 5), it also provides what the Commission on Freedom of the Press (1947), also known as the Hutchins Commission, noted more than six decades ago when the parents of the Millennial Generation were born:

> Our society needs an accurate, truthful account of the day's events. We need to know what goes on in our own locality, region, and nation. We need reliable information about all other countries. We need to supply other countries with such information about ourselves. We need a market place for the exchange of comment and criticism regarding public affairs. We need to reproduce on a gigantic scale the open argument which characterized the village gathering two centuries ago. We need to project across all groups, regions, and nations a picture of the constituent elements of the modern world. We need to clarify the aims and ideals of our community and every other. (p. 21)

Unfortunately, too often news is not at its best, especially in the projection of "a picture of the constituent elements" (Commission on Freedom of the Press, 1947, p. 26).

There have been almost two centuries of criticisms of news for failing to project a representative picture of constituent groups; much of that criticism has focused on the news media's shortcomings in the coverage of women and people of color (Report of the National Advisory Commission on Civil Disorders, 1968; Poindexter, 2008.)Although news media has deserved criticism for its sub-standard coverage of the youngest of each generation, criticism has been rare. Without criticism to raise awareness, there's little incentive to improve coverage. And from the vantage point of young people, being cropped out of the picture, whether consciously or unconsciously, there is little incentive to pay attention to news.

How Millennials feel about being left out of the news is only one of many factors contributing to minimal news consumption by their generation. In fact, until the multitude of factors, good and bad, positive and negative, are fully understood, news consumption among Millennials will likely not increase. If news consumption does not increase and continues to decline, future news consumption will not only be endangered, a society without news consumers becomes a real possibility. In an effort to reverse the present course leading toward endangered news consumers, Chapter 2 will help us better understand who Millennials are and why they are not into news. Chapter 3 will examine how Millennials feel about the way the news media portrays their generation in the news, followed by Chapter 4, which uses data from The National Survey for News Engagement to sketch a portrait of Millennial engagement with news and social media. Chapter 5 looks at news engagement from the perspective of race, gender, and political identity and finds some troubling trends. Chapter 6 reminds us that just like every generation, there are two distinct groups representing the older and younger members. In this chapter, we'll meet the younger cohort of the Millennial Generation known as Wave II Millennials. The final chapter, Chapter 7, will focus on recommendations to engage Millennials with the news so they can be removed from the endangered species list before it's too late.

· 2 ·

WHY MILLENNIALS AREN'T INTO NEWS

Extensive research shows that if people aren't news consumers by the time
they become adults, they're not likely to develop much of a news habit later.
—NEWSPAPER ASSOCIATION OF AMERICA FOUNDATION

Who is the Millennial Generation and what will it be known for when historians, demographers, sociologists, journalism scholars, and journalists analyze this generation's contributions? Will Millennials be characterized as the first generation on Facebook or as the first generation to be added to a list of endangered news consumers? Whether or not Millennials engage with, or turn away from news, is dependent on a range of generational, individual, societal, and media factors that contribute to consuming or avoiding news.

Millennials, like generations that preceded them and generations that will follow, do not exist in a vacuum; growing up, generations are first influenced by the generation their own parents belong to. The time period that a generation grows up in, as well as when they come of age into adulthood, are also influencing factors. While historical and economic factors may leave a permanent imprint on a generation, when it comes to developing into news consumers, a host of other factors, including media, may intervene.

For example, when the first Baby Boomers were born in 1946, TV had not yet become wildly popular; TV had been invented, but World War II delayed its development (De Fleur & Ball-Rokeach, 1982). Once TV became commercially available, however, it didn't take long for it to be in every Baby Boomer home. Even so, the first Baby Boomers did not begin life with a TV set already present in the home, but for Baby Boomers born between the mid-1950s and 1964, TV was there to welcome their arrival into the world. The distinction as to whether TV was like a family member because it was always present is where I draw the line between what I call Wave I and Wave II Baby Boomers (Poindexter, 2008c). Because of TV, Wave II boomers are more like the generation that followed—Generation X, born between 1965 and the early 1980s (Poindexter, 2008c). Wave II Baby Boomers and Generation X literally grew up on TV.

Generation X, sandwiched between the Baby Boom and Millennial generations, has also been called the MTV Generation, but that label is misleading. The popular cable music channel wasn't founded until 1981, around the time that the oldest Gen Xers were about to graduate high school (Music Television, n.d.). Further, when MTV started, cable was primarily used to improve reception, especially in rural areas—not bring original programming into homes. While only a fraction of Generation X would have watched MTV, watching MTV by the Millennial Generation might have been different, except for one thing. By the time Millennials were old enough to become MTV fans, the home computer and AOL with its kid-friendly Internet activities had arrived, often pushing TV and cable programs aside. During Millennials' teenage years, IM (instant messaging) and downloading music were all the rage. But it was the social media that emerged during the college years that may have determined the fate of news engagement for Millennials and future generations.

While Facebook may have intervened to make Millennials the Facebook generation—not the generation engaged with news—non-media factors may also have characterized this generation. *The New York Times*, for example, said Millennials are "more interested in making a difference than making a dollar" (Rampell, 2011) and The Pew Research Center said Millennials were "more ethnically and racially diverse," "less religious," and "on track to become the most educated generation in American history" (Pew Research Center-Millennials, 2010, p. 1).

As the most educated generation ever, one would expect Millennials to be enthusiastic news consumers, because education level strongly correlates with consumption of news. The fact that Millennials will have the highest education attainment and the lowest level of news consumption may also become a defining characteristic of this generation.

If the correlation between education and news consumption has been a predictable pattern over the past three decades, why are news consumers endangered in this highly educated cohort? The answer lies somewhere in the mix of individual and household characteristics, socialization influences, likes and dislikes, attention competitors, and generational markers.

In 2008, after compiling the various factors that had been linked to news consumption over the past several decades, I developed a model that showed how individual and societal factors connected to produce enthusiastic news consumers or disinterested news avoiders (Poindexter, 2008e). But that news consumption explanatory mock-up that I developed was when Facebook was in its infancy, available to college students only, and Twitter was so new that most people had never heard of it. Now that Facebook has been emancipated from college campuses and tweeting is not just what baby birds do, any previous effort to explain news consumption is obsolete. Social media has changed everything when it comes to understanding why some engage with news and others reject it.

What exactly is social media, which has left such a large imprint on the news media landscape and the lives of Millennials in such a short time period? Merriam-Webster.com defines social media as "forms of electronic communication such as Web sites for social networking and microblogging through which users create online communities to share information, ideas, personal messages, and other content such as videos." While social media can be used for professional networking and as a platform for breaking news and communicating marketing and political messages, it's the *social* in social media that has turned upside down our understanding about the factors facilitating and impeding engagement with news.

But it's not social media alone that's affecting news engagement; it's the unprecedented anytime, anywhere access to social media through mobile devices such as smartphones, tablet computers, and laptops. Whether in a coffeehouse, riding in a car or on a subway, waiting at the airport, even sitting in a college classroom, connecting to and interacting with social media is easy and quick. That's what makes social media such a potentially powerful impediment to news engagement, especially for Millennials. Social media not only eats up time; it can consume attention and render traditional socializing agents ineffective when it comes to engagement with news.

But how can social media be more powerful than all other factors that traditionally have contributed to news engagement? Figure 2.1 provides some insight into that question by displaying the factors that have been identified as contributing to a generation's news engagement. Now that social media is part of the media landscape, social media engagement has been inserted as an intervening force that can serve as a gateway or barrier to news consumption.

[handwritten marginal note:] don't discuss news in person

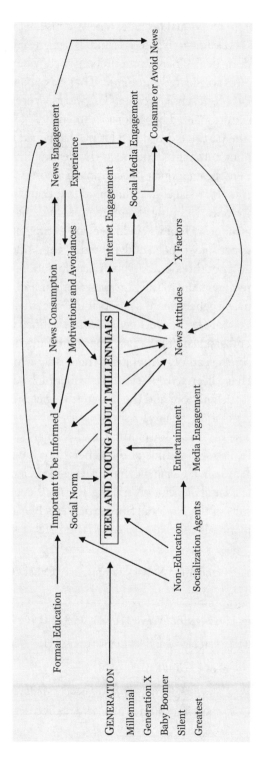

Figure 2.1 Factors Contributing to Millennial Generation's News Engagement after Emergence of Social Media.

Whether or not an individual becomes a news consumer or avoider is due to at least nine factors according to Figure 2.1, and this process appears to be messy, chaotic, and not a done deal. There was a time, though, when the development of a news consumer was considered automatic. That was a half century ago in the 1960s when two journalism scholars called daily newspaper reading "one of the most thoroughly institutionalized behaviors of Americans" (Westley & Severin, 1964, p. 45). Over the past five decades, a lot has happened to make news consumption anything but automatic. Although the decline in news consumption began as Baby Boomers became adults and continued among Generation X adults, it wasn't until Millennials' passage into adulthood that there were signs that news consumption was not only declining at a more rapid rate but that there also was a danger that engagement with news could become a thing of the past.

Why have news consumers been endangered in the Millennial Generation, but news consumption not threatened in previous generations? There's no simple answer, but there are some clues in the historical markers and media that defined each generation. Since a generation is a group bound together by the time period in which its members were born, every generation is defined by the first and last birth years of its members. Despite the fact that there is no universal agreement on the first and last birth years of a generation, there is agreement that during the 20th century, there have been five generations: Millennials, Generation X, Baby Boomers, the Silent Generation, and the Greatest Generation. Listed from the youngest to oldest generation, Figure 2.2 shows how the five generations are connected, as well as some historical and cultural markers that have come to symbolize them. The figure also shows three of the generations have been called more than one name. Millennials, for example, have been called Generation Y and Gen Y. Names such as the Digital Generation and the Texting Generation did not stick. As we learn the results of the National Survey of News Engagement in Chapter 4, we'll see that Millennials could also be called the Facebook Generation.

FIGURE 2.2 Millennial, Generation X, Baby Boomer, and Other 20th-Century Generation Facts

---

Millennials Born 1983–1999 (Wave I-1983–1991; Wave II-1992–1999)

~ Label coined by: Neil Howe and William Strauss (Howe & Strauss, 2000)

~ Also called: Generation Y, Gen Y

~ Coming of Age Historical/Cultural Markers: Columbine, 9/11, Wars in Afghanistan and Iraq, Hurricane Katrina, Virginia Tech shooting rampage,

FIGURE 2.2 (*continued*)

Teach for America, Election of first African American President, BP Gulf Coast Oil Spill, Same-Sex Marriage, Great Recession, Healthcare Reform, Immigration, Arab Spring

~ U.S. Presidents: None yet

~ Kid and Coming of Age News, Media, and Technology: Gameboy, Nickelodeon, the Internet, AOL, IM, music downloading, iPod, MySpace, teen magazines, Harry Potter, cell phone, texting, *American Idol*, blogging, Wikipedia, YouTube, Google, *The Daily Show with Jon Stewart*, *The Colbert Report*, Facebook, smartphone, apps, Twitter, iPad, lol, omg

Generation X born 1965–1982

~ Label coined by: Canadian author Douglas Coupland

~ Also called: 13th Generation

~ Coming of Age Historical/Cultural Markers: Challenger Explosion, Fall of Berlin Wall, O.J. Simpson trial, hip hop, latchkey kids, AIDS

~ U.S. Presidents: None yet

~ Kid and Coming of Age News, Media, and Technology: MTV, CNN, *USA Today*, Mac computer, *The Cosby Show*, *Oprah*, VCRs, renting movies, reality shows

Baby Boomers born 1946–1964 (Wave I-1946-1956; Wave II-1957-1964)

~ Label coined by: Unknown

~ Also called: History's Wealthiest and Most Influential Generation

~ Coming of Age Historical/Cultural Markers: Civil Rights Movement, Vietnam War, Feminist Movement, Civil Rights Act of 1964, Voting Rights Act of 1965, Assassination of Dr. Martin Luther King, Jr., Assassination of Sen. Robert Kennedy, man walks on the moon, Roe v. Wade, birth control pills, Gay Rights, Woodstock, hippies, sexual revolution, smoking marijuana, Peace Corps, 18-to-20-year olds given right to vote, Watergate, Richard Nixon resigns as president

~ U.S. Presidents: Bill Clinton, George W. Bush, Barack Obama

~ Kid and Coming of Age News, Media, and Technology: TV, radio, movies, *Seventeen* magazine, comic books, *The Ed Sullivan Show*, *American Bandstand*, Motown Sound, *Roots*

FIGURE 2.2 *(continued)*

Silent Generation born 1925–1945

~ Label coined by: *Time* Magazine in 1951

~ Also called: Unknown

~ Coming of Age Historical/Cultural Markers: Korean War, Brown v. Board of Education, Cold War, Fallout Shelters, Russians launch Sputnik, First American orbits earth, Assassination of President John F. Kennedy

~ U.S. Presidents: None

~ Kid and Coming of Age News, Media, and Technology: radio, newspapers, movies, newsreels, comic books

Greatest Generation born 1901–1924

~ Label coined by: Tom Brokaw

~ Also called: GI Generation

~ Coming of Age Historical/Cultural Markers: Great Depression, Social Security, GI Bill, World War II

~ U.S. Presidents: Seven presidents including John Kennedy, Lyndon Johnson, Richard Nixon, and Ronald Reagan

~ Kid and Coming of Age News, Media, and Technology: radio, newspapers, movies, newsreels, comic books

---

Usually when generations are reported on or talked about, the descriptions are referring to a group born during years spanning a decade and a half to almost two decades. These reports rarely emphasize that within a generational birth period, there are two distinct groups that I call Wave I and Wave II. This distinction is important because a closer look at these two sub-generational groups reveals differences that can both distinguish within a generational birth period and overlap a portion of a generation that preceded or followed it, especially when it comes to the adoption of new media. Case in point: The media environment that Wave II Baby Boomers grew up in was more similar to Generation X's media environment than Wave I Boomers (Poindexter, 2008c, p. 49).

Even if the start and end dates of a generation vary by several years, depending on the individual or organization defining the generation, membership in a generation never varies: once a Millennial always a Millennial. But over a generation's life span, changes do take place in an age cohort. So, as indicated on the far left of Figure 2.1, the 20th century generations are fixed, but over a lifetime, the age cohorts change as they move through the stages of life from birth to maturation to death. Each age cohort, whether pre-teens, teens, 20-somethings, 30-somethings, retirees, etc. will have a unique perspective as it experiences rites of passage, historical events, popular culture, styles, technology, and media.

During the first decade of the 21st century, the first Millennials or Wave I Millennials, started turning 20. During the second decade of the 21st century, Millennials will age through their 20s and mature to the 30-something cohort, which will bring if not 30-something experiences, a 30-something vantage point. It's also important to keep in mind that within each age cohort there are individual and social-economic-cultural background differences, including race, ethnicity, gender, and income, that may define an age cohort and even a generation. For example, as noted earlier, the Millennial Generation has been called the most racially and ethnically diverse generation ever (Pew Research Center-Millennials, 2010). We'll see in Chapter 5 that this racial diversity matters in how news is perceived.

Moving from left to right in Figure 2.1, you can see that both education and non-education socialization agents contribute to an age cohort's news consumption. As noted earlier, education is a key influencing factor on an age cohort because historically, higher educated people are more likely than individuals with less education to consume news, whether by reading newspapers, watching news on TV, or getting news through other means. And since typically the more highly educated consume more news, the expectation should be that as the most educated generation, Millennials will have an abundant supply of news consumers. But indicators suggest otherwise; news consumers are expected to be in short supply in the Millennial generation.

Non-Education Socialization Agents

If level of education is related to news consumption, what role then is played by non-education socialization agents identified in Figure 2.1? Non-education socialization agents can be as powerful, if not more powerful, than formal education, especially because the influence is strongest during the formative years.

> Although socialization is a life-long process, much of socialization takes place during the formative years. Families, schools, media, textbooks, children's books, peers, reference groups, religious institutions, governmental, non-profit and political organizations are some of the direct and indirect socialization agents that can shape values, norms, beliefs, attitudes, and behaviors. (Poindexter, 2008e, p. 11)

If socialization is "the social process by which individuals come to belong to a society and acquire some of its values, beliefs, perspectives, knowledge, social norms, and preferences" (Wright, 1986, p. 185), and families, schools, media, peers, children's books, textbooks, reference groups, religious institutions, governmental, non-profit, civic, and political institutions are directly and indirectly teaching the values, norms, and preferences, then it's easy to see the influence of these non-education socialization agents in news engagement. Sometimes, of course, the messages are mixed and the rules are contradictory, and this can matter for different age cohorts of a generation. When parents and schools tell children it is important to be informed of the news, that can make a difference, but what happens if peers think being informed of news is "uncool?" Even within the same family, there can be different messages. In fact, a study that examined parental socialization about newspaper reading observed: "it usually is expected in our society that boys will become concerned about public affairs....Girls usually are not expected to become absorbed with political developments" (Clarke, 1965, p. 545)

Entertainment Media Engagement

In Figure 2.1, it can also be seen that every generation is engaged with entertainment media on some level. In some cases the medium may have offered some news and information, but it is still predominantly an entertainment platform. The Greatest Generation experienced movies, radio, and comic books. Commercial radio started in the 1920s; comics and the first talking movies were in the 1930s (Campbell, 1998). As a new entertainment medium was added to the media mix, its novelty may have heightened initial interest, but that initial fascination may have waned as the next new thing replaced it.

By the time the first Baby Boomers started elementary school, TV had been added to the mix of entertainment-oriented media. And because TV was in the home, unlike movies, it was always there just like a member of the family. Before TV's arrival though, radio "commanded a central position in most American living rooms in the 1930s and 1940s" (Campbell, 1998, p. 101). With its variety shows, situation comedies, and quiz shows, radio was entertainment central, that is, until the arrival of TV.

Each generation's teenagers have been smitten with entertainment media that may have been obstacles to engagement with news. In fact for almost every generation of the 20th century, parents, politicians, policy-makers, and scholars have fretted over the influence that some of these entertainment-oriented media—movies, radio, comic books, magazines, TV, music, games, Internet—may have had. For those concerned as to whether a generation would grow up to become an informed generation, the entertainment media may have seemed like unwelcome intruders, especially during the formative and coming-of-age years when as socialization agents they may be as influential, if not more so, than parents and schools.

While previous generations expressed concern about the negative socialization influence of movies, comic books, and TV during the 20th century, the jury is out on the 21st century's social media. It's too new to know its exact role in socialization. Still, social media, as shown in Figure 2.1, can influence. At the very least, spending time with social media can mean less time spent on news, unless, of course, social media are being used to follow news. When social media take time away from news, they are more a barrier to news consumption; when facilitating engagement with news, social media are the news gateway.

Social Norm on Importance of Being Informed

If socialization is, as sociologist Charles Wright (1986) asserted, the process of acquiring a society's values and social norms, Figure 2.1 shows that one of society's norms focuses on the importance of being informed. Traditionally in a democratic society, being informed is something a good citizen does (McCombs & Poindexter, 1983). Where does this social norm about the importance of being informed come from? Since parents are the first teachers, children first learn the importance of being informed from their parents. Parents may teach the importance of being informed directly by explicitly telling their children or indirectly by example: Newspapers are in the home and they are being read, the TV in the living room is turned to the news and it's being watched, the radio in the car is tuned to the news and it's being listened to. Even if parents do not explicitly tell their children that being informed is important, their actions do. Learning through observation is a powerful teaching tool. Just as growing up in a home with visible signs of the importance of being informed can instill this social norm in children, growing up in a home with no visible signs of engagement with news can lead to a weak social norm about the value of being informed.

Of course, believing that it is important to be informed is not a guarantee that people will actually inform themselves; still, if being informed isn't valued, it's unlikely that engagement with news will be a high priority. In fact, that's what my colleague and I found when we tried to link the social norm that being informed is important with reading newspapers and watching news on television (Poindexter & McCombs, 2001).

Parents, of course, are not the only ones responsible for passing on this social norm to the next generation. Schooling also plays a pivotal role, whether through the required K-12 curriculum, or through teacher-led elective initiatives emphasizing news in classroom activities. Regardless of curriculum requirements or elective news-in-the-classroom activities during the formative years, studies show that as education increases, the belief in the importance of being informed becomes stronger, and when the belief is stronger, there is increased engagement with news (McCombs & Poindexter, 1983; Poindexter & McCombs, 2001).

While the belief that being informed can lead a person to engage with news, the actual news engagement experience, and the attitudes about it have played important roles in whether news consumption continues or is discontinued. At least, that was the case before social media became a force in the media landscape. But between the social norm to be informed and the news engagement experience, researchers have identified a variety of motivations and avoidances that contribute to consuming or avoiding news.

Motivations and Avoidances

Over the past several decades, researchers have tried to understand why some people engage with news and others don't. For some news consumers, engagement with news is part of a daily routine that is taken for granted. Like breathing, news engagement just happens. In addition to habit, news consumers are motivated by a desire to keep up with what's going on and even to do something to pass time (Weaver et al., 1979). Non-news consumers by definition are not engaged with news, but they may have engaged with news in the past. For those who formerly engaged with news, their news engagement experience may explain why they no longer read, watch, or listen to news. In fact, "it was not until after newspaper reading declined as a thoroughly institutionalized behavior that scholars began to ask *why* some individuals ignore newspapers" (Poindexter, 2008a, p. 28).

The reasons behind avoiding news or a specific news medium generally fall into four categories: preference for other news medium; perceived constraints such as not having time to consume news; real constraints such as a time conflict or cost; rejection of news or news medium (Poindexter, 2008f). When news is the source of the rejection, it is often due to dissatisfaction with content, format, or presentation (Poindexter, 2008f), but it can also be a rejection of the medium such as the newsprint and ink used to print a newspaper.

Though it's not required to engage with news prior to rejecting it, the news engagement experience can lead to positive or negative attitudes. Despite the fact that some attitudes and avoidances overlap, attitudes about news differ from avoidances; attitudes are positive or negative evaluations of the news-centered object that is comprised of multiple dimensions. For older generations that grew up in a traditional news media landscape, there were essentially 12 dimensions of the news-centered object that might be evaluated, ranging from the institution and content to complexity and feel. But for Millennials, who have come of age in a media landscape bubbling with social media, smartphones, and tablet computers, there are new dimensions of the news-centered object that weren't factors for Generation X, Baby Boomers, or the Silent and Greatest generations (see Figure 2.3).

FIGURE 2.3 Dimensions of the News-Centered Object in a Social Media, Smartphone, Tablet Computer World

- Anytime-anywhere accessibility

- Perpetual updating

- Search-ability

- Share-ability

- Link ease and reliability

- Comment-ability

- Contribute-ability

- Coolness

- Other dimensions that have yet to emerge

Note: Previously identified dimensions of the news-centered object include: "institution, medium, content, experience, expectation fulfillment, contact, cost, time, access, complexity, multi-tasking capability, feel" (Poindexter, 2008a).

Other than updating news reports, these new dimensions of the news-centered object seem unrelated to the quality of news content or organization producing it; these facets of the news-centered object are more about what the news consumer is doing with news content. Is it accessible 24/7? Is it tagged for easy searching? Can you share it? Can you dig deep by clicking on links? Are the links reliable and helpful? Can you comment on it or contribute to it? Is it cool? For older generations that grew up evaluating traditional dimensions of the news-centered object such as cost and time, these new dimensions do not re-define news. But for Millennials, anytime-anywhere accessibility, search-ability, share-ability, link ease and reliability, comment-ability, contribute-ability, and coolness may re-define what news is, and expectations of it.

What is news? Carl Bernstein defined news as "what journalists say it is" when he participated in a discussion on one of the biggest news stories of the 20th Century, held April 21, 2011, at the University of Texas at Austin College of Communication complex. The Watergate discussion also featured Bob Woodward, the other half of the *Washington Post* reporting team that won a Pulitzer Prize for their Watergate stories, and Robert Redford, who played Woodward in *All the President's Men*, the film that inspired a generation of young Baby Boomers to take up the profession of journalism.

News has also been described as perishable (Park, 1940; Stephens, 1997) and distinct from history (Park, 1940). A distinction has also been made between news and other types of content, such as opinion, analysis, and advertising, that might be bundled with news in a newspaper (McQuail, 1983). In fact, news is seen as providing "the component which elevates or distinguishes something called a newspaper....(McQuail, 1983, p. 138). News' First Amendment protection has also been emphasized (McQuail, 1983), and news has been called product, process, and culture (Campbell, 1998). News as culture was described as "...the process of gathering information and making narrative reports—edited by individuals in a news organization. . . ." (Campbell, 1998). In these narrative reports, "selected frames of reference" were created, which helped "the public make sense of prominent people, important events, and unusual happenings in everyday life" (Campbell, 1998, p. 388).

"A window on the world," is how Gaye Tuchman, author of *Making News: A Study in the Construction of Reality*, explained the meaning of news (Tuchman, 1978, p.1). A sociologist who studied how news is constructed, Tuchman said "news aims to tell us what we want to know, need to know, and should know" (Tuchman, 1978, p.1).

In the 21st century, telling us what we want to know, need to know, and should know is no longer the exclusive domain of the news media and news values and the purpose and principles of journalism remain unchanged, except, perhaps, in the eyes of Millennials.

As far as news values are concerned, conflict often seems to be the only criterion used for judging news value, but there are other criteria that determine what becomes news: timeliness, impact, proximity, unusualness, prominence, and audience. Traditionally, TV news included visual impact as part of its news value criteria and radio included audio impact, but today, with news stories expected to be published across platforms, visual and audio impact criteria are no longer news values relied on by broadcast news alone.

While news values address what might be reported as news, they do not deal with the quality of news reporting, which encompasses journalistic ideals of truthfulness and fairness. Concerns about the quality of the reporting of news date back to long before the Greatest Generation was born. In fact, the first African American newspaper *Freedom's Journal* was founded in 1827 because of extreme dissatisfaction with the quality of reporting by the mainstream press.

The standard that defines quality journalism today was unknown to the early U.S. press, which was most known for partisanship. The 19th-century press wasn't known for quality journalism either, but by the late 1800s, journalism standards began to change when "'objectivity' became codified as the great law of journalism" (Mindich, 1998, p. 114).

Some three decades later in 1922, two years before the first members of the Silent Generation were born, quality journalism standards received further attention when newspaper editors created an association and an ethics code that emphasized the ideals that symbolize quality news and ethical journalism: responsibility; freedom of the press; independence; sincerity; truthfulness; accuracy; impartiality; fair play; and decency.

Almost a quarter of a century later, when the first Baby Boomers were born, the quality of news and press performance were called into question by The Hutchins Commission. After concluding that the press had failed to meet society's needs, the Commission, which was headed by the president of the University of Chicago and funded by the founder of *Time Magazine*, Henry Luce, set forth what society needed and expected from the press.

The Hutchins Commission not only criticized the press as a whole, it criticized reporters, the first gatekeepers in the process of reporting news. The criticisms could very well have been an outline for a lecture for Journalism 101. The Hutchins Commission stressed that reporters must be "careful and competent," "must estimate correctly which sources are most authoritative," "must prefer firsthand observation to hearsay," and "must know what questions to ask, what things to observe, and which items to report" (Commission on Freedom of the Press, 1947, p. 21).

The Commission added that equally important as accuracy is "the identification of fact as fact and opinion as opinion, and their separation, so far as possible." Furthermore, accuracy is everyone's responsibility from the first gatekeeper "to the final, published product" (Commission on Freedom of the Press, 1947, p. 23).

Almost two decades after the Hutchins Commission's report, the first Generation Xers were born, and it wasn't long after that the Kerner Commission, a new national Commission appointed by President Lyndon Johnson in the wake of riots across American cities, released a report that included a stinging criticism of the press, which seemed to echo some of the complaints of the first black newspaper almost a century and a half before. The Kerner Commission criticized the press for its lack of understanding or appreciation of black culture, thought, or history; for its negligence in reporting on race relations and African American frustrations and difficulties; and for its failure to hire black journalists (*Report of the National Advisory Commission on Civil Disorders*, 1968).

Despite six decades of emphasizing criteria for achieving quality journalism through the ASNE and Hutchins and Kerner Commission reports, a reporter at one of the most highly respected newspapers in the nation won a Pulitzer Prize for what turned out to be a fabricated news story about an eight-year-old heroin addict named Jimmy. Once the editors at *The Washington Post* determined the story was fabricated, the Pulitzer Prize was returned (Griffith, 1981). This high-profile ethical misconduct at the same newspaper that had won a Pulitzer for its Watergate reporting that helped bring down the president of the United States was the first of a series of newsroom ethical breaches that were publicly exposed. Although the Janet Cooke scandal at *The Washington Post* happened in 1981 before the first Millennials were born, more scandals hit newsrooms and newspaper front pages as the Millennial Generation began to come of age. From Stephen Glass at *The New Republic* (Bissinger, 1998) to Jayson Blair at *The New York Times* (Berry et al., 2003) and Jack Kelley at *USA Today* (Morrison, 2004), the Millennial Generation has grown up during a time that journalistic malpractice has scandalized some of the most prestigious newsrooms in the country, damaging those organizations and chipping away at the credibility of the press everywhere.

It was, perhaps, the 19-point credibility decline between 1985 and 1996 that, like a front-page headline, got the attention of journalists (Pew Research Center -Americans spending more time, 2010). In fact, some journalists began to worry that "something was seriously wrong" with journalism (Kovach & Rosenstiel, 2007, p. 2). Instead of "serving a larger public interest," they had begun to believe that journalism was "damaging it" (Kovach & Rosenstiel, 2007, p. 2).

It is conceivable that part of the reason journalism was not perceived as serving the public interest was because of its failure to "teach" the public what its purpose and principles are and how it conducts its journalistic business. This failure to teach the public about the process of journalism may have worked in a pre-Internet era, but in a media landscape that offers unlimited ways to get information 24/7, blurring of fact and opinion, misinformation, sensationalism, rumors, and political and business spin passing as news, withholding information about how journalism works is not only bad for the profession, it's dangerous for a democracy that requires an informed public to thrive. If it is the case as media analyst Ken Doctor (Farhi, 2011, p. 27) asserts in *American Journalism Review* that "there is abysmal ignorance among citizens about what journalists do to inform the citizenry," it is not surprising that the public has been skeptical and often cynical about journalism and the news it produces. And who has, perhaps, been most skeptical and cynical about journalism? The generation that came of age during the Civil Rights Movement, the Viet Nam War, and the Women's Movement: Baby Boomers, the parents of Millennials.

As Baby Boomers became adults, the newspaper industry expected they would become newspaper readers, like the generation before them. Over seven-tenths (71%) of adults read a newspaper according to a 1965 Gallup poll, and journalism scholars were asserting newspaper reading was a "thoroughly institutionalized" behavior (Westley & Severin, 1964, p. 45). But Baby Boomers weren't picking up the newspaper, and to the dismay of the industry, circulation started trending downward only to accelerate as Generation X grew into adulthood.

It was about the time that their Millennial children were growing into their adolescent years that journalists started looking inward, evaluating their profession. In the 1990s, there was the civic or public journalism movement that questioned journalists' aloofness from the public, and by the late 1990s, there was a focus on "principles that journalists agree on—and that citizens have a right to expect" (Kovach & Rosenstiel, 2007, p. 5). Called the "elements of journalism," these principles provided an opportunity for journalists to re-dedicate themselves to their responsibilities and "educate" the public about journalism's mission of providing "people with the information they need to be free and self-governing" (Kovach & Rosenstiel, 2007, p. 5). And to achieve this mission, which is the cornerstone of the press's First Amendment protection, nine elements were identified followed by a tenth element six years later. Without any effort on the press's part to communicate to the public that these elements are the core principles of journalism, the public will likely remain suspicious of the press and its role in society, further weakening each generation's engagement with news.

FIGURE 2.4. What the Public Should Expect of Journalism According to Kovach & Rosenstiel (2007, pp. 5–6)

- Journalism's first **obligation** is to the **truth**.

- Its first **loyalty** is to **citizens**.

- Its **essence** is a discipline of **verification**.

- Its practitioners must maintain an **independence from those they cover**.

- It must serve as an **independent monitor of power**.

- It must provide a **forum for public criticism and compromise**.

- It must strive to make the **significant interesting and relevant**.

- It must keep the **news comprehensive and proportional**.

- Its practitioners must be allowed to exercise their **personal conscience**.

- Citizens, too, have rights and responsibilities when it comes to the news.

Note: I have added italics and bold to emphasize the aspects of the elements that are key to elevating journalism's credibility in the eyes of the public.

Reviewing the elements, it's easy to understand the public's skepticism and cynicism about the press because in some cases, news values appear to be at odds with the elements necessary to "provide people with the information they need to be free and self-governing" (Kovach & Rosenstiel, 2007, p. 5).

How, for example, can the news value of timeliness be reconciled with the elements of truth and verification? This disconnect was obvious in the initial reporting of the shooting at Fort Hood, the military base in Central Texas where 12 soldiers and one civilian were killed, the shooting of Arizona Congresswoman Gabrielle Giffords, and the killing of Osama bin Laden. In the rush to get the news out, facts were wrong and truth and verification took a back seat. Furthermore, when unusualness is out of proportion to its value as news, news consumers may be left shaking their collective heads, wondering why news coverage is being devoted to such un-newsworthy topics. Most troubling is the public's declining belief that the press protects democracy. In 1985, over half (54%) of the public agreed the press protects democracy, but by 2011, only 42% agreed that the press protected democracy. Is this decline due to press performance, the public's failure to understand the purpose, principles, and process of journalism, or the declining sense that the press is moral, gets the facts straight, and is careful to avoid bias (Press widely criticized, 2011)?

Clearly the public is more negative than positive toward the press; unfortunately, these negative attitudes undermine the merits of a free press in society, weaken the social norm that values the importance of being informed, and erode news consumption, especially among Millennials, who are already distracted by social media.

Compared to other technologies that deliver news, information, and entertainment, social media is the new kid in the media landscape, and unlike legacy news media, which was established to inform the public of the important news of the day, social media were created to emphasize the social. It's that emphasis on social that has, perhaps, most distracted Millennials away from news. But despite having come into being to enhance social life, Facebook and Twitter have emerged as players in the news landscape. Legacy news media have co-opted them as platforms for reporting, updating, and personalizing news, and some social network users have extended the social networking purpose to include sharing and reporting news. But still, because Facebook emerged as the next new thing on the scene just as Millennials were entering into adulthood, this social networking site became a huge distraction that was fun and exciting and really, really cool, unlike the news that their parents, read, watched, and listened to. With declines in news credibility, failures by the news industry in creating news consumers, and such fun things to do with social media, I predict that unless there is some intervention on the part of socialization agents, society, or the news industry, by the third decade of the 21st century, news consumers will not just be endangered; they will become extinct in the generations to come.

· 3 ·

HOW MILLENNIALS *REALLY* FEEL ABOUT NEWS AND COVERAGE OF THEIR GENERATION

Insulting. Patronizing. They [news media] look down on us. They [news media] are shining a bad light on our generation. They never interview anyone…from our age group.
—Opinions expressed by Millennials at the
Millennials and News Summit

Thu Pham, one of five Millennials who critiqued news media coverage of their generation at the Millennials and News Summit, an event I organized as part of Journalism, Society, and the Citizen Journalist, a news literacy course I created, emphasized that despite being so busy, her cohort wants to get news, and she applauded news media efforts that make getting news easy. But what does getting news mean and what is the news that Thu and her Millennial peers are getting? Is it news about the economy and politics, or stories about sports and celebrities? Or for Thu's generation, which is unlike any previous generation as far as accessing the most up-to-date news with mobile devices anytime, anywhere, does getting news mean paying attention when their generation is the news subject? News is all of that and more, but it's the news that's perceived as relevant that may ultimately dictate whether getting news is worth the effort, or engaging with news is a waste of time. News relevance may be in the eyes of Millennials, but news for and about them is high on their relevance scale, which is why their inclusion in the news can influence their attitudes about news and whether or not they spend time getting it.

Do Millennials find stories about their age group in the news? Do they feel the news media treats them respectfully or do they feel the news media looks down on them in coverage about them? Do Millennials feel news coverage about their age group is fair? Is it in context? Is their generation stereotyped? Can their voices be heard, whether the story is about them, the economy, or the presidential election? According to Millennials who critiqued news coverage at the Millennials and News Summit, held at the University of Texas at Austin, the media does a lousy job of covering their generation. And compared to TV, newspapers get low marks for gaining their attention.

The Millennials speaking out at the Millennials and News Summit were not unique in their opinions about news media coverage of their generation. Millennials participating in the National Survey of News Engagement were also critical of the news media's coverage of their generation. In fact, Millennial comments in the survey underscored the fact that the Millennial generation does not consider news its BFF (Best Friend Forever).

What do Millennials think when you say news to them? Does the word news conjure up positive, neutral, or negative words? Do the words Millennials associate with news explain current levels of news consumption? If Millennials have negative images of news now, what does that mean for future news engagement? Because these words reflect Millennial attitudes about news, exploring these words can provide insight into one of several factors influencing Millennial news engagement.

While there are a variety of ways to measure attitudes about news, I asked Millennials a simple, straightforward question to capture their perception of news. Specifically, I asked: When you think about news, what words come to mind?

Figure 3.1, which displays the words that come to mind when Millennials think about news, shows that words with a negative subtext far outweigh positive words such as important, honest, or fair. The fact that the word news evokes so many negative word associations for Millennials is troubling and does not bode well for future news engagement by this generation.

Scrutiny of these negative words also suggests the existence of a negativity continuum; one end of the continuum captures how news makes Millennials feel with words such as depressing, sad, disheartening, while the opposite end of the continuum appears to represent a perception of news. It's that perception that this young generation has of news that is most concerning: useless, boring, biased, propaganda, lies, garbage, crappy. Why would Millennials want to engage with a product that they describe with such negative terms?

FIGURE 3.1 Words Millennials Use to Describe News

POSITIVE	NEUTRAL	NEGATIVE
Important	Current/current events (7)	Crime/Killings (5)
Honest	True stories	Crises
Fair	Information/Informative (5)	Violence
Informed	Government	War (5)
Community	Weather	Death
	Traffic	Disasters
	Reports	Trouble
	Media (20)	Debauchery
	What's happening	Politics (11)
	Economy	Bad
	World affairs	Depressing
	24 hours	Sad
	Breaking	Troubling
	Local	Devastating
	Up-to-date	Scandals
	Drama	Biased
	Keeping up	Crappy
	Knowledge	Garbage
	Reporters	Lies
	Reports	One-sided
	Worldwide	Propaganda
		Bull

FIGURE 3.1 (*continued*)

POSITIVE	NEUTRAL	NEGATIVE
		Useless
		Repetitive
		Boring (4)
		Disheartening
		Fear
		Kingmakers

Note: Number in parentheses represents number of times word was mentioned.

The column of negative words not only reveals a negativity continuum, it also shows that independent of the words that describe how news makes Millennials feel or the perception of it, there is news content that has more of a negative than neutral connotation. Weather, for example, would be neutral, but the content words in the negative column are not associated with positive things: crime, war, disasters, violence, death, scandals, even politics.

Why are the words that Millennials associate with news more likely to be negative than positive? Is this due to how they were socialized about news while growing up? Socialization, as you'll recall from Chapter 2, is "the social process by which individuals come to belong to a society and acquire some of its values, beliefs, perspectives, knowledge, social norms, and preferences" (Wright, 1986, p. 185). To better understand the socialization process, Millennials were asked seven questions about growing up with news (see Table 3.1). Because Millennials, especially those in the Wave I group, represent the children of Baby Boomers, their experience with news while growing up is also compared with Boomers.

It's clear from Table 3.1 that when it comes to news, teachers may be the dominant socialization agent in the lives of Millennials as they grow up. In fact, two-thirds (67%) of the Millennials said a teacher included news in their classroom at least once weekly. "The teachers' ability to influence student attitudes toward newspapers should not be underestimated, especially in the absence of parental influence" (Grusin & Stone, 1993, p. 16). Having news in the classroom can be positive, but it can also be negative if the classroom expe-

TABLE 3.1 Growing Up with News: Millennials and Baby Boomers

	MILLENNIALS	BABY BOOMERS
Teacher included news at least once weekly in classroom	67%	55%
Newspapers were around home most or all of the time	61%	84%
Growing up, news was around most or all of the time	59%	61%
Growing up, someone said being informed about news was important	43%	42%
Growing up, TV was tuned to news around dinner most or all of the time	42%	52%
Growing up, something in the news was discussed at home most or all of the time	33%	27%
Growing up, discussed news with friends often	17%	10%

rience is not enjoyable. A negative experience with news in the classroom can lead to a life-long turn-off (Poindexter, 2008a).

According to Table 3.1, news was also present in the homes in which Millennials grew up; three-fifths of Millennials said newspapers and news were around most or all of the time. Perhaps one of the most important statistics in the chart is the 43% of Millennials who said that while growing up, someone told them explicitly or implicitly about the importance of being informed about news. A follow-up question determined that parents, grandparents, and teachers were the primary sources of this information about the value of being informed about news. Despite this positive statistic related to socializing young people about the importance of being informed, it is concerning that for the majority (57%) of Millennials, no one told them that it was important to be informed about news.

Though TV news appeared to take a backseat to newspapers while growing up, the TV was tuned to news around dinner time most or all of the time, according to two-fifths of Millennials surveyed. For one-third of the Millennials, discussions about something in the news were also taking place at home all or most of the time, but far fewer news discussions were taking place with friends. Seventeen per cent said there were often news discussions with friends.

Since the news media landscape that Millennials grew up in was nothing like the news environment of previous generations, does that also mean there was a difference in the presence of news in their classrooms and homes? By comparing the experiences growing up with news for Millennials and Baby Boomers, some dramatic differences become apparent. The biggest difference between Millennials and Baby Boomers was the presence of newspapers in the home. For Baby Boomers, the generation that grew up in the late 1940s through early 1960s, newspapers were around most or all of the time for over four-fifths (84%) of those surveyed. This percentage reflects why during the early 1960s, newspaper reading was considered a "thoroughly institutionalized" behavior (Westley & Severin, 1964, p. 45). But when this statistic is compared with Millennials growing up, it is apparent that Baby Boomers were less likely to continue the tradition of newspapers in the home. While newspapers were in a whopping 84% of homes that Baby Boomers grew up in, that was not the case for Millennials. According to the National Survey of News Engagement, newspapers were in only 61% of the homes that Millennials grew up in.

Baby Boomers and Millennials also had different experiences growing up when it came to TV news and dinner time. Baby Boomers (52%) were more likely than Millennials (42%) to grow up with TV tuned to news around the dinner hour most or all of the time. Despite the newspaper and dinner time TV news differences, there were similarities between these two generations while growing up. For approximately three-fifths of both generations, news in general was around all or most of the time. Millennials and Baby Boomers were also similar as far as being socialized about the importance of being informed about news; slightly more than two-fifths of both generations said someone told them being informed about news was important. While that statistic has held steady for the two generations, it does not mean Millennials will tell their children that being informed about news is important, especially because of the pervasiveness of social media that has re-defined news engagement for this generation.

In two areas—classrooms and discussions—news was more a part of growing up for Millennials than Baby Boomers. Millennials were more likely than Baby Boomers (67% vs. 55%) to have a teacher include news in the classroom at least once a week. Millennials were also more likely than Baby Boomers (33% vs. 27%) to discuss news at home most or all of the time while growing up. Millennials were also more likely than Baby Boomers (17% vs. 10%) to discuss news with friends most or all of the time.

While it is known from the questions asked that news was present in the lives of Millennials while growing up, attitudes about the presence of news cannot be pinpointed from these questions. Still, since research suggests that engagement with news while growing up matters, Millennials were asked to describe their feelings about news during this period of their young lives. Figure 3.2 shows that feelings about news while growing up differed from the negative-oriented words that Millennials associated with news once they had grown up. The feelings expressed about news make one wonder what happened to turn Millennials against news. In fact, a careful examination of Figure 3.2 shows an abundance of positive feelings about news while growing up. News, for example, was perceived as educational, important, and interesting. While growing up, news was also viewed as helpful, intriguing, and fascinating. Even the negative feelings expressed about news while growing up weren't *that* negative. While being called boring is negative, it's a typical and expected feeling that youngsters express about news. While 17 survey participants recalled that they thought news was boring while growing up, almost as many (16) recalled news as interesting. If intriguing (2), fascinating (2), and informative (13) are added to interesting, it would be fair to say that almost twice as many survey participants recalled news as interesting rather than boring.

Even if some of the negative feelings about news while growing up are not surprising, they should be viewed as a warning, particularly among those concerned that Millennials are endangered as a generation engaged with news. If while growing up Millennials felt apathetic, disconnected, and disinterested when it comes to news, that speaks to socialization about news and the job journalists do reporting the news. While there's not a lot that can be done about scary news, because news *is* sometimes scary, it is of concern when news is recalled as difficult to understand. Whereas it is not particularly surprising that news might be difficult for young people to understand, it is concerning if the difficulty comprehending the news is due to the news writing process that fails to include context and answer the "so what" question that is critical to connecting with the audience (Zerba, 2008, p. 167). These issues will be discussed in more detail in Chapter 7.

FIGURE 3.2 Words That Best Describe Millennials' Feelings about News While Growing Up

POSITIVE	NEGATIVE
Confident	Apathetic (4)
Curious (2)	Biased
Entertaining	Boring (17)
Fascinating	Crap
Fun	Depressing (5)
Great	Disconnected
Helpful	Disinterested
Important (6)	Dislike
Informative (13)	Frustrating
Interesting (16)	Harsh
Intriguing (2)	Hassle
Like	Incomprehensible (6)
Necessary (2)	Mindless
Unbiased	Negative
Useful	Scary (7)
	Sensational
	Whatever
	Worrisome

Note: Number in parentheses represents number of times word mentioned.

Benefits of Engaging with News

Since the 1940s, researchers have tried to determine the value and benefits of various news media, especially newspapers. Today, the specific news medium is less important because news is reported in a variety of ways through multiple platforms. That's why in my National News Engagement Survey, I asked Millennials about the benefits of engaging with news rather than specific news media, and compared their responses with those of Baby Boomers.

By first looking at the column of Millennials in Table 3.2, it is obvious that the majority of this young generation does not strongly endorse the benefits of engaging with news. Only one-fifth of Millennials (20%) strongly agree with the statement that they enjoy keeping up with news, and only 13% strongly agree that they like discussing news with others. Being informed of the news is not viewed as empowering; only 12% strongly agree with this idea. News is not even viewed as helpful in daily life by the vast majority of Millennials; a mere 9% strongly agree with the statement that they depend on news to help with daily life. While the majority of Millennials do not perceive engaging with news as enjoyable, empowering, or helpful in daily life, they do not completely dismiss the benefits of news, either. Only 4% of Millennials strongly agree with the statement that keeping up with the news is a waste of time.

TABLE 3.2 Benefits of Engaging with News for Millennials and Baby Boomers

	MILLENNIALS % Saying Strongly Agree	BABY BOOMERS % Saying Strongly Agree
Enjoy keeping up with news	20%	36%
Like discussing news with others	13%	15%
Being informed is empowering	12%	13%
Depend on news to help with daily life	9%	11%
Keeping up with news is a waste of time	4%	0%

Except for the 16-point news enjoyment gap, Baby Boomers' perceptions of the benefits of engaging with news are not that different from Millennials'. With more than one-third (36%) of Baby Boomers strongly agreeing that they enjoy keeping up with news, they are far more likely than Millennials to perceive an enjoyment benefit from news engagement.

While Boomers and Millennials may differ on enjoyment benefits, the older and younger generations are similar in their assessment of the benefits of discussing news; approximately 13% of Millennials and 15% of Baby Boomers strongly agree that they like to discuss news with others. The idea that being informed of news is empowering appears to be a foreign concept to Baby Boomers and Millennials; fewer than 15% of both generational cohorts strongly endorse this view. Just as few in both generations consider being informed of news empowering, only a small percentage of Millennials (9%) and Baby Boomers (11%) strongly agree that they depend on news to help with daily life.

A review of Table 3.2 is a reminder that of the five benefits of engagement with news examined, enjoyment of news was at the top of the list of benefits strongly endorsed. Yet, with only one-fifth of Millennials and slightly more than one-third of Baby Boomers strongly agreeing with the statement, only a minority of both generations enjoy keeping up with news. In terms of liking discussing news, feeling empowered when informed, and news helping with daily life, only a very small percentage of each generation was passionate about these benefits that news had the potential to deliver. While these benefits may not represent all benefits of engagement with news, there appeared to be strong sentiment when both Millennials and Baby Boomers were asked if news was a waste of time. None of the Baby Boomers and only 4% of Millennials strongly endorsed the statement, "Keeping up with the news is a waste of time."

Grading News Coverage of Millennials

The words Millennials use to describe news, their relationship with news growing up, and the perceived benefits of news no doubt play supporting roles in Millennial news engagement. It is possible, though, that one factor—news coverage of their generation—may play the leading role in whether or not Millennials engage with news, especially because some of the grades that Millennials gave the news media for covering their generation were barely passing. For 68% of Millennials surveyed, the news media's grade did not rise above a C. While 44% assigned a grade of C, one quarter gave D or F grades to news coverage of their age group (see Table 3.3).

TABLE 3.3 How Millennials Grade News Coverage of Their Generation

A	6%
B	26%
C	44%
D	18%
F	6%

What's Behind the A and B Grades?

Of the 6% who gave a grade of A to news coverage of Millennials, a 24-year-old male with some college said his A grade was because the news was "informative." A 21-year-old female who also gave the news media a grade of A said her grade was because "They're always talking about celebrities or things they think young people are interested in." But for an 18-year-old female, the news media's "use of Twitter, Facebook, various apps, etc." was the reason for the A.

The B grades reflected both a touch of criticism and a touch of praise; over a half-dozen Millennials who assigned the news media a B grade said the news media's coverage of their age group was "pretty good." In fact, a 21-year-old male's observation was more nuanced: "I haven't seen anything that makes me feel that news reporting on young people is bad overall, but some stories do certainly miss the mark somewhat and there is always room for improvement." While on the surface, a B is a good grade, a close examination of the explanation shows that in the minds of some Millennials, a B does not mean the news media is doing a good job. A 27-year-old female college graduate observed: "They usually only focus on the bad things happening." A different Millennial female who was the same age but had less college said: "…many young people in the news are in it for negative reasons—then again, most news is negative to begin with."

A Grade of C is Below Average

Many who gave a grade of C were giving the grade because young people were not covered in the news, stories about, or of interest to, young people were lacking, or stories about young people were negative. In fact, a 26-year-old male said the news media "do not understand young people." A 24-year-old female with some graduate education was more direct in her assessment: "A lot of the coverage is about how we're either completely screwed in the economy and can't get jobs, or we're lazy and refusing to work and move out of mom's house." A 26-year-old male with some college said his C grade was because of the celebrity focus when young adults are in the news. He called this type of coverage "pointless gossip and garbage." A 21-year-old male college graduate said his C grade was because "they just like to bash us."

D and F Grades Reveal News Coverage of Millennials is on the Wrong Track

Explanations for the failing, or almost failing, grades varied, but there were some recurring themes. First, Millennials who gave Ds and Fs to the news media for coverage of their age group were keenly aware of being excluded from the news. Additionally, they observed that if they were covered at all, the news coverage was negative or primarily focused on celebrities. Finally, there was a sense that the news media did not care about them.

"We are overlooked," said a 19-year-old female with some college who gave the news media a D grade. "All they ever talk about are celebrities," she added. A 26-year-old female college graduate said she gave the news media a D because there wasn't much reported about her age group other than "graduations or crimes."

A 20-year-old male said the news media deserved a failing grade because news coverage "makes my age look awful; not all people between 18 to late 20s are killers, robbers, etc. I strongly dislike the image the news puts out there about my age group." A 28-year-old female college graduate who said the news media deserved a D agreed that news coverage about Millennials is heavily about crime—"crimes they have committed or are accused of committing." A 24-year-old female college graduate echoed that opinion when she explained the reason for giving the news media a D: "The only time I see young people in the news is when they are in trouble with the law or have been in an accident. There is never any coverage of the positive things that young people are doing, so older generations are given a very skewed perception. . . ."

A 26-year-old male's D grade was because, in his view, the news media aren't even trying to engage young people. "...besides *The Daily Show,*" he said, "nobody makes an effort to even try to talk to young people." A 28-year-old female with a master's degree explained her D grade by pointing out the news media's overall failure when it comes to Millennials: "They do not give young people compelling reasons to follow their stories."

These grades represent Millennial perceptions about news coverage, but what is the reality? Does news coverage exclude Millennials? Or if Millennials are included in the news, is the coverage negative? Or are they included because they are celebrities or have been accused of a crime? A close look at news coverage for a 40-day period found some truth to Millennials' criticisms.

Every day for 40 days, *The New York Times*, NPR, Google News, *USA Today*, and CNN, among other news outlets, were monitored to identify stories about Millennials, stories that affected Millennials, stories that might interest Millennials, and news that Millennials should know. These stories were posted on a Facebook page created to aggregate news stories for Millennials. Over the course of 40 days, several thousand published and broadcast news stories were reviewed, and of those, approximately 250 stories were posted because they fit the Millennial news criteria: Stories were explicitly or implicitly about Millennials or could have an impact on Millennials. If it was determined the story was news Millennials should know or might want to know, it was also posted. Additionally, stories providing insight and context on stories in the news were posted. Finally, stories that might enchant, or elicit a Millennial lol (laugh out loud), regardless of topic, were added to the posted stories. (Detail about the process of aggregating news stories for Millennials can be found in Appendix D.)

After reviewing several thousand stories published or broadcast to determine if they qualified as Millennial news, it became clear that Millennials who gave the news media low grades for not including Millennials in the news were correct in their assessment. There just weren't that many stories about Millennials over the 40-day period examined. Of explicitly Millennial stories identified, the criminal and celebrity connection that Millennials complained about was evident. Examples included: the trial of the Millennial mother Casey Anthony accused of killing her two-year-old daughter Caylee; the visit to California by the newly wed Millennial royal couple Prince William and Kate Middleton; Bristol Palin, the daughter of former governor of Alaska and vice presidential candidate Sarah Palin; Facebook co-founder Mark Zuckerberg; kids of celebrities who were attending college.

There were also stories from *The New York Times*, NPR, and CNN explicitly about Millennials unrelated to celebrity or criminal activity. But just because Millennials are referenced in the headline and discussed in the story does not mean Millennials are actually heard from in the story. In fact, the complaint that "nobody makes an effort to even try to talk to young people" was found to be true in *The New York Times'* "College Students Don't View Debt as Burden" (Carrns, 2011). Although the headline was explicitly about Millennials, there were no quotes from anyone in that age group. The article included eight direct and indirect quotes; half of the quotes were from a study and the remaining half were from the study's lead author; none were from college students or even recent college graduates who were now faced with paying back their student loans.

The headline and photo made it clear that CNN's "The Changing Face of America's Youth" was about Millennials, but after reading the story, it was obvious that Millennials, although discussed in the story, were barely heard from except through a token quote (Sutter, 2011). While the U.S. Census Bureau, the think tank researcher who analyzed the census data, unidentified demographers and residents, and a University of California professor were the sources for seven of the eight quotes, only one quote was attributed to a Millennial, and that was the seventh quote included in the story.

While some stories may lead you to believe, through the headline and photo, that Millennials will be heard from, a *New York Times* story, "Job Jugglers, on the Tightrope" did not include any reference to Millennials in the headline, but there was a Millennial in the photograph (Seligson, 2011). Despite the fact that the article failed to explicitly reference Millennials in the headline, four of the nine sources were Millennials. Additionally, the reporter used many Millennial quotes to not just illustrate this part-time job-juggling trend but to let Millennial voices be heard. Beginning with the first line of the second paragraph, references to the Millennial Generation could be found throughout the story: ages 26, 23, 28, young, young college graduates, young people, Gen Y, young women, and 20s. Even though references to Millennials appeared throughout the story, surprisingly none of the four eye-catching photographs that captured Millennials doing one of the part-time jobs they juggled included any reference to their age in the caption.

News impacting Millennials may be thought of as a continuum. On one end of the continuum is news such as a presidential election or depressed economy that affects, or is at least applicable to, each and every generation; on the other end of the continuum is news affecting Millennials exclusively.

A *USA Today* story, "Americans doing more work on weekends," is an example of a story applicable to every generation, especially because the Bureau of Labor Statistics American Time Use Survey, upon which the article was based, included data from 13,200 people 16 years or older (St. John, 2011). Comparisons were made between women and men and part-time and full-time workers, and there was one quote from the author of *168 Hours: You Have More Time Than You Think*, but there were no quotes, references to, or examples from Millennials to see if they were spending less or more time relaxing and watching TV than Americans in general.

Two other *USA Today* stories would be applicable to all generations but especially Millennials. "Distracted-driving programs show success" used a young person in the silhouette driving and texting, but in the story, there was no reference to young people or quotes from young people (Copeland, 2011). Sources quoted were government and quasi-government officials and agencies. The *USA Today* story "Study: Even one glass of beer, wine boosts car crash risk" is also applicable to every generation, especially Millennials, but they are not mentioned or quoted in the story (Dallas, 2011). Only the study and the study's author were quoted.

Some news impacts Millennials exclusively, but one wouldn't know that from the headline in NPR's "An Affliction of the Cornea Gets a Closer Look" (Neighmond, 2011). In the third paragraph, it's obvious that this eyesight-threatening disease called Keratoconus affects teens and young adults, but this important information is excluded from the headline. The story even emphasizes the impact of this cornea disorder on Millennials in the closing paragraph by telling this age group: "Experts suggest that if you're a teen or 20-something whose vision is changing so quickly that you find you need to switch the prescription of your glasses or contacts every few months, check with your doctor. You may need to have the shape of your eyes examined" (Neighmond, 2011). Yet, the age group affected directly would likely miss the story because there is no reference to them in the headline.

Despite the failure to include Millennials in the headline, Millennials were referenced in the story and Millennial quotes were used throughout the story. For example, when Millennial Kaley Jones first realized something was wrong with her vision while sitting in her high school history class, she was quoted as saying: "It was really scary. It was kind of like looking through plastic wrap. I could see color, but no real detail" (Neighmond, 2011).

Millennial News that Insults and Hurts

Excluding or barely including Millennials in the news is not just a lost opportunity; it's journalism practicing tokenism. Unfortunately, the way Millennials have sometimes been covered, as well as the tone used to report on them, is not only patronizing and disrespectful; this type of coverage is insulting and hurtful.

An editorial cartoon published in a section of the Sunday *New York Times* captured what Millennials meant in some of their criticisms of news. As shown in Figure 3.3, the editorial cartoon is a take-off on Dr. Seuss's beloved *Oh, the Places You'll Go!* "Go out there. You are going to be great," said Dr. Seuss's editor as he described the message of the "popular gift for graduates from kindergarten to col-

Figure 3.3 Editorial Cartoon Published in the Sunday *New York Times*. © Tribune Media Services, Inc. All Rights Reserved. Reprinted with permission.

lege" (Blais et al., 2007). But the message of the editorial cartoon is that nothing great is waiting for the new college graduates. What's waiting after graduating college, according to the editorial cartoon, is delivering pizza, returning to your old bedroom at home, unpaid internships, and debt counseling (Davies, 2011).

Perhaps the news story that most insulted Millennials was broadcast by *60 Minutes* in 2007 but, thanks to the Internet, is still available today. When Millennials discussed news coverage of their generation during the Millennials and News Summit they cited *60 Minutes'* "The Millennials are Coming" story as an example of how *not* to cover Millennials unless the purpose is to insult them. Morley Safer, who is a member of the generation that would be grandparents or great-grandparents of Millennials, introduced the story by describing Millennials as a "new breed of American worker" (Safer, 2007).

> Stand back all bosses! A new breed of American worker is attacking everything you hold sacred: from giving orders, to your starched white shirt and tie. They are called, among other things, "millennials." There are about 80 million of them, born between 1980 and 1995, and they're rapidly taking over from the baby boomers who are now pushing 60. They were raised by doting parents; played in little leagues with no winners or losers, they are all winners. They are laden with trophies just for participating and they think your business-as-usual ethic is for the birds. And if you don't like it, you can take your job and shove it.

During the 60 *Minutes* Millennial segment, Morley Safer used interviews with experts to tell the story of Millennials invading the workplace, which he called a "psychological battlefield" in which "millennials have the upper hand . . ." (Safer, 2007). The first three experts interviewed on camera were Baby Boomers; halfway through the segment, two Millennial brothers, who advise 20-somethings, were interviewed. Among the first three Baby Boomer experts was a *Wall Street Journal* columnist who blamed Mr. Rogers for telling Millennials when they were pre-schoolers that they were special. During the 60 *Minutes* piece, Millennials were the target of unabashed criticism. The experts said this generation had not been trained "how to eat with a knife and fork, or how to work in an office because they have never held a summer job" (Safer, 2007). Safer called Millennials "narcissistic praise-hounds" and criticized them for moving "home after graduation" (Safer, 2007). The two Millennial experts who "advise" fellow 20-somethings on how to cope with work asserted: "No longer is it bad to have four jobs on your resume in a year" (Safer, 2007).

Millennials participating in the Millennials and News Summit were not the only ones critical of the 60 *Minutes* segment. Although a review of the dozens of program comments found that Baby Boomers and Generation X were thanking 60 *Minutes* for what they considered eye-opening journalism, Millennials were appalled by the piece, which they viewed as a hatchet job on their generation.

Among the comments posted on the 60 *Minutes* Web site was 23-year-old "cubator23,"[1] who expressed genuine disappointment in the 60 *Minutes* piece because it was "one-sided" and failed to include challenges this young generation has faced, and what the writer called "victories" they had won despite their young age. Cubator23 said: "We came of age post-9/11, we understand that life is delicate and to stand for what we believe in, we signed up to fight in Iraq, applied for Teach for America in record numbers and in 2004, represented the strongest young voter turnout since 18–20 years olds won the right to vote in 1972. 60 *Minutes*, I expected a lot more."

Another commenter, "maythirty,"criticized 60 *Minutes* for calling the Millennial Generation self-absorbed and spoiled and for ignoring the Millennials who have chosen "public service professions—teachers, social workers, police officers, etc.—and where the focus is not on salary and a feeling of entitlement, but on helping others."

A person with the user name "recentgrad" also complained that 60 *Minutes* had ignored the many Millennials fighting a war and the "rising costs of college tuition." In contrast to Baby Boomers, the writer said that she and her sister "will be paying back student loans of over $150,000" and added that because "starting salaries are ridiculously low, Millennials have no choice but to live at home."

"Vellinge" called the 60 *Minutes* story "one-sided, inaccurate, and completely irrelevant." The writer said that he kept waiting for Morley Safer to address the economic realities facing most Millennials as they enter the workforce, but he never did.

For "alanalana," the 60 *Minutes* story was "one of the worst and most one-sided, I have ever seen" on 60 *Minutes*, and alanalana defended the Millennial generation as:

> arguably the most competitive, hard working generation in history. Universities are harder to get into requiring more sacrifice at earlier ages to get competitive for college. Meanwhile the manufacturing sector of the economy that used to provide less educated young people with working wages have all but disappeared. The pressure is on for my generation, who has the highest educational debt in history, and who is already paying for the mistakes of previous generations (social security, the environment, etc.). We are a forward thinking hard working generation, saddled with the mistakes of the past and struggling to make a living in the modern economy. Shame on 60 *Minutes* for this trite and misleading story.

"A worthless piece of non-scientific psycho-babble that has no basis in the real world" was the way "redelefnt2" described the 60 *Minutes* piece. "Zerocharismo"pointed out that the 60 *Minutes* segment was the reason they [60 *Minutes*] were "behind in teen and 20s viewership" and added that there was no reason "to insult the few younger viewers you have left."

"Imwitheband" expressed that it was "pretty sad" that an influential company like CBS would produce such "biased material" to represent a "generation of emerging adults" as lazy and dependent on their parents.

"Misslynn81" was emphatic in the criticism and concerns about the consequences of the 60 *Minutes* story: "I am a Millennial who is extremely offended by the report I just watched. I believe that 60 *Minutes* has given a very biased opinion of the Millennial Generation, and, as I feared, previous generations are already using this report against my generation."

The fear that "misslynn81" expressed was evident in some of the comments from Baby Boomers who also watched the 60 *Minutes* story. These comments were not just caustic; some of the comments were openly hostile toward the Millennial Generation.

After watching the 60 *Minutes* segment, "mississa1" said: "They [Millennials] never really worked hard for anything in their lives." From "backlin1's perspective, Millennials are a "bunch of selfish pampered do-nothings…" An individual using the name "gsu0599" called Millennials "self-righteous, self-centered, spoiled brats." And "wmalex59" observed "the spoiled rotten generation of I want it now has come home to roost…literally."

Several viewers from older generations predicted the Millennial Generation's future impact. "Hillary1973" said: "In the future when historians look back at the downfall of the USA like many great civilizations I would not be surprised if lack of hard work, over-involved parenting and entitlement plays into the analysis." "Thinkamerica" commented: "Our society and country are in grave danger." "Nauseatic" was even more dramatic in his comments when he said that because of the Millennial Generation, "We're all doomed if this is the future!"

Almost four years after the original airing of the 60 Minutes report, the segment was still being resented and debated. Millennials at the Millennials and News Summit resented the report, and some non-Millennials still believe the report is an accurate representation of that generation. That's what I observed at my faculty retreat, which was held a couple of days before the first day of class of a new school year. The focus of the retreat was on effective teaching, and item number one on the agenda was the Millennial Generation, in recognition of the fact that college students today are different from college students of past generations. Actually, we never really discussed the characteristics that make Millennials unique because one of my colleagues mentioned the 60 Minutes report as evidence that this generation is less competitive because while growing up they received participation certificates and there were no losers—only winners. The majority of my faculty colleagues are Baby Boomers with a smattering of Generation X, and some, like me, are parents of Millennials. Although there were no Millennials in the room to stand up for their generation, I tried to represent their point of view by sharing the criticisms of the Millennials who participated in the Millennials and News Summit and the criticisms posted after the 60 Minutes segment aired. Because the 60 Minutes franchise is almost sacred in the halls of journalism schools, it's hard to undo their reporting even four years later. That's why it's so important to get it right the first time when reporting on Millennials. It's not just about responsible journalism; it's also about the perceptions that are left among non-Millennials and the loss of a generation of future news consumers because they know first-hand that the reporting is inaccurate. In Chapter 7, we'll explore how to get it right the first time when reporting on the Millennial Generation.

Note

1. Comments were identified by user names rather than real names. User names and original quotes can be found at Comments on the Millennials are coming (2007).

· 4 ·

TOO BUSY FOR NEWS;
UNLIMITED TIME FOR SOCIAL MEDIA

We're so busy that we don't have time for newspapers but we do want to get the news and we want it fast and we want it on our phones.
—THU PHAM, MILLENNIAL COLLEGE STUDENT SPEAKING AT
MILLENNIALS AND NEWS SUMMIT

Not all Millennials are disengaged with news—yet. And the engagement that Millennials have with news looks nothing like past generations at the same age. In 1964, when the first Baby Boomers were almost 20 and reading newspapers was called a "thoroughly institutionalized" behavior (Westley & Severin, 1964, p. 45), engagement with news was primarily consumption-oriented, such as reading newspapers and weekly newsmagazines, watching television news, and listening to news on the radio. Occasionally the news audience might write a letter to the editor and the editor would select some of the letters and publish them in the newspaper or news magazine.

Today, news engagement is consumption and so much more. News engagement might include reading a newspaper, reading a story on Yahoo News, posting a story on Facebook, clicking a link, tweeting a story, or uploading a video to the local TV news station. News engagement can also mean reading news received in an e-mail, texting a news story, or watching Jon Stewart's *The Daily Show*.

In the past, news engagement was more passive. Today, with social media, smartphones and apps, and a wireless landscape, engaging with news is quick, easy, and anything but passive. News engagement can also be unintended. While reading a newspaper is purposeful engagement with news, getting TV or cable news might be accidental or coincidental, due to the fact that someone else may have tuned the TV to the 6 o'clock local news. Accidental news consumption might also happen when going online to check e-mail. Engaging with news on a smartphone or iPad is more purposeful when a news app is used; with a light touch to the app, you're taken directly to the news. Without an app, getting news might be purposeful, but it also might be serendipitous.

Whether intended, unintended, or serendipitous, traditional news consumption measures (frequency of reading newspapers, watching local TV news, etc.) are inadequate to capture the news engagement in today's news environment. The Pew Research Center underscores this point by noting in its 2010 news consumption survey that "instead of replacing traditional news platforms, Americans are increasingly integrating new technologies into their news consumption habits" (Americans Spending More Time, 2010). A consequence of this traditional and digital news integration, according to Pew, is that over four-fifths (83%) of Americans "get news in one form or another as part of their daily life" (Americans Spending More Time, 2010). Still, almost one-fifth (17%) "got no news yesterday" (Americans Spending More Time, 2010), that is, when the traditional measurement of news consumption was used. But the relationship between the audience and news today is nothing like the past; furthermore, today's relationship requires an expanded set of measures to capture what is taking place in a news media landscape that has been redefined by the addition of social media, mobile devices, and digital platforms.

The addition of social media, mobile devices, and digital platforms to the news media landscape has expanded the relationship between news consumers and news. In the past, we read, watched, and listened to news. Today, we still read, watch, and listen to news, but we also click, post, text, like, comment, and upload. To capture this transformation in the news media landscape, a distinctly different term is needed to encompass both traditional news consumption and the news consumer experience in today's news and social media landscape. That's why I recommend that we replace the term news consumption with the term news engagement to reflect the different types of news content as well as the platforms and social media that consumers now use to connect with news.

While social media alone did not contribute to the need for a different term to reflect how consumers now connect with news, social media has enhanced the variety of ways to engage with news. When Facebook was exclusive to college campuses, the news media and other non-college news content providers could not use Facebook as a platform for sharing news. But once Facebook was liberated from college campuses, its adoption by journalists, news organizations, and news aggregators provided a new opportunity for news engagement.

In addition to the news media's adoption of Facebook, and later Twitter, the news media landscape has undergone a digital, wireless, and mobile transformation. There are not only many new ways to engage with news, but news engagement can occur anytime, anyplace, on the go, or at home. Engaging with news is as simple as touching an app on a smartphone or iPad.

Getting News

Despite the myriad and anytime, anyplace ways to engage with news, the end result remains the same: Consumers are getting news in some form or fashion up to seven days a week. To establish a baseline for the news that consumers are getting, participants in the National Survey of News Engagement were asked: Approximately how many days in an average week do you get news?

TABLE 4.1 Number of Days Per Week Millennials and Baby Boomers "Get" News

	MILLENNIALS	BABY BOOMERS
0 to 1 Days	15%	3%
2 to 4 Days	27%	5%
5 to 6 Days	20%	17%
7 Days	39%	75%

Although later we'll be able to see the specific platforms from which consumers are engaging news, in terms of getting news, news is often gotten even if that was not the intention. If you're checking your e-mail, news can pop up. Watching a non-news program, news can crawl across the bottom of the screen. Going on Facebook, news may be viewed on a friend's Facebook News Feed. Sitting in an airport waiting for your flight, CNN is on the screen, bringing the airport version of news. News is even shown on a flight, to a captive audience. Even when your iPad is in rest mode, news can break through if a news app is installed. News in some format or mode is literally everywhere, which is why the vast majority get news at least two days a week. Still Millennials are five times more likely than Baby Boomers to get news only one day or less (15% vs. 3%). Perhaps, more importantly, Millennials are far less likely than Baby Boomers to get news seven days a week; 39% of Millennials compared to 75% of Baby Boomers get news every day of the week.

Reasons Millennials Get News

With over six decades of studies consistently showing that the need to keep up with what's going on motivates news consumption, it's not surprising that most Millennials get news for the same reason (Berelson, 1949; Weaver et al., 1979). The exact wording may vary from "to keep up with stuff" to stay "abreast of all current events," but the meaning was the same in the National Survey of News Engagement, which asked Millennials their main reason for getting news. While some variation of keeping informed was the reason that the vast majority of Millennials engaged with news, Millennials noted other reasons for getting news: boredom, curiosity, to know if there's anything to be concerned about, specific content such as crime, weather, gossip, entertainment, coupons, taxes, horoscope, sports, and to see who died. For some Millennials, getting news is inevitable because news just "pops up!" While no Millennials explicitly said they got news because it was part of their job, a separate question made it clear that news can be beneficial for jobs. Millennials (63%) were more likely than Baby Boomers (56%) to say that getting news was not a job requirement; nevertheless news was beneficial for their jobs.

News Preferences

By asking if participants in the National Survey of News Engagement get news and the reasons for getting it, we're able to sketch news engagement in broad strokes; by following up with more pointed questions about getting specific types of news, we can add detail to the meaning of news engagement. One such follow-up question on the type of news Millennials paid most attention to provided insight about news categories, ranging from hyperlocal news about the neighborhood to international news that reports what's happening around the globe (see Table 4.2).

TABLE 4.2 Type of News Most Paid Attention to by Millennials and Baby Boomers

	MILLENNIALS	BABY BOOMERS
Local	39%	42%
National	31%	37%
International	17%	8%
State	11%	10%
Neighborhood	3%	3%

While the distinction between local and neighborhood news may be in the eyes of news consumers, local is the most popular type of news and neighborhood is the least popular, not just for Millennials but also for Baby Boomers. Whereas there's not much difference between Millennials and Baby Boomers in paying attention to local and state news, there is a difference between these two generations regarding international news. When the five news types are compared, international news may get a lower ranking overall for the younger and older generations, but international news ranks higher for Millennials, who are twice as likely as Baby Boomers to pay attention to news from around the world (17% vs. 8%).

Keeping Up With Important Issues

While traditional news categories provide some insight into engagement with news, they don't tell us much about other factors driving news engagement. Do news consumers keep up with news about problems facing the country? What about issues personally important to them? Table 4.3 suggests that while issues of personal importance and important problems facing the country may contribute to engagement with news, it is far less the case for Millennials, despite the fact that almost half (47%) said there was an issue personally important to them.

Issues of personal importance to Millennials such as the economy, the environment, illegal immigration, jobs, health care, and the war are regularly covered in the news, but that does not mean Millennials are regularly following these issues in the news. In fact, fewer than two-fifths (37%) said they often get news about these personally important issues. In contrast, almost two-thirds (64%) of Baby Boomers indicated that they had an issue of personal

TABLE 4.3 Get News to Keep Up with Personal Issues and Country's Problems

	MILLENNIALS	BABY BOOMERS
Often get news about issue of personal importance	37%	65%
Often get news about problem facing country	35%	64%

importance, and almost two-thirds were actually getting news about these personally important issues. A similar pattern can be seen for getting news about the most important problem facing the country. With only one-third (35%) of Millennials regularly getting news about the most important problem facing the country, it appears that whether you're talking about the most important problem facing the country or an issue of personal importance, Millennials are not using the news to engage with these issues.

Transforming the News Landscape and Engagement with News

Scanning Table 4.4, which displays statistics from more than three dozen questions on news engagement, reminds us of the vast difference between the news media landscape today compared to the time when the first Baby Boomers were becoming adults. Not only does the Millennial Generation have significantly more platforms for getting news, it also has more roles in the news media landscape to play. When the first Baby Boomers became adults in the 1960s, news media was comprised of newspapers, local and network TV news, news magazines, and news on the radio. It would be almost another decade and a half before the first 24-hour cable news network would be added to the news media landscape. When the first Baby Boomers came into adulthood, *The Daily Show* and *The Colbert Report* did not exist. Additionally, the relationship of Baby Boomers to the news media was primarily that of passively consuming news.

In contrast to Baby Boomers, the Millennial Generation has emerged into adulthood in a news media environment in which the availability of news is seemingly limitless, engagement with news is wide-ranging, and social media's presence gives new meaning to news engagement and the news media landscape.

When did the transformation of the news media landscape actually begin? Was it 1980 when CNN, the 24-hour cable news network, was launched? Or was it the frequently updated online newspapers that emerged during the late 1990s and early 2000s? Was it a big breaking news story such as the 1995 Oklahoma City bombing or 9/11 that drove news consumers to the Internet and awakened the potential of the Web as a platform for news? Or was it the adoption of broadband, which speeded up the process of getting news stories that included more than text? With broadband, news consumers could get "media-rich content such as audio, video, and flash movies from news Web sites to their computer (or other devices)" (Schmitz Weiss, 2008, p. 120). Or did the transformation of the news media landscape begin with the creation of *The Daily Show* that unleashed the idea that watching *The Daily Show* was "even better than being informed" (About The Daily Show, n.d.).

Or, perhaps, the news media landscape's transformation began when bloggers arrived and, like squatters, claimed a patch of the landscape despite the fact that journalists, until they co-opted blogging, thought bloggers had no right to lay claim to anything remotely journalistic. It's impossible to pinpoint the precise moment that set off the transformation, but there's no question a transformation of unprecedented scope has taken place, and the addition of Facebook has not just altered the landscape, it has upended it. As Table 4.4 shows, Facebook is not just a domineering aspect of the news media landscape, it is so dominant in the lives of Millennials that Facebook is a part of their identity. In fact, it would *not* be inaccurate to label Millennials the Facebook Generation. It's not just that a whopping 85% of Millennials report they are on Facebook; it's also that almost three-quarters spend a minimum of one hour on Facebook every day!

No one could have predicted that Facebook would become the ubiquitous and dominant force that it has become in the lives of Millennials. Facebook's Millennial co-founder Mark Zuckerberg couldn't even have predicted the future impact of this social network (Kirkpatrick, 2010).

The speed with which Facebook reached over 900 million users (Facebook, n.d.) since its 2004 launch is unprecedented in the history of adoption of media and technology. Though Facebook's roll out across the world began on a college campus, within two and a half years, anyone over 12 years of age could join the social networking site, and many of them did, which is why if Facebook were a country, it would be three times as large as the population of the United States and ranked the third-largest country in the world behind China and India (Grossman, 2010). Despite the fact that every generation, including Millennials, Generation X, Baby Boomers, Silent, and probably the Greatest,

TABLE 4.4 Engaging with Social Media and News: Millennials vs. Baby Boomers

	MILLENNIALS	BABY BOOMERS
Currently on Facebook	85%	62%
Facebook active 1 hr+ Daily	72%	44%
Read mostly non-news magazines	68%	70%
Get news while online doing something else	53%	49%
Get news primarily from TV	53%	51%
Access news online with laptop	51%	34%
Read e-mailed news links often	46%	43%
Purposely search for news while online	45%	46%
Have news apps on cellphone	39%	16%
Get news daily	39%	75%
Get news primarily from online	38%	21%
Access online news with desktop	28%	61%
Use news apps on cell phone often	28%	18%
Currently on Twitter	27%	9%
Read news on Twitter daily	23%	24%
Read readers' comments on news stories	23%	8%
Watch video on news Web sites often	20%	7%
Spend 10% of Facebook time getting news	19%	8%
Access news with smartphone and apps	17%	2%
Watch slideshows posted on news Web sites	17%	6%
See news on friends' Facebook page often	16%	6%

TABLE 4.4 (*continued*)

	MILLENNIALS	BABY BOOMERS
Read news on friends' Facebook page often	16%	9%
Watch *Daily Show* often	15%	4%
Watch *Colbert Report* often	13%	4%
Text a news story often	11%	1%
Have iPad or tablet computer	11%	5%
Click on most news links	9%	6%
Post news on Facebook page often	9%	3%
Comment on news story often	9%	5%
Read non-journalist blog often	9%	0%
Tweet a news story often	8%	3%
Read journalist blog often	8%	2%
E-mail news link often	7%	4%
Upload photo to news Web site often	6%	0%
On news media Facebook page daily	6%	7%
Upload video to news Web site often	6%	0%
Someone you know e-mails news link often	4%	3%
Get news primarily from hard copy newspaper	4%	18%
Get news primarily from radio	4%	3%
Access news with iPad or tablet	2%	1%
Access news with cell phone but no apps	2%	1%

is on Facebook, Millennials dominate Facebook in the U.S., and Facebook, unlike news, is a major force in their young lives (Grossman, 2010). News, though, is not inconsequential in the lives of Millennials. Yet compared to Facebook, calling news anything but a minor player in Millennial lives would be an overstatement.

While according to Table 4.4 two-fifths (39%) of Millennials get news daily, that does not translate into news consumption as we knew it in the past. Just like the transformed news media landscape, getting news varies from consuming traditional news such as reading newspapers or watching news on TV to engaging with news on platforms that did not exist prior to 2004. For traditional news consumption, TV ranks first (53%) while hard copy newspapers (4%) and radio news (4%) are not even present on Millennials' radar. While almost two-fifths (38%) of Millennials primarily get news online, over half (53%) make it clear that news is not their destination; they're getting news while online doing something else. Still, 45% of Millennials insist they are purposely searching for news while online. But news is also searching out Millennials and it's effective. Almost half (46%) say they often read news links e-mailed to them.

In some ways, Millennials are not very different from their parents' generation of Baby Boomers when it comes to traditional news consumption, but in other ways Millennials are distinctly different. The biggest difference is in getting news daily. Baby Boomers are almost twice as likely as Millennials (75% vs. 39%) to get news daily. While getting news for the two generations differs, the rankings for where news is gotten are the same. Just like Millennials, Baby Boomers rank TV first (51%) followed by online (21%), hard copy newspapers (18%), and radio (3%). Despite the fact that hard copy newspapers ranked third in terms of absolute percentages, the difference between getting news online and getting news from hard copy newspapers was not significant. Baby Boomers, though, are not very different from Millennials in purposely searching for news. They are similar to Millennials in getting news while online doing something else. And just like Millennials, Baby Boomers often read news links e-mailed to them.

To engage with news, news first has to be accessed, and accessing news online is different from accessing news offline. To access news offline, one might pick up a newspaper and scan the headlines on the front page or turn on the TV and flip to the network news, or tune the car radio to a station that announces the latest news headlines. That's how Baby Boomers grew up accessing news. Millennials, though, have come of age with a choice in accessing news—offline or online—and to the extent that Millennials are engaging with news at all, accessing news online is winning. A close look at how

Millennials and Baby Boomers access news online reveals the difference is primarily in the mobility of their entryway to the online news world. In general, Millennials are more likely than Baby Boomers to access online news using a device that is mobile, such as a laptop computer or smartphone with apps; Baby Boomers, though, are more likely to use the trusted non-mobile desktop computer. As can be seen from Table 4.4, over half (51%) of Millennials use a laptop to access news online while one-third (34%) of Baby Boomers do so. Additionally, Millennials are eight times more likely than Baby Boomers (17% vs. 2%) to access news using a smartphone with apps to get news online. Plus, Millennials are more likely than Baby Boomers to use the news apps on their cell phones often (28% vs. 18%).

Although the desktop computer ranks second for the Millennial method of getting news online, Millennials are half as likely as Baby Boomers (28% vs. 61%) to use this stationary computer equipment to get news online. Not surprisingly, a cell phone with Internet access but no apps is barely a factor in getting news for both Millennials and Baby Boomers; the same can be said for iPads and other tablet computers, but that is expected to change in the near future as the price comes down and more tablet computers are adopted.

Has the transformed news media landscape changed the relationship with news for both Millennials and Baby Boomers? Does the more encompassing term news engagement also better explain Baby Boomer activity in the altered news media environment, or are Baby Boomers sticking with traditional news consumption as we've known it? According to the National Survey of News Engagement results, Baby Boomers are, indeed, engaging with news beyond traditional news consumption, but not as much as Millennials, whether it's multimedia or opinion platforms.

With the changed news media landscape, multimedia platforms and digital tools, such as video, photo galleries, and hyperlinks, have not only added value to the news available to consumers, but in some cases have blurred the lines between news produced by print and broadcast. Video is no longer the exclusive domain of TV news; video can also be found on a newspaper's Web site. The same is true for a printed story; a TV station and the public radio station post text versions of stories broadcast on their Web sites. While this added value has the potential to enhance consumer engagement with news, it is not a given that consumers will actually engage with news using these platforms. By scanning Table 4.4, it becomes clear, for example, that Baby Boomers are less likely than Millennials to engage with news by watching videos (7% vs. 20%) and slideshows (6% vs. 17%) posted on the Web site.

Baby Boomers and Millennials, though, are not that different when it comes to clicking on links to dig deep for background and context in news stories. Even so, clicking on links appears to have little appeal for both generations. Only 9% of Millennials and 6% of Baby Boomers click on most links integrated into news stories.

Engaging with Opinion Platforms

In addition to the multimedia platforms and hyperlinks that offer new opportunities to engage with news, a variety of platforms for engaging with opinion have also emerged over the past decade and a half. These opinion platforms include reader comments, fake news programs, and blogs.

Traditionally, letters to the editor were the platform for readers to offer their opinions on the news. Although an unlimited number of opinion letters might be mailed to the editor, only a small sample would be published in the newspaper. After newspapers expanded their reach on the Web, they would often publish additional letters that did not make it to print. Today, online comments are edited for a new type of opinion feature (McElroy, 2012). The opinions that news consumers offer on news stories appear to appeal more to Millennials than Baby Boomers. In fact, according to results from the National Survey of News Engagement, Millennials were three times (23% vs. 8%) more likely than Baby Boomers to read readers' comments.

In today's news media setting, there is a different kind of opinion platform that did not exist in the traditional news media landscape—the fake news show. By satirizing the news and poking fun at newsmakers who are often politicians, and showing actual clips from the real news, *The Daily Show* and *The Colbert Report* are not shy about sharing their opinions. The clever editing and Jon Stewart's "reporting" on citizens protesting Wall Street's excesses and reckless behavior that led to the U.S. economic meltdown made politicians and pundits look silly, selfish, and out of touch (Parks and Demonstration, 2011).

While some believe that Millennials get their news exclusively from these programs that have made satirizing the news an art form, statistics reveal little evidence to support that notion. According to the National Survey of News Engagement, only 15% of Millennials watch *The Daily Show* often and 13% watch *The Colbert Report* often.[1] Still, these fake news shows are more popular with Millennials than the older Baby Boomers, who are far less likely to watch them. Regardless of the low regular viewership by Millennials and Baby Boomers, these satirical news programs have an impact that extends beyond actually watching them. Not only are segments of *The Daily Show* and *The Colbert Report*, which originally air on Comedy Central, often posted on YouTube for everyone to view and share, it's also not unusual for the network evening news, and the Sunday morning talk shows, such as *Meet the Press* and ABC's *This Week*, to incorporate segments of the satire in their own news content.

In addition to reader comments and fake news shows, blogs offer an opportunity to engage with opinion in the news media landscape. When blogs first emerged in the news media landscape, journalists initially dismissed them but later embraced them out of, perhaps, a blend of survival and recognition that blogs might represent a new source for news on one hand and a unique platform that allowed journalists to update ongoing news and even offer analysis and perspective not allowed in traditional news formats (Meraz, 2008).

Despite the lack of an across-the-board blogger code of ethics, for some news consumers, blogs are considered more credible than traditional news media (Meraz, 2008, p. 131). Though a part of the transformed news media environment, blogs, whether written by non-journalists or journalists, are not particularly popular among Millennials, and they are even less popular among Baby Boomers. Still, Millennials are more likely than Baby Boomers to read non-journalist blogs often (9% vs. 0%), and this younger generation is more likely than the older Baby Boomer generation to read blogs produced by journalists (8% vs. 2%).

Is Facebook Facilitating or Obstructing News Engagement?

With the dominance of Facebook in the lives of Millennials and their engagement with news online as a result of accidentally running into news, reading news links e-mailed to them, or purposely searching for news, one would expect that Facebook would facilitate connecting Millennials to news. Several questions in the National Survey of News Engagement attempted to test this idea by identifying elements connecting Facebook, news, and Millennials. A careful look at Table 4.4 reveals Facebook has barely been a factor in connecting Millennials with news. Despite the News Feed feature—a "constantly updating list of stories from people and pages" followed on Facebook—there appears to be little connection between Facebook and news (News feed basics, n.d.).

Fewer than one-fifth (19%) of Millennials spend 10% of their time on Facebook getting news. In fact, the mean percentage of Facebook time spent getting news is 8.63%, with a median of 4.0%; that is, half of Millennials surveyed said they spent more than 4% of their Facebook time getting news and half spent less.

Despite the small percentage of Facebook time devoted to news, Millennials could engage with news more because there are several opportunities to do so, beginning with the News Feed feature, added two years after Facebook was founded (Kirkpatrick, 2010). With the News Feed, Millennials can easily notice or even read news posted on a friend's Facebook page. Additionally, Millennials can post news on their own Facebook page or get news from the news media's Facebook. Although more needs to be understood about the news on a News Feed, the results of the National Survey of News Engagement suggest that only a small percentage of Millennials are taking advantage of these Facebook opportunities to engage with news.

Facebook co-founder Mark Zuckerberg may be disappointed to learn the News Feed has not had the hoped-for results. According to *The Facebook Effect*, the News Feed was designed to engage Millennials with news. In fact, Zuckerberg saw the News Feed as "a real source of relevant news, both about your friends and about the world" (Kirkpatrick, 2010, p. 295).

Former Facebook President Sean Parker envisioned Facebook's potential for "altering the landscape of media" (Kirkpatrick, 2010, p. 296). The idea was that on Facebook you could become an editor, similar to the local newspaper editor; you would essentially have the "same power that mass media has had to beam out a message" (Kirkpatrick, 2010, p. 296).

Just as hoped, Millennials do notice news and actually read the news, but it is not an overwhelming percentage. Only 16% of Millennials in the National Survey of News Engagement said they often notice news on a friend's Facebook page or often read the Facebook-posted news. Further, only one-tenth (9%) of Millennials post news on their own Facebook pages and even fewer (6%) read news on the news media's Facebook page every day.

Twitter's emergence in the news media landscape in 2006 has also provided an opportunity to have the power of a local news editor (Kirkpatrick, 2010). Despite the fact that Twitter is included in the social networking site genre, Twitter asserts that it is not a social networking site:

> Twitter facilitates social networking, but it's not a social networking website. In fact, Twitter works quite differently from social networks: when you accept friends' requests on social networks, it usually means you appear in that person's network and they appear in yours. Following on Twitter is different, because instead of indicating a mutual relationship, following is a one-way action that means you want to receive information, in the form of tweets, from someone. Twitter allows people to opt-in to (or opt-out of) receiving a person's updates without requiring mutual following. (Following rules and best practices, n.d.)

Despite the parsing of the definition, at the moment Twitter appears to be evolving as a medium for reporting and commenting on news. Though far fewer Millennials are on Twitter than Facebook (27% vs. 85%), Twitter users are slightly more likely to read news on Twitter than Facebook users are to read news on a friend's Facebook page often (23% vs. 16%). Whether posting a news story on Facebook or tweeting a news story, this type of engagement with news is not very popular; fewer than one-tenth of Millennials engage with news by Facebook posting and news tweeting.

New Roles for Millennial News Consumers?

The myriad ways to engage with news in the transformed news media terrain make it possible for consumers to assume roles beyond that of traditional news reader, viewer, and listener. The altered news environment now makes it possible for non-journalists to assume the role of journalist and contribute to the news. Blogging, texting, and mobile devices with still and video cameras and editing apps opened the door to non-journalists being able to post and share newsworthy information and photographs. With the addition of the microblog Twitter in 2006 to the news media landscape, news reporting by non-journalists has gained momentum and, perhaps, achieved some of the goals that Mark Zuckerberg tried to achieve with the Facebook News Feed. Whether called citizen journalism, participatory journalism, or a host of other names, citizen journalism appears to have taken up permanent residence in the news media landscape. Citizen journalists are inspired to report news, and traditional news organizations are embracing citizen journalists, whether due to necessity or recognition of the added value to their own news content.

The idea of citizens reporting news is, of course, not new; what is new is the variety of ways that citizen journalists can report the news and the extent to which the news media has embraced this new form of reporting. From CNN's iReports to *The New York Times'* requests for photos of Hurricane Irene damage, news organizations have additional sources of news and, in a way, expanded their news staffs in times when newsrooms have been downsized. While citizen journalists may not consider themselves journalists, organizations try to instill journalistic standards in them. For example, when *The New York Times* requested photos of Hurricane Irene, the hurricane that in 2011 went up the East Coast killing 44 people, shutting down the subway in New York City, and causing more than $7 billion of damage, it did not throw journalistic guidelines to the hurricane winds—it laid down some journalistic rules for reporting news and submitting photos (Hurricane Irene death toll, 2011; Cooper, 2011).

The New York Times posted the following request to its readers: "As Hurricane Irene makes landfall on the East Coast this weekend, send us photographs of early evacuations, storm scenes and damage in your area. Please include the time and location of the photo" (Scenes from the storm, 2011). Upon submitting photos, readers were informed of the following journalistic guidelines:

> By submitting to us, you are promising that the content is original, doesn't plagiarize from anyone or infringe a copyright or trademark, doesn't violate anybody's rights and isn't libelous or otherwise unlawful or misleading. You are agreeing that we can use your submission in all manner and media of The New York Times and that we shall have the right to authorize third parties to do so. And you agree to the rules of our Member Agreement, found online at http://www.nytimes.com/ref/membercenter/help/agree.html. (Scenes from the storm, 2011)

With citizen journalism now part of the news media environment, the question becomes: Are Millennials adopting the role of citizen journalist? Results from the National Survey of News Engagement suggest that Millennials are indeed participating in citizen journalism; furthermore, citizen journalism is not homogenous. According to the survey results, there appear to be four types of citizen journalists: citizen reporters, citizen photojournalists, citizen commentators, and citizen editors. If uploading photos and videos to news Web sites often constitutes being a citizen photojournalist, then according to Table 4.4, 6% of Millennials would fall into this category. None of the Baby Boomers (0%) said they had uploaded a photo or video to a news Web site. Almost one-tenth (9%) of Millennials would be classified as citizen commentators; half as many Baby Boomers (5%) indicated they comment on news stories often.

Just as newsrooms have editors who determine what ultimately gets published, broadcast, or posted, the transformed news environment has citizen editors who serve a similar role by texting, posting, tweeting, and e-mailing news stories. As can be seen in Table 4.4, Millennials are more likely than Baby Boomers to perform these editorial roles in the altered news terrain; Millennials are more likely than Baby Boomers to text a news story often (11% vs. 1%), post news on Facebook often (9% vs. 3%), and tweet a news story often (8% vs. 3%). As far as e-mailing a news story, Millennials have a slight edge over Baby Boomers (7% vs. 4%).

While these citizen journalism functions have been made possible by the transformed news media landscape, mobile devices such as smartphones and tablet computers with apps have made this editorial function easy and fast. Using a smartphone, it literally takes seconds to text or e-mail a story. Posting news on Facebook and tweeting a news story may take longer, but not much.

The idea of a citizen editor is not new; in yesterday's news media environment, it wasn't unusual to read the newspaper, find an article of interest, clip it, and share it with a neighbor or mail it to a friend or relative. That very act of sharing the news said the news was important. Now, with the convenience of a mobile device, within seconds you can share a news story by texting, e-mailing, posting, or tweeting. Through Facebook's News Feed and Twitter's 140 characters, one could function like an editor and let those connected to you know that the news you are texting, e-mailing, posting, or tweeting is important and worth paying attention to.

As Table 4.4 reminds us, there is no shortage of platforms for accessing news, and the opportunities to be exposed to news, whether intentionally or unintentionally, are unlimited. News can be connected to anytime of the day or night and from wherever one might be. News can even find us when we think we're disconnected. CNN and *The New York Times* will break through an iPad in the off position to deliver the big news story of the moment. And for those with a citizen editor in their inner circle, there is no escape from news. Citizen editors will deliver the news to their friends and followers whether by text, e-mail, Facebook, or Twitter.

While lack of availability of news may have been a legitimate excuse for older generations who did not read, watch, or listen to news, that is not an excuse Millennials can use. Despite the fact that today news is available, accessible, and unavoidable, too few Millennials are enaged with it. Additional insight into why Millennials do not engage with news will be addressed in Chapter 5; how to engage Millennials with news before it's too late will be addressed in Chapter 7.

Note

1. The results of the National Survey of News Engagement are similar to the Pew Research Center findings on viewership of *The Daily Show* and *The Colbert Report*. In the National Survey of News Engagement, 15% of Millennials (ages 18–29) reported watching *The Daily Show* often; the Pew study found 13% of 18–29-year-olds watched *The Daily Show* regularly. Regular 18–29-year-old viewership of *The Colbert Report* in the Pew Research Center study was 13%; in the National Survey of News Engagement, 13% of Millennials (18–29-year-olds) reported watching *The Colbert Report* often (Americans spending more time, 2010, p. 94).

· 5 ·

RACE AND ETHNICITY, GENDER, AND POLITICAL IDENTITY IN MILLENNIAL NEWS ENGAGEMENT

Racial and ethnic diversity may get the headline when the Millennial Generation is described but gender and political identity are at least as important when news engagement is the focus of the discussion.
—PAULA POINDEXTER

Millennials are different from generations that came before them, and within their own generation, they are not the same. Peter Levine, director of CIRCLE (The Center for Information & Research on Civic Learning & Engagement) underscored that point at the Millennials and News Summit held at the University of Texas at Austin when he said: "When we talk about Millennials as if they were a group, we obscure enormous differences among them, differences which by far dwarf the differences between them and previous generations." Three areas in which Millennials differ from previous generations include: racial and ethnic composition, women surpassing men in attaining college educations, and voters who connected with the 2008 presidential election through the Internet and turned out in record numbers. Racial and ethnic diversity may get the headline when the Millennial Generation is described, but gender and political identity are at least as important when news engagement is the focus of the discussion. We will therefore closely examine race and ethnicity, gender, and political identity to determine their role in this generation's relationship with news. The question then is: Are race and ethnicity, gender, and political identity facilitators or obstacles to the Millennial Generation's engagement with news?

Race, Ethnicity, and News

The Millennial Generation is called the most racially and ethnically diverse because when compared with Generation X, Baby Boomers, the Silent Generation, and the Greatest Generation, there are far fewer whites and far more people of color. According to the National Survey of News Engagement, whites are slightly more than a majority of the Millennial Generation and African Americans, Hispanics, Asian Americans, and others represent over two-fifths (see Table 5.1).

With such a robust representation of racial and ethnic groups, the question is: What role, if any, do race and ethnicity play in news engagement and attitudes toward news? An analysis of the National Survey of News Engagement reveals in the news engagement arena, races and ethnicities are more alike than different; yet, there are some differences that are noteworthy and in some cases, troubling.

TABLE 5.1 Millennial Portrait: Race and Ethnicity

RACE AND ETHNICITY:	
White	55%
African American	14%
Hispanic or Latino	14%
Asian American	13%
Native American	1%
Other	3%

One noteworthy difference is the racial identity of one type of citizen journalist; a troubling difference is the racial identity of Millennials assigning failing grades to the news media's coverage of their generation. For Millennial citizen journalists, it is noteworthy that race and ethnicity matter for one of the four citizen

TABLE 5.2 The Role of Race and Ethnicity in News Engagement and Attitudes

	WHITE	AFRICAN AMERICAN	HISPANIC	ASIAN AMERICAN
Upload photo often	7%	5%	0%	14%
Upload video often	5%	5%	0%	18%
Agree most news is biased	40%	29%	8%	22%
Grade F for coverage of young people	4%	25%	0%	4%

journalist types introduced in Chapter 4. Specifically, Asian Americans were more likely than whites, African Americans, and Hispanics to act as citizen photojournalists by uploading photos and videos to news Web sites (see Table 5.2). For the other three types of citizen journalists—citizen reporters, citizen editors, and citizen commentators—there were no racial or ethnic distinctions.

It is also noteworthy that when the Millennial Generation was asked to express its feelings about news, race tapped into the very essence of what journalism should be: unbiased. Specifically, when Millennial participants in the National Survey of News Engagement were asked to agree or disagree with the statement, "Most news is biased," whites (40%) were most likely to agree with that statement followed by African Americans (29%) and Asian Americans (22%); less than one-tenth of Hispanics agreed that most news is biased.

Though three of the four racial/ethnic groups thought news was biased, only one group assigned the news media a failing grade for coverage of its cohort. In fact, African Americans were at least six times more likely than whites, Asian Americans, and Hispanics to give the news media an F grade. The reasons for the F grade included lack of interest by their generation, the news media's failure to include them in the news, and the news media's emphasis on negative stories about them.

A 20-year-old African American male best articulated the reasons news media coverage of his age group deserved an F when he said: "I strongly dislike the image the news puts out there about my age group." He emphasized that "not all people between 18 to late twenties are killers, robbers, etc." This young man was likely knowledgeable about the news media's coverage of his age group because he is an avid news consumer. Not only does he get the news daily, he also prefers state news followed by local news. While this Millennial primarily gets his news from TV, he also gets news while on his laptop. He doesn't purposely search for news but he still gets it on Yahoo.com, perhaps, because that's his homepage. Also, he gets news online because someone he knows e-mails news to him. Additionally, he often sees news on a friend's Facebook page that he occasionally reads. And, he added, one day a week, he gets news from the media's Facebook page. Answers to several questions made it clear that this young man's engagement with news is as a consumer—not a citizen journalist. He said that he does not text news or post news on his Facebook page, and he does not upload video or photographs to news media Web sites. Also, this young man said he is not on Twitter.

While it's impossible to say with any certainty that the news environment in which this Millennial grew up has played a role in his news engagement today, research suggests a likely correlation. His exposure to news, though, was not in the classroom but at home. This young man said his teachers did not include newspapers in his classroom, but news was around him at home all of the time. Most of the time, the TV was tuned to news around dinner time; news discussions took place at home some of the time, and occasionally, newspapers were around. Perhaps the most powerful news socialization agent in this Millennial's life was his father, who told him being informed about news is important.

This young African American man's negative assessment of news coverage was not very different from most of the young African American men who shared their opinions about how news represented them at the one-day summit "Evolving the Image of the African American Male in American Media," organized by University of Pittsburgh Vice Chancellor for Public Affairs Robert Hill and funded by The Heinz Endowments. This first-of-its-kind summit held up a mirror to the news media's coverage of African American males and what was reflected back was unsettling, if not alarming. Following the summit, Vice Chancellor Hill described the essence of the research, and summit criticisms of news media coverage of young African American men, in an op-ed column published in the *Pittsburgh Post-Gazette*: "…young black men and boys rarely appear in daily national and local American news media. But, when they do, the tendency is to present them as the focus of crime coverage, replete with mug shots and perp walks" (Hill, 2011).

One summit panel titled "A Conversation Among Young African American Males" gave voice to Millennial criticisms about news media coverage and echoed the F grade that African American Millennials were more likely to give the news media in the National Survey of News Engagement. Ironically, the complaints of the Millennial panelists about negative portrayals of African Americans were not only similar to criticisms in the 1968 Kerner Commission Report (Report of the National Advisory Commission on Civil Disorders, 1968), they were consistent with negative portrayals documented in four decades of scholarly research, which show that African Americans are excluded from the news, or that when they are included they are mostly stereotyped as criminals, impoverished, entertainers, or athletes (Dixon & Linz, 2000; Entman, 1994; Gilliam & Iyengar, 2000; Poindexter, 2011; Poindexter, Smith, & Heider, 2003).

The majority of the young African American men who spoke on the summit panel were in college and one, Ashton Gibbs, was both a basketball star and an honors student. Gibbs (2011), who plays for Pitt's varsity men's basketball team, observed that the news media only wants to report on players' activities on the basketball court, thus reinforcing the African American athlete stereotype: "We're doing even better things off the court," he said, "but that doesn't get covered" (Gibbs, 2011).

It's one thing to omit off-the-court contributions in news coverage; it's another thing, and far more disturbing, to portray young African American males as what another Millennial panelist described as "prime suspects" who are "automatically guilty." Unfortunately, this young man's criticism is not new or unique; this criticism is consistent with what scholars who study news coverage of African Americans have documented for decades:

> Beginning in the 1970s, the most frequently reported news story that included African Americans "concerned possible crime or past criminal activity on the part of blacks" (Roberts 1975, 2). The criminal stereotype of African Americans has been particularly salient in broadcast news, whether local or national. Images have not been of just any type of criminal but of violent and menacing criminals. Studies have found African Americans were significantly more likely than Anglo Americans to be shown in stories about violent crime (Entman 1992). African Americans were also more likely to be shown as suspects in murder stories despite the fact that "blacks do not account for the largest number of murders" (Gilliam & Iyengar 2000, 562). African Americans were also "more likely to be portrayed as perpetrators of crime even though arrest statistics do not support that representation" (Dixon & Linz 2000, 145). Finally, African Americans were "more likely to be portrayed as felons on television news than to be arrested for felonies (44 percent vs. 25 percent)" (Dixon & Linz 2000, 146). (Poindexter, 2011, pp. 110–111)

Since more than four decades ago when researchers first documented the negative images of African Americans in the news, three generations—Baby Boomers, Generation X, and Millennials—have completed or begun the passage through young adulthood. Despite increased racial and ethnic diversity for each successive generation, the negative image of African Americans in the news has remained the same. The news media's tendency to portray African Americans in a negative light is not only inconsistent with responsible journalism and bad for African Americans and society as a whole; this type of coverage creates another obstacle to Millennial news engagement that may be impossible to overcome.

Gender and News

Just because gender gets less attention when the Millennial Generation is discussed, it does not mean gender is less important in the news engagement equation. As results of the National Survey of News Engagement show, in some areas of engagement with news, the gender gap is as pronounced among Millennials as some of the entrenched gender gaps that can be found in salaries and hourly wages, in corporate boardrooms and executive suites, among university full professors and administrators, in Congress and the White House, in the fields of science, technology, engineering, and mathematics, and in newsrooms and online and offline news stories. But for Millennials, there is one area in which the gender gap not only closed, it flipped: education attainment. "In the Boomer and Silent generations, men exceeded women in college attendance and graduation rates" (Pew Research Center - Millennials: A portrait, 2010). The beginnings of this gender gap reversal were first evident as Generation X began to go to college. Now that Wave I Millennials have gone to college, more women than men are "graduating from or attending college" (Pew Research Center-Millennials: A portrait, 2010). To put this in a generational context: Among Baby Boomer parents of Millennials, fathers were more likely than mothers to have attended and graduated college; for Millennial children of Baby Boomers, daughters are more likely than sons to have gone to college and graduated.

Despite the gender gap in attending and graduating college that exists among Millennials, Millennial males and females are more similar than different when it comes to engagement with news and social media. Still, in a few key areas, a pronounced gender gap is evident, starting with a 17-point difference in news consumption (see Table 5.3). Millennial females are far less likely than Millennial males (36% vs. 53%) to consume news six or more days a week. The gender gap in news consumption, regardless of age, was the focus of

Women, Men, and News: Divided and Disconnected in the News Media Landscape (Poindexter, Meraz, & Schmitz Weiss, 2008), but that gender gap pales in comparison when the focus is on young adults in the Millennial Generation. The National Survey of News Engagement data suggests that Millennial females may be even more endangered as news consumers than their male counterparts.

Because education is highly correlated with news consumption, Millennial women who surpass Millennial men in attending and graduating college should also surpass men in news consumption. But that is not the case. Furthermore, if young educated women are not consuming news, what will they do as they grow older, and what are the implications for the children of this generation if a child's first role model for news consumption becomes extinct?

The reasons behind the seemingly persistent gender gap with women consuming news less than men include: exclusion of women from the news pages, and second-tier news coverage when they are included (Poindexter, 2008a; Desmond & Danilewicz, 2010). This exclusion and second-tier coverage may be a reflection of fewer women among newsroom personnel. Yet, even when women run newsrooms, their editorial decision-making is similar to men's, so the news content doesn't change, at least according to the first study to look at women as the gatekeeper (Bleske, 1991). In fact, two decades later when Jill Abramson was appointed executive editor of *The New York Times*, becoming the first woman to hold that post in the 160-year history of that venerable newspaper, she virtually agreed with that research finding about female gatekeepers when she said: "The idea that women journalists bring a different taste in stories or sensibility isn't true" (Brisbane, 2011).

While college-educated Millennial women may not care whether the newsroom is led by a woman or a man, they likely care whether the news is in touch with and respectful of the lives they lead and the opportunities they have. Not only are women's voices not included in the news, newsmakers don't look like them. In other words, the gender gap in the news pages may appear far wider than the gender gap that actually exists in today's society.

A gender gap is also apparent when the focus is on *The Daily Show* and *The Colbert Report*. Millennial males were five times more likely than Millennial females to watch *The Daily Show* often, and four times more likely to watch *The Colbert Report* often. Millennial males were also far more likely than Millennial females to read a journalist's blog, and they were more likely than Millennial females to say that someone they knew e-mailed them a news link often.

Females are not just less likely than males to consume news regularly, watch fake news shows, or read a journalist's blog, they also prefer different news. While females are half as likely as males to rank national news as their preferred category of news (19% vs. 44%), they are almost twice as likely as males to prefer local news (54% vs. 28%).

Despite their higher level of engagement with news, Millennial males appeared to be more cynical about news than females. Millennial males were almost twice as likely as Millennial females to agree that the news media cared little about people like them, and males were less likely than females to *disagree* with the statement that keeping up with the news is a waste of time. While this contradiction between what both males and females do with news and what they think about news is puzzling, it does underscore that beliefs about the importance of news may not lead to engagement with news if social media and other factors are standing in the way.

TABLE 5.3 News Consumption and Attitude Differences of Millennial Males and Females

	MALE	FEMALE
Consume news 6–7 days per week	53%	36%
National news is preferred	44%	19%
Local news is preferred	28%	54%
Watch *Daily Show* often	27%	5%
Watch *Colbert Report* often	23%	5%
Read journalist's blog often	14%	2%
Someone e-mails you news often	9%	0%
Agree media cares little about people like you	33%	18%
Disagree keeping up with news is a waste of time	47%	66%

Political Identity and News

It is, perhaps, rare when the Millennial Generation is discussed that political identity is emphasized. Even for other generations, political identity was rarely referenced except when Baby Boomers and the Silent Generation made the passage into adulthood. For young Baby Boomers as well as the second wave of the Silent Generation, there was both a political and civic identity as those generations fought for civil and voting rights, equality for women, and against the Viet Nam War. While young African Americans, especially college students, were identified with sit-ins, freedom rides, voter registration drives, and some of the most dangerous civil rights marches across the segregated South, young Silent Generation and Baby Boomer women fought for equal rights and equal pay with their male counterparts, and males who were required to serve in the armed forces, whether they wanted to or not, fiercely protested against the war in Viet Nam. No doubt these experiences, both the good and the bad, helped shape the political identities of these generations. It was also at this young age that Baby Boomers became the beneficiaries of the adoption of the Twenty-Sixth Amendment to the U.S. Constitution, which by lowering the voting age to 18 forever linked their generation to the highest turnout ever in a presidential election when they turned out to vote in 1972.

Political identity, unlike race, ethnicity, and gender identities that people are born with, can vary in meaning depending on how individuals identify themselves. For example, individuals who describe themselves as moderate Democrats or conservative Republicans are identifying with a political party and ideology. Political party and ideology are some of the political identities that scholars use to explain political participation, such as voting. But political identity is not just for understanding political participation; political identity when defined by party, ideology, or even turnout during a presidential election can also provide insight into news engagement.

A larger percentage of Millennials identify with the Democratic Party, while Republicans and Independents can each claim one-fourth of this generation. But despite the Millennials who identify with Republicans and Independents, according to the Pew Research Center: "Millennials have come of age professing an allegiance to the Democratic Party and profoundly little identification with the GOP" (The generation gap and the 2012 election, 2011, p. 5). As far as ideology, most Millennials identify with the middle, according to the National Survey of News Engagement. The ends of the political spectrum about equally appeal to Millennial conservatives and liberals (see Table 5.4).

TABLE 5.4 Millennials' Political Party Identification and Ideology

POLITICAL PARTY IDENTIFICATION:	
Democrat	38%
Republican	27%
Independent	27%
Other	8%
IDEOLOGY:	
Conservative	24%
Middle of the Road	42%
Liberal	28%
Other	5%

Because some groups have a history of turning out to vote more than others, turnout has also come to signify political identity. Senior citizens, for example, are known for a high turnout during a presidential election, while a low turnout traditionally has been associated with young adults. But in 2008 it was no longer accurate to say young people did not turn out to vote. Just as the turnout in the 1972 presidential election helped define the political identity of Baby Boomers as a generation, the record turnout in the 2008 presidential election helped define the political identity of the Millennial Generation.

> When 23 million young people voted in the 2008 presidential election, they made history. It was the largest turnout of young voters in almost four decades, according to CIR-CLE, the Center for Information and Research on Civic Learning and Engagement. The participation of this young age group, known more for its history of not voting than voting, sent a powerful message: Young voters matter. (Poindexter, 2010b)

Heather Smith, head of the young voter education and registration advocacy group Rock the Vote, which in 1992 helped 350,000 young people register to vote and in 1993 helped the Motor Voter bill become law (Rock the Vote, n.d.), called the 2008 turnout "truly a remarkable moment" (Harris, 2008). The turnout was not only remarkable because of its impact on the outcome of the presidential election, it was extraordinary because it transformed how young voters are perceived: "No longer can pundits and politicians say we don't vote," the Rock the Vote executive director said.

In 2012, this turnout dimension of the Millennial Generation's political identity could, of course, revert to the old image, especially because "more often than not [young voters have] ignored their civic responsibility and skipped elections" (Poindexter, 2010b). What young voters do in the future is not just about how they perceive their own political identity; it is also about how others view them.

Embracing their civic responsibility and turning out to vote in future elections would provide consistency to the Millennial political identity. If Millennials turn out in 2012 like they did in 2008, "it would likely put to rest the conventional political wisdom that young adults are apathetic and fickle" (Poindexter, 2010b). Furthermore, by participating politically in 2012, young voters could shine the spotlight on issues important to them. A high turnout in the 2012 presidential election as well as future elections could also establish a political identity for this generation that says Millennials "are a voting bloc to be respected and even feared by politicians who ignore them" (Poindexter, 2010b).

Why did the conventional wisdom about young voters not apply in 2008? What accounted for the record turnout that re-defined their political identity at least for one presidential election cycle? Was this generation's racial and ethnic diversity a factor because of the historic presence of an African American on the presidential ballot? Were African American Millennials more likely than whites, Latinos, Asian Americans, and others to vote? According to the National Survey of News Engagement, the answer is: No. Gender was also not a factor and neither was ideology. In other words, it didn't appear to matter whether Millennials were African American, Latino, white or Asian American or even male or female. It also didn't matter whether they were conservative, middle of the road, or liberal. What seemed to matter most in the 2008 presidential election was whether a Millennial identified with Democrats, Republicans, or Independents. As Table 5.5 shows, in 2008, over two-thirds of Millennial Democrats and Republicans said they voted in the presidential election while only slightly more than one-third of Millennial Independents did so.

Regardless of the party affiliation dimension of their political identity, the Millennial Generation made history in 2008. While newspapers and newsmagazines, TV newscasts and news Web sites, historians and cable news pundits, as well as voters, teachers, and school children emphasized the historic election of the first African American president, Millennials were making his-

TABLE 5.5 Millennials, Political Party, and Voting for President

	DEMOCRATS	REPUBLICANS	INDEPENDENTS
Voted in 2008 presidential election	67%	69%	35%
Definitely will vote in 2012	68%	56%	37%

tory because their turnout during the 2008 presidential election was the largest turnout of young voters since 1972 when incumbent President Richard Nixon defeated South Dakota Senator George McGovern, the Democratic Party nominee. The youth turnout in the 1972 election benefited from the Twenty-Sixth Amendment to the U.S. Constitution, which, when ratified in 1971, lowered the voting age from 21 to 18, making it possible for 18-year-olds, 19-year-olds, and 20-year-olds to vote in a presidential election.

Thirty-six years later a record number of young voters also voted in the 2008 presidential contest between Democratic Party nominee Illinois Senator Barack Obama and Republican Party nominee Arizona Senator John McCain. While the driving force in the young voter turnout during the 1972 presidential election was the draft and the Vietnam War, the impetus for the turnout in 2008 was less about war—even though the U.S. was fighting two wars—and, perhaps, more about a campaign strategy that expanded the electorate to include young voters, and a digital landscape that facilitated that expansion.

During the 2008 presidential election, one candidate above all others catered to the Millennial electorate; he held many of his rallies on college campuses, where he inspired young voters with speeches that soared, and he communicated with them through the new media they had adopted with gusto. David Plouffe, the mastermind behind the Obama campaign strategy, understood that new media, which Millennials were the first to adopt, would be critical to their success, especially because "political campaigns were in many respects stuck in the Dark Ages technologically" (Plouffe, 2009, p. 36).

Despite the fact that some cynics missed the news in the Millennial turnout during the 2008 presidential election, Obama campaign manager David Plouffe did not. In fact, without the record turnout of Millennials and African Americans, the 2008 election may have had a different outcome:

The reason we won comfortably, with the highest vote percentage for a Democrat since LBJ, was that among people voting for the first time in a presidential election—or for the first time in a long time—we won by a shocking 71–27 percent. Younger voters turned out in huge numbers. African American voters turned out at roughly the same rate as white voters for the first time in the country's history. The share of the electorate over sixty-five actually dropped between 2004 and 2008, not because fewer older voters turned out but because younger ones showed up in droves. (Plouffe, 2009, p. 381)

It is, perhaps, impossible to separate the impact of the strategic use of new media, which young people had adopted as their own, and a strategy to expand the electorate by energizing Millennial voters, but there is no question that activity on the Internet, whether part of or independent of the Obama campaign, got the attention of the generation that was voting for the first time. It was no accident, for example, that the first video for Barack Obama's presidential campaign was released on YouTube, the video-sharing Web site adored by Millennials. Obama's campaign manager Plouffe noted in his book about the 2008 presidential campaign that when they released that video on June 18, 2007, "it instantly became a YouTube phenomenon" (Plouffe, 2009, p. 32). In addition to embracing YouTube, then-presidential candidate Barack Obama sent messages from his smartphone and made campaign promises with Millennial appeal. This intersection of a strategy to expand the electorate by bringing in young voters and the use of new media that Millennials had adopted may have been the difference maker in the outcome of the 2008 presidential election.

While Plouffe credits the Obama campaign's digital strategy for much of candidate Barack Obama's success, Autumn Caviness, a communications instructor who monitors the intersection of social media, race, and culture observed during a discussion we had about the 2008 presidential election that credit must be shared with will.i.am's "Yes We Can" video and the "Obama Girl" video for attracting the attention of Millennials.

will.i.am's "Yes We Can" video, which was uploaded to YouTube during the first week of February, 2008, was described by MTV as "one of the biggest Obama-boosting efforts" (Kaufman, 2008). Within one week of its YouTube posting, the video had 10 million views (Kaufman, 2008). While the use of celebrities was reminiscent of the 1985 multi-Grammy-winning "We Are the World," written by Lionel Richie and Michael Jackson and sung by "46 top recording artists in America" (Jet, 1985) to raise money to help famine victims in Africa, the black-and-white "Yes We Can" video, which also won awards and ultimately exceeded 23 million views, was distinctly different from "We Are the World." The New York Times described the format of the "Yes We Can" video as a layering of the glitterati singing and speaking the words to Mr. Obama's New Hampshire speech simultaneously (Barack Obama's New Hampshire primary, 2008) over Mr. Obama's voice. It's set to a simple guitar melody and, especially considering the amount of young pop stars involved, probably wouldn't seem too out of place on the radio. (Alexovich, 2008)

The New York Times underscored the impact that the Internet and Millennial content can have on young voters during a presidential election when it observed that will.i.am's "Yes We Can" song

> is a prime example of how the Web's user-generated content sites are undeniably affecting voter engagement this election cycle. Purchasing four and a half minutes of national TV airtime would have been near impossible, but the Internet can reach that highly sought youth audience gratis. (Alexovich, 2008)

While will.i.am's "Yes We Can" video was star-studded and professionally produced, "Obama Girl" had the look of a video that any YouTube-loving Millennial might produce. *The New York Times'* description of the video might help explain why it received over 23 million views: "The music is totally pop, though the video is all chest and cleavage, and well, a pair of red boy pants with OBAMA across the back" (Phillips, 2007). The Millennial actress featured in the video lip-syncs "I got a crush on Obama. Baby, you're the best candidate" and pictures of Obama are shown throughout: Obama in the nation's capital; Obama on the campaign trail; a shirtless and swim trunks-clad Obama vacationing in Hawaii.

The New York Times, Fox News, *Newsweek*, ABC News, as well as other news outlets extended the Obama Girl video's reach beyond YouTube by reporting it as news. After the video was posted on YouTube, *ABC News* described it as "an amusing, risqué music video, featuring a nubile young woman breathlessly singing her love for presidential candidate Sen. Barack Obama, D-Ill." (Tapper, 2007). The Obama campaign denied involvement with the video; *ABC News* reported that the "song and video took the Obama campaign by surprise" (Tapper, 2007). ABC further noted that the song and video "demonstrated how the democratic nature of the Internet—specifically Internet video on sites such as YouTube—is affecting politics in unpredictable ways" (Tapper, 2007).

Viewer comments on ABC's Obama Girl story confirmed the impact of the Internet on politics and revealed why some Millennial viewers and even parents of Millennials were as smitten with the video as Obama Girl was smitten with presidential candidate Barack Obama in the video.

> This video was fun. I went to Obama's web site after and found out more about him. I was worried about him not having enough experience but he has been in politics all his life basically. The website is awesome. I think I found my favorite candidate. (Comments, 2007)

As a young college educated female I liked the video....Obama is smart and that makes him attractive...it is time out for "Politics as usual."...Get A GRIP!!! WE have to begin to reach our younger and more urban populations and if that means videos then I am in!! I want a shirt and will order enough for other young ladies that I know. While everyone else is talking about how "BAD" the video is, I will be able to have that "conversation" about Obama and things will CHANGE!!!! Thanks Obama Girl Team....Tell your momma VOTE OBAMA!! (Comments, 2007)

Go OBAMA GIRL Go! We love the video! My 13 year old immediately bookmarked it in her favorites...followed by "Who is Obama?" FUN, FUN, FUN! This video is Americana at its finest! Definitely at its latest, up to date and freshest for American politics. You Tube is today, you tube is where every candidate wants to rock the vote and OBAMA Girl rocks it in the most refreshing hip way to come in a long time. Good for her, good for Obama! Good for the usual boring, on snooze control robotic political garbage we are fed. In our household we got a crush on Obama Girl's sense of business and marketing. We like her cute "dance" moves too. Go Obama Girl Go! (Comments, 2007)

One comment even reflected the relationship between the Obama Girl video and connecting to young voters:

Talk about 'rock' the vote. How else do you get the demographic? (Comments, 2007)

While YouTube may have been effective in getting the attention of Millennial voters during the 2008 presidential elections, it should not be forgotten that youth-targeted cable TV channels have also played important roles in educating, registering, and shaping the political identity of young voters. Over two decades ago, the music cable channel MTV focused young voter attention on the 1992 presidential race with election news reports, public service announcements, and special programming that included the appearance of then-presidential candidate Arkansas Governor Bill Clinton. This "Facing the Future with Bill Clinton" installment of MTV's "Choose or Lose" special presidential election programming not only got the attention of young voters, it made the young music cable channel a player in the presidential election. The Chairman and CEO of MTV said the goal of the program was to "'demystify' the political process by making 'young people the king of the show'" (Ifill, 1992, p. A12).

Young people were definitely in control of the town hall-style program as they asked what *The New York Times* described as "blunt" and "impolite" questions of the presidential candidate (Ifill, 1992, p. A12). The questions and heartfelt answers by then-presidential candidate Bill Clinton not only paid dividends at the polls when young people turned out to vote, but MTV's reach multiplied exponentially when traditional news organizations such as *The New York*

Times reported the unprecedented event. The news about MTV's Choose or Lose segment with Bill Clinton likely was even bigger because his opponent refused MTV's invitation to participate in a similar town hall. Calling MTV the "teeny-bopper network," Bush 41, the first George Bush to be elected president, may have thought MTV wasn't a dignified forum for an incumbent president despite the fact that he was running for re-election (Miller, 1992).

While the appearance of presidential contender Bill Clinton on MTV received lots of attention from mainstream news media, MTV was not the only cable channel delivering presidential election programming to a youthful audience. Black Entertainment Television (BET) cable network "provided two-minute updates throughout both conventions and aired live 30-minute specials from the convention floor on the last day of each convention" (Dennis, 1992, p. 56). Additionally, Comedy Central provided nightly convention satire called Indecision 92. With its limited and focused presidential election coverage in 1992, Comedy Central was a bit player in the election coverage arena, but that has since changed with the emergence of *The Daily Show*.

Created in 1996 and hosted by Craig Kilborn until 1999 when Jon Stewart became the anchor, *The Daily Show* is now a major player in presidential election coverage, and its reach extends far beyond the comedy cable channel despite the fact that its brand of news is "unburdened by objectivity, journalistic integrity, or expensive graphics" (About the Daily Show, n.d.).

While *The Daily Show* may not take itself seriously, political scientists and journalism scholars have taken it seriously as they have sought to understand the fake news show's attraction and impact, especially during a presidential election season. For example, an Annenberg Public Policy Center (2004) study during the 2004 presidential contest between Massachusetts senator John Kerry and incumbent president George W. Bush found *The Daily Show* attracted viewers who were "more interested in the presidential campaign, more educated, younger, and more liberal than the average American…" (2004).

But just because it doesn't take itself seriously, it doesn't mean *The Daily Show* doesn't take coverage of the presidential campaign trail seriously. *The Daily Show* not only devotes countless programs to the presidential election, it also brands its presidential election coverage just like network news and cable news programs brand their election coverage. But in keeping with its image, *The Daily Show*'s presidential election coverage slogan of "Indecision" plus the year of the presidential contest is less serious than the more staid news networks. As a result of devoting so many hours to the 2008 presidential election, "Indecision 2008" likely had more of an impact on young voters in 2008 than MTV's 1992

"Choose or Lose" town hall with presidential candidate Bill Clinton. But it's also likely that *The Daily Show* had more of an impact on young voters because of the format of its presidential election coverage. In real journalism, *The Daily Show*'s method of editing real news footage would get a journalist fired, but *The Daily Show* is not doing real journalism; it's making fun of and exposing presidential candidates and the real journalists who cover them. Even if you didn't get that *The Daily Show* was making fun, Jon Stewart's facial expressions and impeccably timed pauses would clue you in. In fact, *The Daily Show*'s clever editing of journalists' comments from the varied network and cable news shows often reveals that the real journalists are frequently more "over the top" than the presidential candidates or even *The Daily Show*.

For example, "Baracknophobia," episode #13079, which aired June 16, 2008 and received over 330,000 views, exposed the news media for outrageous and unfounded reporting about Barack Obama (Baracknophobia, 2008). "Headlines-Gaffe-in" (2008), which aired April 14, 2008, and received over 400,000 views, made fun of Barack Obama, Hillary Clinton, the media, the American people, and hypocrisy in the same episode.

Although it received far fewer views than "Baracknophobia" and "Headlines-Gaffe-in," episode #13094 "Press Favors Obama" (2008) didn't just make fun of the press; *Daily Show* anchor Jon Stewart leveled a stinging criticism at the press. With its clever editing of comments made by news anchors and reporters, this episode exposed a press failing in its responsibility to deliver unbiased reports on the contenders for president of the United States in 2008.

No One Factor Can Take Credit for the 2008 Turnout That is Associated with Millennials' Political Identity

It was likely a multitude of factors—Millennial-appealing candidate, Obama campaign strategy to expand the electorate and use the power of the Internet for communications, the will.i.am and Obama Girl videos posted on YouTube, *The Daily Show*'s laugh-out-loud mocking of presidential candidates, campaign trail silliness and news media coverage, and young voter education and advocacy groups such as Rock the Vote—that interacted to produce a potent effect, because according to analysis by the U.S. Census Bureau, "citizens between the ages of 18 to 24 were the only age group to show a statistically significant increase in turnout." In 2008, turnout among Millennial voters 18 to 24 was

49%, a two-percentage point increase from 2004's 47%. Commenting on the increased turnout, the U.S. Census said:

> This represents the second straight presidential election where young citizens significantly increased their voting rates. Over the last two presidential elections, young citizens have increased their voting rate by a total of 12 percent, compared to 4 percent for 25 to 44-year-olds and 1 percent for 45 to 64-year-olds. (Voting and Registration, 2010)

One factor that makes this increase in the 2008 presidential election among the youngest adults even more remarkable is what Peter Levine, Director of CIRCLE, calls the "delay" dimension in the "developmental trajectory." Speaking at the Millennials and News Summit held at the University of Texas at Austin, Levine said that voting is one of several rites of passage that young people now start later in life. According to Levine: "the average age of first marriage has gone way up. The average age when people become financially independent of their parents goes way up. So it's not too surprising that the age when they start voting should go up."

The "delay" factor, though, must have been dormant in 2008, because turnout did increase among the youngest voters, strengthening the argument that the multitude of factors identified thus far were at play in Barack Obama's successful presidential election. Will similar factors have an effect in 2012? Will young voter turnout increase for a third presidential election? Will political identity as defined by political party play a role in 2012 as it did in 2008? The same percentage of Millennial Democrats and Independents who voted in the 2008 presidential election say they intend to vote in 2012. But for Millennial Republicans, a smaller percentage plans to vote, according to the National Survey of News Engagement. Still, over half of Millennial Republicans intend to vote, which is far more than the 37% of Millennial Independents who said they will likely vote in the 2012 presidential election.

While it is not surprising that political identity, when defined as political party, is a factor in presidential election voting, it is somewhat surprising that political party plays a role in some types of news engagement. For example, political party correlates with consuming news about the most important problem facing the country. Millennial Democrats (45%) are far more likely than Millennial Republicans (27%) and Independents (29%) to say they often keep up with news about the most important problem facing the country (see Table 5.6).

While Millennial Democrats, Republicans, and Independents can keep up with news about the most important problem facing the country online or offline, two avenues for engaging with news are only possible online. Both

TABLE 5.6 Millennials, Political Party, and News Engagement

	DEMOCRATS	REPUBLICANS	INDEPENDENTS
Often keep up with news on most important problem	45%	27%	29%
Click on most links	11%	13%	2%
Someone you know e-mails news often	7%	2%	2%

Democrats and Republicans were more likely than Independents to click on most links, presumably to get more background and context about the most important problem facing the country. Furthermore, Democrats were slightly more likely than Republicans and Independents to receive a news story e-mailed from someone they knew.

What is the connection between political identity, when defined as political party, and growing up with news and attitudes about news? Of the half dozen questions asked about the presence of news, whether at home or school, only two questions found differences based on which political party Millennials identified with (see Table 5.7). In the National Survey of News Engagement, Millennials who identified with Republicans were more likely than Millennials who identified with Democrats and Independents to have newspapers around growing up. But growing up, Millennial Democrats were the most likely and Republican Millennials were the least likely to be told being informed of news is important. Even though over half of Millennial Democrats and over one-third of Millennial Republicans were told news was important while growing up, that lesson did not seem to translate into a belief about a responsibility to keep informed once they became adults. Only Millennial Democrats and Millennial Republicans strongly agreed that they had a duty to keep informed; for Millennials who identified themselves as Independents, a sense of duty to keep informed was near zero.

Political identity as defined by political party also revealed differences in attitudes about the objectivity of news and the free availability of news on the Internet. Millennials who identified with the Republican Party were almost

TABLE 5.7 Millennials, Political Party, Socialization, and Attitudes

	DEMOCRATS	REPUBLICANS	INDEPENDENTS
Newspapers were around growing up	34%	39%	31%
Growing up someone said news is important	52%	35%	44%
Strongly agree have duty to keep informed	27%	27%	2%
Agree most news is biased	24%	44%	23%
Strongly agree all news on Internet should be free	44%	29%	35%

twice as likely as Millennial Democrats and Independents to agree that most news is biased. When it comes to the free availability of news on the Internet, a reversal of opinion between Millennial Republicans and Democrats emerged. Millennial Democrats (44%) were far more likely than Millennial Republicans (29%) to strongly agree that news on the Internet should be free. The attitude of Independents about free news on the Internet hovered between Democrats and Republicans; slightly more than one-third of Millennial Independents strongly agreed news on the Internet should be free.

Political party is one measure of political identity, but it's not the only or even most important one. Ideology is also a dimension of political identity, and it appears to matter most for socialization about news and attitudes toward news. Liberals were far more likely than conservatives to recall that while growing up, news was included in their classroom at least once a week (see Table 5.8). Millennial conservatives were more likely than Millennial liberals and Millennials who considered themselves middle of the road ideologically to agree that we have a duty to keep informed. Not surprisingly, Millennial conservatives were more likely than middle-of-the-road and liberal Millennials to agree that most news is biased.

TABLE 5.8 Millennials, Ideology, Socialization, and Attitudes

	CONSERVATIVE	MIDDLE OF THE ROAD	LIBERAL
Teacher included news at least once weekly	55%	77%	85%
Agree we have a duty to keep informed	63%	49%	58%
Agree most news is biased	42%	23%	28%

This chapter began by asking whether race and ethnicity, gender, and political identity are facilitators or obstacles to the Millennial Generation's engagement with news. By chapter's end, it is evident that if we treat all Millennials the same, we risk concealing crucial information that may help us fully understand individual factors such as race and ethnicity, gender, and political identity that may stand in the way of Millennials engaging with news. The fact that the Millennial Generation is more racially and ethnically diverse, contains more educated females, and is more cognizant of its political identity and power because of the 2008 presidential election, suggests that for this generation, race, ethnicity, gender, and political identity may indeed help explain why this generation is endangered as news consumers. In other words, when Millennials are analyzed by race, gender, and political identity, dissatisfaction with news coverage emerges as a common complaint. The data in this chapter suggest that to some degree, African American, white, female, Republican, Independent, and ideologically conservative Millennials may be less likely to consume news because they view it as negative, uncaring, biased, and without value. The good news, though, is that the news media determines what news coverage looks like, so it has the power to do something about this criticism. If, though, news organizations fail to address this negative perception about their news coverage, the news media must share responsibility for not just a generation of endangered news consumers but a future society in which news consumers no longer exist.

· 6 ·

WHAT WAVE II MILLENNIALS (KIDS) SAY ABOUT NEWS

I think people should know but kids don't NEED to know everything.
—13-YEAR-OLD GIRL WHO BELIEVES KEEPING INFORMED IS
SOMEWHAT IMPORTANT

Wave II Millennials, born approximately between 1992 and 1999, were in middle school and high school at the start of the second decade of the 21st century. Except for, perhaps, some good and bad memories about braces, learning to drive, after-school and summer jobs, and first dates, most of us can't remember, or prefer to forget, what it was like to be a kid at that age.

During the preteen and teenage years, changes abound—physical, psychological, and social, including relationships with socialization agents, whether parents, teachers, peers, or media. Of all relationships, the news media have had the weakest relationship with kids of all ages, diminishing the potential of any socializing influence. Except for some school-based programs to "grow" future news consumers or unusual goings-on that might attract a journalist's attention, the news media, especially the newspaper industry, has rarely covered kids.

It's not clear why, over the years, the newspaper industry in particular has ignored kids, especially teenagers, at the same time that many of its advertisers and the industries they cover have embraced them. Simply put, teenagers are and have been a market powerhouse. In fact, the spending power and consumption potential of the teen cohort was reported more than 50 years ago in *Businessweek, Esquire, Cosmopolitan, Time,* and *Life* magazine. *Life* magazine even compared the teenage market to General Motors, noting that teen buying power exceeded GM sales: "Counting only what is spent to satisfy their special teenage demands, the youngsters and their parents will shell out about $10 billion this year, a billion more than the total sales of GM [General Motors]" (*Life* cited in Osgerby, 2008, p. 35). Although the newspaper industry snubbed the $10 billion teen market, it's unlikely that it would have slighted a $10 billion company in its own news pages.

Unlike the newspaper industry, though, the founders of *Seventeen* magazine grasped the potential of the teenage market. "Conceived as a publication geared to college girls," only three years after its 1944 launch, *Seventeen*'s circulation was "over a million a month" (Osgerby, 2008, p. 33.); today, *Seventeen*'s audience is more than 4.7 million among girls ages 12 to 19 (*Seventeen,* n.d.). *Seventeen*'s closest competition is *Teen Vogue,* the teenage sibling of *Vogue* magazine, which has an audience of 3.6 million (*Teen Vogue,* n.d.).

In hindsight, the newspaper industry could have embraced teenagers, a cohort that could grow up to become its future readers; instead the industry at best stood on the sidelines and at worst ignored teenagers, while magazines and non-news media industries such as fashion, music, film, entertainment, cable TV, and fast-food reached out to them with enthusiasm.

Even the burgeoning computer industry understood the importance of the teenage market. By the 1980s, when computers were shrinking to fit on the tops of desks and the home computer market was exploding, the teen market was part of the computer industry's business model. Computers were discounted to schools, they included games software, and they were in family rooms and kids' bedrooms, often supplanting the TV set. Gameboy, the hand-held computer game console created by the Japanese company Nintendo, was wildly popular, and as kids passed from childhood into adolescence, a greater variety of computer-based games awaited them (Nintendo company history, n.d.).

As the computer and gaming industries targeted youth, kids responded with gusto. Ironically, the news media added beats to cover these exciting new technologically based industries that included youth in their business plans, but ignored this young cohort that was important to its future and journalistic responsibilities. Ignoring an individual, group, or cohort in the case of teenagers works both ways; the news industry didn't seek out teens and the young cohort ignored them back, except when newspapers were in classrooms and they were required to pay attention to them as part of their school work.

As newspaper reading declined as a "thoroughly institutionalized" behavior (Westley & Severin, 1964, p. 45) and fewer homes subscribed to newspapers, the classroom became more important as a gateway to news consumption, especially reading newspapers.

Historically, the inclusion of news content in the classroom has depended on state curriculum requirements, teacher initiative, textbook author approach, and news industry commitment. More and more states are adding media literacy to their curriculum requirements, which means that textbook authors are adding media literacy sections. A state requirement for media literacy or a section in an approved textbook, though, does not necessarily mean news literacy.

Perhaps one of the largest recent efforts to increase news literacy is at Stony Brook University in New York where a Center for News Literacy has been established. A separate program directed at middle and high school students and started by a retired *Los Angeles Times* journalist is the News Literacy Project. Both the Stony Brook Program and News Literacy Project seek to elevate critical thinking about news among Millennials (News literacy expands to DC, 2011). In fact, the founding dean of Stony Brook's School of Journalism, former editor of *Newsday* Howard Schneider, said their mission was to "teach the next generation of students how to separate legitimate news accounts from misinformation, propaganda, spin, and uninformed assertion" (McCormick Foundation, 2011).

Another vehicle for learning about journalism has been middle and high school journalism programs. But while middle and high schools may offer journalism as an elective, a journalism elective affects only a small percentage of students, and a middle or high school journalism course is not the same as news literacy, even though learning the purpose, principles, and process of journalism is a key dimension of news literacy. Without understanding the purpose, principles, and process of journalism, it's difficult to distinguish between legitimate news and stuff that passes for news. That's why teacher initiative and news industry commitment are so important in bringing news content to the classroom.

News enters the classroom through many doors. In fact, when I asked over a dozen middle school teachers in Austin, Texas, about news sources, other than newspapers, that they used in their classrooms, the teachers named a variety of news sources, including the Internet, local magazines, monthly publications, YouTube, blogs, *Junior Scholastic Magazine*, the Associated Press wire service, and network and local TV. Teachers use these news sources to illustrate concepts they're teaching, or they may be participating in a program that provides news content and teacher resources. Although many of these news-in-the-classroom programs are sponsored by news organizations, more often than not, the newspaper programs are originating from circulation departments rather than newsrooms.

According to the Newspaper Association of America Foundation, the idea of newspapers in schools dates back to June 8, 1795, when *The Portland* [Maine] *Eastern Herald* published an editorial extolling the benefits of reading newspapers in schools:

> Do you wish your child to improve in reading solely, give him a newspaper—it furnishes a variety, some parts of which must infallibly touch his fancy. Do you wish to instruct him in geography, nothing will so indelibly fix the relative situation of different places, as the stories and events published in the papers. In time, do you wish to have him acquainted with the manners of the country or city, to the mode of doing business, public or private; do you wish him to have a smattering of every kind of science useful and amusing, give him a newspaper—newspapers are plenty and cheap—the cheapest book that can be bought, and the more you buy the better for your children, because every part furnishes some new and valuable information. (History of NIE, n.d.)

About a century and a half after the publication of *The Portland Eastern Herald* editorial, Iphigene Ochs Sulzberger, wife of the publisher of *The New York Times*, "lent her support to requests of New York teachers for delivery of the newspaper to school classrooms," making *The New York Times* one of the first news organizations to provide newspapers to classrooms for instructional purposes (History of NIE, n.d.). But Mrs. Sulzberger, whose father Adolph S. Ochs bought *The New York Times* in 1896, did more than lend her support to teacher requests for delivery of the newspaper. According to Mrs. Sulzberger's obituary published in *The New York Times* after her death at age 97, "she also encouraged the paper to develop its potential as a classroom aid to teachers, which helped to make it the most widely circulated daily newspaper in schools and colleges" (Iphigene Ochs Sulzberger, 1990).

By the early 2000s, over 950 news organizations delivered "newspapers and educational programs to nearly 40 percent of all public school students in the United States" (History of NIE, n.d.). These newspaper programs, which became known as NIE (Newspaper in Education), provide lesson plans, training, teacher resources and recognition, as well as classroom sets of newspapers so that each student would have a newspaper to read.

While teachers ultimately decide how newspapers will be incorporated in their classrooms, Table 6.1, which displays the results of a national survey I conducted of NIE managers, shows that NIE programs produce materials to influence not just learning in the classroom, but also the society that these young

TABLE 6.1 Focus of Newspaper in Education (NIE) Curriculum Materials

% SAYING NIE PROGRAM HAS CURRICULA EMPHASIZING:	
Being a good citizen	89%
Reading comprehension skills	89%
Being an informed citizen	84%
Character education	82%
First Amendment	78%
Meeting state educational requirements	74%
Public or community service	74%
Connecting work with the "real" world	68%
Connecting global news to local community	66%
Health	66%
Purpose and principles of journalism	60%
Sports	60%
Leadership development	55%
Providing the context for news	51%
Meeting NCLB Requirements	47%
Navigating rites of passage that young people experience growing up	45%
21st-century skills	45%
Analyzing news coverage for bias	42%
Analyzing news coverage for diversity	40%

people will inherit. NIE programs, through their curricula offerings, seek to help develop good citizens with character who are informed and public-service minded. NIE programs also seek to strengthen reading comprehension skills as well as to help young people understand journalism, its purpose and principles, and First Amendment underpinnings. Although 84% of the NIE programs emphasize the importance of being informed, and 78% put the focus on the First Amendment, only 60% of the programs have curriculum materials that might qualify as news literacy, that is, emphasizing the purpose and principles of journalism. Understanding the purpose and principles of journalism, though, is not sufficient to make one news literate; the process used to produce journalism must also be understood because process answers the question: How do journalists know what they know and how do they independently verify the news they report?

With news consumers endangered in the Millennial generation, what middle and high school teachers do in their classrooms is more important than ever. Incorporating newspapers and other news sources in these middle and high school classrooms may be the last defense against a future without news consumers. When curriculum materials are considered along with the newspapers that are used in classrooms, and teacher initiative and commitment, newspapers can be more than sources of news; they can also be agents of socialization, molding young minds, helping them develop into not just future news consumers but contributors to the public good.

Public good benefits of newspapers in classrooms may not be quantifiable, but they certainly are observable. NIE managers have observed them, and so have teachers and parents. When asked in my national survey of NIE managers, "In what ways, if any, do you think newspapers in classrooms contribute to the public good," NIE managers responded that newspapers in classrooms connect, elevate, empower, transform, and protect.

Newspapers *connect* students to the real world because, as one NIE manager explained: "newspapers at school are very often the only opportunity to see what is happening in the world, in the U.S., the state…and the local community." Additionally, newspapers connect students with their families. As another NIE manager observed: "Students go home and discuss what they have read in the paper with their parents."

Newspapers in classrooms also *elevate* skills; they polish reading skills, sharpen critical thinking skills, and hone decision-making and leadership skills.

Additionally, newspapers in classrooms *empower*; as another NIE manager emphasized: "students take pride in being well-informed." This empowerment is a consequence of the role that newspapers play in *transforming* lives. As observed by another NIE manager, newspapers in the classroom contribute to the public good by helping kids become "literate, informed, voting adults." Being informed makes students "more involved in their community" and "more caring about issues." And when they are more involved, they make the "community a better place to live."

Finally, newspapers contribute to the public good because they *protect* "our First Amendment freedoms." As one NIE manager asserted: "…EVERYONE needs to understand what role the free press plays in our democracy."

Though teachers may include news in their classrooms and the benefits to individuals and the public good may be apparent, that does not mean Millennials will pay attention to news beyond their classroom requirements. There are simply too many competitors for Millennials' attention. This is particularly true for Wave II Millennials, born in the 1990s. Unlike Wave I Millennials and previous generations, Wave II Millennials have never known life without personal computers, the Internet, and the Web. Wave II Millennials are authentic Digital Natives. And unlike Wave I Millennials, who first experienced social media in college, social media such as MySpace was part of the media landscape when Wave II Millennials were in elementary school. In other words, in terms of media offerings and access, Wave II Millennials are more different than adolescent cohorts of previous generations. This difference offers news organizations, especially the newspaper industry, an opportunity for a "do-over" in its relationship with adolescent cohorts. Embracing instead of ignoring adolescents may be the difference maker in whether news consumers in the future thrive or cease to exist. As Northwestern University's Management Center, and the Newspaper Association of America Foundation found in their study of teens and online news, time is running out.

> . . . today's young people are more disengaged from news than their counterparts in previous generations were. Extensive research shows that if people aren't news consumers by the time they become adults, they're not likely to develop much of a news habit later. (Teens Know What They Want from Online News, n.d.)

Although Wave II Millennials may be more disengaged than previous adolescent cohorts, there is a relationship with news, albeit a weak one. More often than not, Wave II Millennials are "News accidentals," "news consumers who have a weak connection to the news; their exposure to news, which is non-purposeful, usually happens while not looking for news" (Poindexter, 2008e, p. 9). News accidentals are one of seven types of news consumers in the news media landscape; the other news types are: News enthusiasts, News monitors, News betweeners, News eclectics, News intenders, and News avoiders (Poindexter, 2008e). News accidentals offer more hope than News avoiders for a future relationship with news. News accidentals may not seek out news but they don't avoid it, either. If there are to be news consumers in the future, the mission should be to establish a path for Wave II Millennials that bypasses news avoidance and shows them the way to news engagement.

The task of developing Wave II Millennials into news consumers is both daunting and urgent. There is simply no more time to waste, especially because—as the Northwestern and NAA study on teens and news found—news as presented on the Internet "frequently and quickly turns them off, overwhelms them and makes them click away." Fortunately, this young cohort is "somewhat interested in news" (Teens Know What They Want from Online News, n.d.).

This study also found this adolescent cohort "would like to be 'informed,' but don't want to spend too much time on getting information" (Teens Know What They Want from Online News, n.d.), which is why the study concluded that there was a "mismatch" between what's offered and what this teenage cohort wants (Teens Know What They Want from Online News, n.d.). To engage this age group with news, the study asserted, "news organizations must offer something different" (Teens Know What They Want from Online News, n.d.).

Though the presentation of news should be improved for Millennials and every generation, the fact remains that there is more diversity than ever in the news that's offered. Furthermore, offering something different is simply not enough to engage adolescents with news. The something different that is needed is how adolescents are socialized about news at home and in school. The process in the past that has socialized generations of adolescents into news consumers is broken. But how does one fix a broken process? It's a little like fixing a broken newspaper business model. First, you have to stop denying there's a problem; then you have to commit to trying something new—not once but as many times as is necessary to find the right socialization model for cultivating future news consumers.

In an ideal world, cultivation of news consumers would start at home and be reinforced at school by teachers, the curriculum, and news-in-the-classroom programs that have newsroom involvement. Unfortunately, when it comes to developing future news consumers, the world is anything but ideal.

While some of the efforts to increase news and media literacy are not explicitly cultivating future news consumers, future news consumption is a likely outcome. These programs are so young that it's much too early to evaluate their long-term impact; however, any effort is better than no effort at all. Even the long-term impact of the program I developed as a different approach to developing Millennials into future news consumers is also unknown, but some of the early pretest results, which were showcased at the Millennials and News Summit at the University of Texas at Austin, look promising.

This approach to socializing Wave II Millennials into adults who will consume news is now in its fourth year of pretesting. So far 50 teachers and over 1,000 students from over 50 schools representing 10 school districts have participated in the news-in-the-schools program that I call mynews@school.

Four principles guided me in the creation of mynews@school:

- understanding that the purpose, principles, and process of journalism matters
- engagement with news in the classroom should be real world
- journalists and future journalists must be involved in the process of socializing future news consumers
- a democratic society demands involvement from everyone

Since understanding the purpose, principles, and process of journalism is so important, it's unclear why historically the news media has not educated the public about its methods of doing journalism. The public as a whole knows little about how journalism gets done. Understanding journalism's purpose, principles, and process not only serves as a foundation for distinguishing real news from stuff that passes for news, it has the potential to improve attitudes toward news and increase news consumption.

The second principle, that engagement with news in the classroom should be modeled after real world news consumption, is also critical, because in the real world of getting news, there are no textbooks to read, worksheets to fill out, or tests to take. In the real world, people search for news, scan headlines, stop and read stories that get their attention, and ignore stories that have no relevance to their lives. In the real world, news is discussed, debated, and shared.

While the news industry has a rich history of cultivating future journalists through internships and summer workshops, when it comes to cultivating future consumers of their own news product, journalists and journalism schools have been missing in action. The third principle in developing mynews@school is, therefore, based on my belief that if there are to be news consumers in the future, journalists and journalism schools must become engaged in the process of cultivating future consumers of the news they produce. In recognition of the fact that Millennials, especially Wave II, are different from previous generations, journalists, teachers of journalism, and future journalists should become more knowledgeable about this young cohort, which potentially will improve news coverage.

The fourth principle that guided the development of mynews@school is that to safeguard our democratic society, it's everyone's responsibility to nurture future news consumers. It can't be as Vivian Schiller, the former head of NPR, former senior vice president and general manager of NYTimes.com, former executive vice president of CNN, and now NBC executive in charge of online operations, asserted in a Q&A following her keynote address at the 2011 International Symposium on Online Journalism. After Ms. Schiller spoke eloquently about the importance of news literacy, I asked her what the news media can do to improve news literacy. While she indicated that the news media had a responsibility to produce quality journalism, she didn't feel the news media had a responsibility to increase news literacy. That responsibility, she said, belongs to parents and schools. With news consumption at its lowest level and Millennials barely engaging with news, responsibility cannot and must not rest solely with parents and teachers. All of society, including the news media and journalism schools, civic, business, political, and education leaders, foundations, state boards of education, curriculum associations, and parents and teachers must accept responsibility for cultivating news literacy in the youngest of each generation if news consumers are to exist in the future.

Everyone has a responsibility, but everyone does not know how to socialize the youngest among us into news-literate adults who regularly pay attention to news. If attempts at socialization are done incorrectly, young people may just as easily be turned off by news and socialized into future news avoiders instead of future news consumers. That's why teachers are so important—but not just any teacher. That's one of the most important lessons I've learned while pretesting mynews@school in public, private, and charter schools over the past four years.

Although mynews@school, like other news literacy programs, is a young program, its roots go back to my graduate school days when I found an academic study that was both shocking and troubling. The study was about non-newspaper readers, and many of them were young adults. In my master's thesis, I tried to understand why non-readers didn't read newspapers, and in my Ph.D. dissertation I tried to identify factors that might contribute to news consumption. Later, after graduate school, I worked for *The Los Angeles Times*, where one of my responsibilities included overseeing the development of a Newspaper-in-Education Program that provided newspapers, teacher training, and supplemental classroom materials. The program contributed to circulation, and it encouraged the development of future newspaper readers. Despite news literacy efforts on the part of *The Los Angeles Times* and other news organizations around the country, news consumption has continued to decline. As computers, the Internet, and social media transformed the news media landscape, the decline in news consumption accelerated, and news consumers appeared to be on the brink of disappearing. I knew something was seriously wrong and an intervention was needed, but wasn't sure exactly what type of intervention was needed until I had the opportunity to explore the issue in a new course I created as part of the Carnegie-Knight Initiative on the Future of Journalism Education. That was six years ago.

Designed for journalism and liberal arts majors and titled Journalism, Society, and the Citizen Journalist, the course was one part news literacy and one part current and future audience for news, including news consumption behavior and attitudes toward news and journalists. In the liberal arts students in this class, who were learning the purpose, principles, and process of journalism for the first time, I recognized a news media landscape transformation occurring right before my eyes. It was this classroom filled with Millennials, and a final group project that explored ideas about creating the next generation of news consumers, which helped me realize that the news consumption socialization model of the past would not work for a generation that was nothing like generations of the past at the same age. Not only was a new socialization model needed if there were to be news consumers in the future, but past assumptions about socializing future news consumers should be discarded; these assumptions were now obsolete.

mynews@school was initially created as a partnership because of my belief that if there are to be news consumers in the future, everyone had to be involved. The idea was to start the partnership with the local newspaper, middle and high schools, and journalism schools, and eventually expand beyond those three partners. mynews@school was launched with the blessing of the editor of the local newspaper, coordination with the educational services manager in charge of NIE, willing teachers who had been identified using the NIE manager's teacher database, and reporters and journalism professors willing to visit one of the participating classrooms to discuss the purpose, principles, and process of journalism.

mynews@school activities revolved around 10 minutes of free reading, small group and classroom discussion, and curriculum materials to help students understand the purpose, principles, and process of journalism. Free reading to simulate real-world news consumption during the first 10 minutes of class was a key component of the mynews@school program. By allowing 10 minutes of free reading time, students were able to explore the newspaper on their own. Following personal exploration, students participated in small group discussions that facilitated understanding some aspect of the purpose, principles, and process of journalism. The final discussion, which was student led, involved the whole class. Through class discussions, teachers gained insight into students' interest in, and reaction to, the week's lesson on the purpose, principles, and process of journalism. A typical mynews@school fall calendar of activities is displayed in Figure 6.1.

FIGURE 6.1 Ten Weeks of mynews@school Activities

Week 1:	Getting acquainted with the e-edition of the newspaper
Week 2:	What is news? What is the process of journalism?
Week 3:	The front page
Week 4:	News story formats and writing styles
Week 5:	News story ideas and quotes
Week 6:	Visuals in the newspaper
Week 7:	Datelines and geography
Week 8:	Holidays, commemorations, and history in the news
Week 9:	Exploring news Web sites
Week 10:	Teachers and students complete end-of-program questionnaires

(The focus on elections is during presidential election years. Activities to be offered in the future include: breaking news, research and fact-checking, diversity in news coverage, kids in the news, etc.)

mynews@school also includes weekly e-mail communication with the classroom teacher. On Monday, I would e-mail teachers a new curriculum activity created to help students understand the purpose, principles, and process of journalism; upon completion of the lesson, the teacher would send me feedback, including examples of student work. (Examples of the e-mails and activities can be found in Appendix B.3) Additionally, during the third year of the program, teachers kept a journal, to be turned in at the conclusion of the 10-week program along with postprogram teacher and student questionnaires. Once everything had been turned in, students received a participation certificate and teachers received a gift check.

Over the course of the 10-week program, some teachers drop out, but the highly engaged teachers go the distance. Since mynews@school is still being refined, there is no comparison control group, but there's no question that highly engaged teachers are putting their students on the path to becoming news-consuming adults. This was apparent when I visited classrooms of three highly engaged teachers. Teaching subjects as diverse as language arts, journalism, and technology, the three highly engaged teachers used mynews@school with a total of 90 middle school students. Since an analysis of the post-program questionnaire responses found no statistical difference in the three different classes regarding interest in news, perceived importance of news, and engagement with news and social media, results from the questionnaires were combined to sketch a portrait of Wave II Millennials who participated in mynews@school during the 10-week program.

The 90 middle school students were in the 7th or 8th grade; most (70%) were in the 7th grade. Ninety-three percent were 12 or 13 and the remaining were 14. Over half (54%) were male, and although they did not match the racial and ethnic diversity of the country, they were still a diverse group: 49% white; 27% Asian; 10% multi-racial; 7% African American; 7% Latino or Hispanic. Eighty-six percent of the 7th and 8th graders said they plan to go to a 4-year college after high school and 13% said they probably will go to college after high school.

Table 6.2 is a reminder of the difference between Wave II Millennials and the older, 20-something Wave I Millennials and even previous generations. Simply put, Wave II Millennials are coming of age digitally. When Wave I Millennials, Generation X, and Baby Boomers experienced middle school, they didn't have cell phones and access to many of the digital activities that Wave II Millennials take for granted.

As far as news consumption, more Wave II Millennials (81%) who participated in the mynews@school got news from TV than other media, but it wasn't an exclusive arrangement. Three quarters had gotten news from a print paper and news on a Web site, and 40% had gotten news from Facebook. One-third had accessed news on a cell phone, and Table 6.2 suggests they may have been in the early stages of adopting Twitter as a place to follow news.

Since there was no control group for comparison purposes, the impact of mynews@school on interest and engagement with news cannot be sorted out, but the post-program questionnaires suggest a higher level of news engagement than one might otherwise expect from 7th and 8th graders. During the final week of the 10-week program, two-fifths of the students said they were very interested or interested in news, and another two-fifths said news was of interest somewhat. These 7th and 8th graders paid attention to news a mean 3.3 days a week. When asked from what source they would *usually* get news, the middle schoolers cited the following sources: TV (57%), other (16%), online (13%), print newspaper (11%), teachers (2%), and parents (1%).

TABLE 6.2 Wave II Millennials (Kids), News, and Social Media

% OF KIDS PARTICIPATING IN MYNEWS@SCHOOL PROGRAM SAYING THE FOLLOWING APPLIES TO THEM:	
Have computer at home	98%
Have Internet access at home	98%
Searched on Google on their own	97%
Taken picture with cell phone	92%
Have own cell phone	83%
Sent text message with cell phone	83%
Watched TV news on their own	81%
Read news on a Web site	74%
Read a print paper on their own	74%
On Facebook	58%
Read news on Facebook	40%
Accessed news on cell phone	34%
Posted a video on YouTube	27%
Own an iPad	10%
Followed news on Twitter	6%
On Twitter	3%

In addition to an interest in news and paying attention to news, an overwhelming majority (92%) discussed news; news discussions averaged 2.36 days per week. Of those who discussed news, 64% discussed news with one person and 36% discussed news with more than one person. As far as discussions with one person, parents were the dominant discussion partner. Over one-third (34%) said they discussed news with their parents followed by friends (16%), classmates (8%), teachers (5%), and other (1%).

Without a controlled experiment, it's impossible to know how much, if any, mynews@school has contributed to the engagement with news displayed in

Table 6.2, but from the questionnaire responses, it's clear that kids participating in mynews@school are thinking about news in ways they might not have before, which, in and of itself, may contribute to their development as news consumers.

Furthermore, as a result of the free reading time in the mynews@school program, these 7th and 8th graders were engaging with news like news consumers in the real world. When asked what part of the paper they turned to first, the vast majority had a specific favorite section, just like adults. About one-third first turned to the front page, while over a quarter (27%) turned to sports first. The comics pages were first turned to by 16%, and almost one-tenth first turned to the lifestyle section of the paper. Other sections mentioned included opinion, editorial cartoon, and horoscope. The fact that 84% of the mynews@school participants first turned to a section of the newspaper other than the comics is another reminder of differences between kids today and previous generations at the same age. For kids from previous generations, the comic strips were often the first introduction to the newspaper, and the "serious parts of the paper" came later (Schramm et al., 1960). But for the kids participating in mynews@school, the "serious parts" such as the front page and sports were turned to first.

Three quarters of the middle-school students said as a result of participating in mynews@school they know more about the "purpose, principles, and process of journalism." And the post-program questionnaires found positive attitudes about the importance of news and intentions to consume news once they grow up. Of the four measures displayed in Table 6.3, most of the kids participating in mynews@school thought keeping informed of news was important to some degree. For example, a 12-year-old 7th grade boy said keeping informed of news and current events is somewhat important because "being informed could save your life some day or waste your time another." A 13-year-old girl in the 7th grade who agreed that keeping informed was somewhat important said: "I think people should know but kids don't NEED to know everything."

The recognition that kids were different was a theme among those who thought keeping informed was only slightly important. "I'm only 13," a 7th grade girl said. Other middle school students echoed similar sentiments: "It kind of depends on your age; I'm 12 and don't need to know most of this." Although a 12-year-old 7th grader thought keeping informed was somewhat important, the relevance of some types of news was questioned: "We don't vote or anything so we don't need to know." Some kids completely rejected the importance of keeping informed: "Who cares what's going on elsewhere? It doesn't affect you." But a 14-year-old 8th grade boy said it best while explaining why it is important to keep informed: "If you're not caught up on the news, you could be in serious trouble."

TABLE 6.3 Attitudes About News from Kids Participating in mynews@school Program

Importance of keeping informed of news	49% say "very important" or "important"	34% say "somewhat important"
Interest in news	40% say "very interested" or "interested"	41% say "somewhat interested"
Likelihood of paying attention to news as adult	35% say "definitely"	42% say "probably"
Enjoy keeping up with news	22% say "a lot"	37% say "some"

While the importance of keeping informed of news was endorsed by the largest percentages of kids participating in mynews@school, enjoying keeping up with news was endorsed by the fewest number of kids. Enjoyment of news, though, matters. What happens with news in the pre-teen and early teen years may affect what happens with news once kids grow up. While importance of keeping informed and interest in news were strongly correlated with intentions to pay attention to news as an adult, enjoyment of keeping up with news correlated most strongly with what kids planned to do about news once they grew up.

In fact, 35% of these Wave II Millennials who participated in the mynews@school program said they definitely will pay attention to news as an adult, and another 42% of the mynews@school participants said they probably will; in other words, over three-quarters (77%) said they definitely or probably will pay attention to news when they grow up.

When kids articulated their reasons for paying attention to news once they grow up, there appeared to be recognition, at least for some, that adults have a responsibility when it comes to news. For example, a 13-year-old 8th grade girl said she'll probably pay attention to news when she grows up "cause when I'm older it will be very important." A 13-year-old 7th grader who is somewhat interested in news and enjoys it a little said: "I care now (a little) and think grown-ups should be informed." Among those who will *definitely* pay attention once they grow up, a 14-year-old 8th grade boy who discusses news with his parents said: "It becomes my responsibility to know."

But while these responses appear promising, it's important to emphasize that these kids also have reservations about news. Among those who have no intentions of paying attention to news as a grown-up, a 13-year-old 7th grade girl was blunt in her explanation. "It's boring," she said.

After spending two and a half months during their class time reading and discussing news and learning about the purpose, principles, and process of journalism, the participants made some sophisticated observations about the news and its presentation; they also had ideas about making news better able to engage their age group. They want more stories that appeal to kids and more and better pictures. They'd also like to see more stories about the daily lives of regular people, especially kids. They want to know what kids are doing to "make a difference in the community." One student suggested a kid forum for kids to post comments. And there was an interest in seeing middle school sports, including football, basketball, and volleyball. Some kids said the stories were too long and some liked the inverted pyramid style of writing because the most important information was at the beginning of the story and the rest of the story could be skipped. They liked the eco-friendliness of the e-edition. They preferred it to paper and ink, which they thought was wasteful. They also liked the fact that they had access to the archives in the e-edition.

It's unlikely that this kid insight about newspapers and news would have happened without their teachers. The teachers shared their observations at the Millennials and News Summit held at the University of Texas at Austin. The middle school journalism teacher emphasized that kids don't have a lot of time, so news must be relevant if kids are to pay attention. She said that if some of the activities at their schools were covered, kids would pay attention. Also, the journalism teacher emphasized that the news media should "try harder to focus on what a 12, 13, 14-year-old would want to know about." The middle school technology teacher echoed this thought when he said: "Pick things kids are interested in and use that as a stepping stone." The middle school social studies teacher emphasized the importance of "having links to learn more" and opportunities for kids "to respond."[1]

The three teachers emphasized other benefits that flowed from the mynews@school program. The kids, the teachers said, are questioning things because they now recognize there might be "another side." Just like adults, students were discussing and sharing stories. Plus, because the program provided both the e-edition and a hard copy of the newspaper, students were taking the hard copy home and discussing news with their parents. For some students, the language arts teacher said, this was the first time they had ever had a newspaper in their home. The teacher observations at the Millennials and News Summit underscored that teachers are not only vital to the implementation of mynews@school, they are vital if there are to be news consumers in the future. As the gateway to future news consumers, teachers' socialization influence should not be underestimated.

Note

1. Teachers participating in the Millennials and News Summit included Paige Hert, Canyon Vista Middle School;Laurie Humphries, Cedar Valley Middle School;Philip Powell, Wiley Middle School.

· 7 ·

ENGAGING MILLENNIALS WITH NEWS IN A SOCIAL MEDIA WORLD: IT'S NOT TOO LATE, YET

...if we do nothing, consuming news will become extinct. This is the dirty little secret of our democracy. Our nation was founded on the principle that there can be no restraints on the press that informs us. But if news consumption continues to decline, being informed will be a relic of the past.

—PAULA POINDEXTER, MILLENNIALS AND NEWS SUMMIT
THE UNIVERSITY OF TEXAS AT AUSTIN, NOVEMBER 11, 2010

At some point between analyzing the news and media habits of three generations of teenagers for a book I was writing on gender differences in news consumption, and preparing a presentation on Millennials and news for the annual conference of state-wide newspaper executives, I had a thought that would have been unimaginable only a decade before: Was it possible that the upcoming generation of youth would reject—not just newspapers—but news in any form?

The consequences of the next generation rejecting news would be devastating on many fronts. Our democracy would suffer. The news media and the newspaper industry in particular, which was already reeling from the loss of classified advertising revenue thanks to Craigslist, the loss of display advertising courtesy of the Great Recession, and the loss of subscribers who were finding free news on the Internet, would suffer. Furthermore, individuals, families, communities, our values, and the public good would suffer if future generations abandoned news. Whether the upcoming generation would be committed to news in any form was unknown, but the warning signs visible in national news consumption data trends produced by the Pew Research Center were not good. The next generation looked like candidates for a list of endangered news consumers.

This unthinkable idea crystallized for me after seeing an editorial cartoon in the Sunday *New York Times*. Three people sat at a kitchen table. The oldest person, who was reading a newspaper, said: "The newspaper says they may stop delivering letters on Saturday." The teenager looked up from his laptop and said: "What's a letter?" A pre-teen who played with a hand-held device asked: "What's a newspaper?" (Stantis, 2010).

What would be the message if we fast-forwarded 20 years? There are still three people but now they're at DFW, waiting to board their flight from Dallas to Kansas City. In the airport waiting area 20 years into the future, there's no airport version of CNN; in fact there's no flat screen suspended from the ceiling. No one is reading a newspaper and no discarded newspapers are on the chairs or in the recycling bin. The three people are seated next to and across from each other. The oldest person, now a 40-something Millennial, opens her laptop and logs onto Facebook. The News Feed pops up and she clicks on a news story a colleague had posted. After reading the story, she announces to her younger traveling companions, her teenage and pre-teen children: "News Web sites will no longer include e-mail as an option for sharing news." Seated directly across from her is her post-Millennial-Generation teen, a college-bound authentic digital native, born 15 years after 9/11. He looks up from his 10th generation iPad and says: "What's e-mail?" In the adjacent seat is her post-Millennial pre-teen. The pre-teen has removed her pink ear buds long enough to hear the conversation. Although her eyes remain fixed on her smartphone screen, her wrinkled forehead suggests she's puzzled by the conversation. "What's news?" she finally asks.

What's the likelihood that this scenario will become our future? It depends on what we're willing to do, beginning today, to solve a complicated problem that demands a shared, long-term commitment from all stakeholders. Who are the stakeholders? We may have different roles to play, but everyone—legacy news media, online-only news and journalism schools, social media, search engines, and fake news, education, business, civic, and political leaders, parents and teachers—has a stake in ensuring that future generations engage with news. Even Millennials have a stake in their own future news engagement.

Solving the Problem Begins with Acknowledging That One Exists

Figure 7.1 is recognition that the solution to a long-term, complicated, entrenched problem requires sustained action on many fronts. But that action cannot begin until there is an acknowledgment that a problem exists by those who can do something about the problem. If stakeholders continue to ignore, discount, or fail to take any responsibility for solving the problem, it will become a problem impossible to fix. Unfortunately, it's hard to persuade stakeholders to acknowledge the existence of a problem when the highly regarded Pew Research Center suggests there is no problem, with the title of its 2010 news consumption survey report, Americans Spending More Time Following the News (2010).

It's only by digging deep into the report and comparison data that warning signs can be found. In 2008, 27% of 18 to 29-year-olds said they got news "at regular times;" two years later, that number had dropped to 21% (Americans Spending More Time, 2010, p. 45). In 2012, will that number decline another six points? Will 15% say they get news at "regular times"? If the trend continues, by 2018, when Wave II Millennials are in the 18 to 29-year-old age group, will there be no one getting news at regular times?

Another red flag in the Pew Research Center news consumption trends is the "sharp decline" from 2008 to 2010 in the percentage of young people who enjoy following news. In 2008, 39% of 18 to 29-year-olds said they enjoyed following the news; in Pew's 2010 news consumption survey the number dropped to 27%. Using a more intense measurement in my own National Survey of News Engagement conducted a year after the 2010 Pew news consumption survey, only 20% of Millennials *strongly* agreed that they enjoyed keeping up with news. And there was a lack of a strong endorsement for some of the other benefits expected from engaging with news. For example, in my National Survey of News Engagement, only one-tenth strongly liked discussing news with others. The same goes for the feeling of empowerment with being informed, and depending on news to help with daily life. The only bright spot in these statistics was that only four per cent strongly agreed with the statement that keeping up with news is a waste of time. In other words, keeping up with news was *not* perceived as wasting time. Still, no passion for news and its benefits was apparent—more evidence that a problem exists.

FIGURE 7.1 Engaging Millennials with News Demands Effort from Many Fronts

1. Stakeholders must admit problem exists.

2. Stakeholders must acknowledge problem matters.

3. Problem must be defined.

4. Consequences of doing nothing about problem must be identified.

5. Stakeholders must educate themselves about Millennials.

6. Legacy news media must become engaged.

7. Non-legacy news media (Web-only for profit and non-profit) must get involved.

8. Social media and search engines must intervene.

9. Fake news (*The Daily Show*, *The Colbert Report*, *The Onion*, *SNL*, etc.) has a role to play.

10. Civic, education, business, foundation, and political leaders must step up.

11. Journalism Schools, journalism organizations, institutes for continuing journalism education and training, and academic journalism associations must become engaged.

12. Parents need to do more.

13. More committed teachers are needed.

14. Millennials have a responsibility, too!

Stakeholders Must Acknowledge Problem Matters

Whether looking at the trends showing a decline in getting news or only a small percentage endorsing some of the benefits of news, Step 2 in solving the problem, according to Figure 7.1, is that stakeholders must acknowledge that the problem identified actually matters. This step underscores the fact that acknowledging a problem exists is not the same as recognizing that the consequences of not fixing the problem will have profound negative effects on society and the public good. If a problem is not perceived to have negative consequences, the odds of fixing it decline significantly.

Though Chapter 1 described a future in which news consumers no longer existed, that does not mean stakeholders who can actually fix the problem agree with this scenario. Psychological processes such as selective exposure, selective perception, selective retention, and cognitive dissonance have been known to stand in the way, enabling and reinforcing denial, causing us to greet the problem with the response: So what?

The Problem Must Be Defined

Once stakeholders are in agreement that we are faced with a very serious problem and the problem matters, we must focus on Step 3 in Figure 7.1, defining the problem. Knowing the exact nature of the problem is the key to buy-in from the many stakeholders required to fix the problem. The problem is simply that news consumption has been on the decline for decades and unless something is done to reverse the decline, news consumption will continue to drop, even with the array of new platforms for news that are populating the news terrain. And now with social media in the news media landscape, social media has managed to intervene at the very point that young adults may otherwise have begun engaging with news. By adopting social media at this critical juncture, social media may have served as a barrier, rather than a gateway to consuming news, accelerating the decline, leaving us to contemplate a future in which news consumers are not only endangered but may cease to exist.

Consequences of Doing Nothing

Step 4 in Figure 7.1 is important to ponder because it helps answer the question: Can we continue to ignore the problem? By answering the question, we are faced with the reality that the stakes are indeed high, and if we continue to ignore the problem, it is at our own peril. In other words, if we do nothing to reverse declining news consumption, we may reach that tipping point and become a nation of news illiterates. The consequences of becoming a nation of news illiterates are far-reaching, and if we reach the point in which being uninformed is viewed as cool, turning the calendar back to a time when some news engagement existed may prove to be an impossible feat.

Educating Stakeholders About Millennials

Becoming educated about Millennials in Step 5 is easy because this generation, born in the early 1980s through the late 1990s, has attracted so much attention from marketers, authors, scholars, social scientists, and research centers such as Pew. In fact, searching for Millennials produces a rich source of Millennial data to mine. Even Wikipedia has a section devoted to the Millennial Generation (Generation Y, n.d.).

Generation experts Neil Howe and William Strauss, who named this cohort, said there were seven characteristics that distinguished the "Millennial persona": "special, sheltered, confident, team oriented, achieving, pressured, conventional" (Howe & Strauss, 2000, pp. 43–44). One of the most comprehensive data sources about Millennials can be found at the Pew Research Center, which has drawn a social and political portrait of Millennials (2010) that not only provides insight into Millennials as a whole, but also shows how Millennials are similar to and different from previous generations at the same age. Millennials, according to the Pew Research Center report, are more likely to have a tattoo, more likely to have supported Barack Obama who became the first African American President in the United States, and more likely to believe that government should do more to help those in need. Furthermore, having come of age and graduated college during the Great Recession of 2008, Millennials are less likely to have found employment and more likely to have moved back home, and these homes that Millennials grew up in are more likely than previous generations to be single-parent households.

There is also a lot to be learned about young adults and news from journalism scholars who have focused their research on this young adult generation. University of Florida journalism scholar Amy Zerba found in her focus groups that young adults say the news is redundant; from their vantage point, "the media are covering the same stories; no new information is given; and/or the lineup of stories on TV newscasts is predictable" (Zerba, 2011, p. 604).

Kelly Kaufhold, a journalism professor at Texas Tech University, found that among college students in this generation, some are informed, but not all. In fact, college students who sought out news were found to be more knowledgeable about news than news avoiders and news finders—those who, despite the fact that they ignore news, news still manages to "find its way to them" (Kaufhold, 2011, p. 88).

Journalism historian and author David Mindich concluded in his must-read book *Tuned Out: Why Americans Under 40 Don't Follow the News* that "our democracy is on the brink of a crisis and the problem will not right itself." He posed the question that should concern all of us who worry about the consequences of our democracy being inherited by a generation in which news consumers are extinct: "Nearing the time when 20- and 30-somethings will be given the tiller of the ship of state, we and they might ask, are they informed enough for the journey?" (Mindich, 2005, p. 112).

As data resources for understanding Millennials are examined, it's important to keep in mind that most of these sources are examining Wave I

Millennials, the older cohort, born between the early 1980s and 1991. This cohort is now college age or has already graduated college and entered, or at least tried to enter, the labor force. Wave II Millennials, as discussed in Chapter 6, are currently in middle and high school. Plus, when Wave II Millennials become young adults they might differ significantly from Wave I Millennials because of the period in which they grew up. While Wave I Millennials were in high school when terrorists flew planes into the World Trade Center in New York, Wave II Millennials were in pre-school and early elementary school on the day of the 9/11 attacks. The Great Recession has hit Wave I Millennials especially hard. Just as they began celebrating graduation from college, they were confronted with an unforgiving job market, requiring them to move back home with their parents—not exactly one's dream after college graduation.

If characteristics and life experiences distinguish Millennials from each other and previous generations, what factors will determine if they will consume news like previous generations? From the perspective of Sandy Woodcock, director of the Newspaper Association of America (NAA) Foundation, who spoke at the Millennials and News Summit held at the University of Texas at Austin, it's not that complicated to develop younger Millennials into life-long news consumers. Woodcock said "their research shows that if you pay attention to young people as an audience that they will come." Paying attention, though, requires a long-term commitment, something the news industry has yet to do. For older Wave I Millennials who have made social media central to their lives, future news engagement will be influenced by many factors, including Millennial attitudes about news and journalism, as well as whether the news media continues along the same path in its news coverage of this generation. That's why the education about Millennials must include their attitudes about journalism.

To find out what Millennials really think about journalism, journalists, and news, I asked their level of agreement or disagreement with nine statements that reflected both positive and negative sentiments about the press. Millennials endorsed two areas that spoke to the heart of journalism, and one expectation the public has for news. Almost one-third (31%) of Millennials agreed or strongly agreed that most news is biased, and one-quarter endorsed the statement: News media care little about you. Since news is expected to be unbiased by both journalists and the news audience, the fact that one-third of Millennials say news is biased is troubling and does not bode well for future engagement with news by this generation (see Table 7.1).

The idea of a caring news media grew out of the public or civic journalism movement, which sought to better engage the news media with the public. With one-fourth of Millennials saying the news media does not care about them, the news media appears to be failing on this front. A different statement tried to gain insight into Millennial expectations as to whether the news media is expected to be caring. The statement asked if the press should act like a good neighbor. The idea of the press functioning as a good neighbor evolved from an earlier survey of the public's expectations of local news (Heider, McCombs, & Poindexter, 2005; Poindexter, Heider, & McCombs, 2006). Although the good neighbor concept was not defined in the National Survey of News Engagement, for the previous study, good neighbor was comprised of four dimensions: caring about the community, reporting on interesting people and groups, understanding the local community, offering solutions. Almost one-third (30%) of Millennials agreed or strongly agreed that the press should act like a good neighbor.

While the press may not place the same value on being a good neighbor as Millennials, the press does place great value on being a watchdog. In fact, past surveys have shown that the press's watchdog function resonates far more with journalists than the public at large. Seventy percent of journalists and 49% of the public have placed high importance on the press as watchdog (Weaver, et al., 2003; Heider et al., 2005). Millennials, though, have a different view of the press. According to Table 7.1, only 35% of Millennials agreed or strongly agreed that the press should function as a watchdog.

While Millennials rejected some past criticisms of the press and endorsed others, such as bias and failure to care about them, a different statement tried to capture how they felt about an emerging business model of paying for news on the Internet. Over half of the Millennial participants agreed or strongly agreed that news on the Internet should be free. This endorsement, combined with other criticisms of the press, will make cultivating and retaining this generation as news consumers even more problematic if more news organizations follow the lead of *The New York Times* and charge for news on the Internet.

Failure to endorse four statements in Table 7.1 by the vast majority of Millennials does provide a glimmer of hope that it's not too late to engage this young generation with news. Less than one fifth agreed or strongly agreed that the news media does not provide context, that journalists lack ethics, that news is boring, and finally that the press has too much freedom.

But the fact that the news media did not get criticized in these areas does not mean there's nothing to worry about concerning the Millennial Generation, especially because in Chapter 3, Millennials barely gave the news media a passing grade for coverage of their generation. News is comprised of and evaluated on different dimensions, but one dimension that can have more influence on

TABLE 7.1 Millennial Perceptions of News and Journalistic Role and Performance % Saying Agree and Strongly Agree

All news on the Internet should be free	56%
News media should be watchdog	35%
News is biased	31%
News media should be good neighbor	30%
News media care little about people like you	24%
News media do poor job of providing context	16%
Journalists lack ethics	16%
Most news is boring	15%
Press has too much freedom	14%

Millennials than others is the perception of how they are covered in the news. That's why part of stakeholders' education about Millennials must include learning what this generation says needs to be done to improve news coverage about them. Whether the news media ignores or responds to these recommendations may ultimately determine whether Millennials engage with news in the future.

Millennial Recommendations for Improving News Coverage

When asked what recommendations they had for improving news coverage about their generation, most recommendations were about content, journalism performance, and personnel. While a few Millennials thought news coverage was fine as it was, a good number had no idea how to improve news coverage. For those who did indeed have opinions about how news coverage of their generation could be improved, recommendations echoed the barely passing grades that Millennials gave the news media in Chapter 3. Millennials wanted less celebrity, gossip, and bad news about their generation. A 21-year-old college female, for example, said: "You don't have to talk about Justin Bieber to get them interested." Another female, a 24-year-old college graduate, endorsed that position with an exclamation point: "Less about celebrities!" Concerning gossip, a 25-year-old male with some college said: "Reduce the gossip and provide more details from around the world."

Millennials also emphasized that the news media needed to have fewer bad stories. For example, a 25-year-old female with some college said: "Show more good than bad; otherwise, it just makes it look like the younger generation is horrible." The flip side of fewer bad stories is more positive stories, which quite a few Millennials endorsed. A 28-year-old African American female said: "Tell more positive things we are doing in our communities." A 25-year-old Hispanic agreed. "Look for the positive in those groups," she said. "Not all of them are running crimes and stuff." In a response by a 28-year-old white male with some college, he addressed the need for more positive stories and fewer celebrity stories: "Do stories on regular people, encourage and reward regular people doing good things, stop wasting our time with stupid celebrity stories."

For some Millennials, it was not just more positive stories; they wanted more stories about their generation. And they wanted more relevant stories. One Millennial said: "report the stories people are concerned about. . . ." For another, relevant meant more stories about the "job situation for students graduating from college." Another gave specific examples of relevant stories: "rising cost of college, how to avoid tremendous debt from an early age, and better ways to find jobs/careers." A 23-year-old female college graduate was to the point in her recommendation: "provide topics that affect us, as well as interest us." But it's not enough to provide topics that affect Millennials; Millennials emphasize that the stories have to make a connection. As a 26-year-old female pointed out: "To engage younger generations…you have to talk about why it affects them. It doesn't have to be blatant or explicit but you should be able to pick up on how it affects your life to get better informed with the news." A 20-year-old male echoed that statement by saying: "Relate the stories in terms they can understand."

Even with doing all of that, a 28-year-old female college graduate emphasized the importance of balance: "Give them both sides of the story in a relevant light so they can make good informed decisions. Both sides would not only conform to what's expected of news but would, perhaps, address the fact that some of the recommendations called for the news media to be "less biased."

Not surprisingly, some of the recommendations emphasized that journalists needed to include more young people as sources. A 27-year-old male college graduate said: "Do more research, get out there and communicate with the young crowd." A slightly younger male said: "More first-hand interaction and interviews with people from this age group when reporting on them. It's always better to go straight to the source rather than assume things. Of course, people vary widely so it is important not to think that what one young person is like is how all young people are, so a large sample size is important."

For some, there would be an improvement in news coverage if the news media simply used reporters from the Millennial Generation: "Have reporters of their age…vs. outsiders who don't know what they're talking about." To achieve this, a 19-year-old male suggested they could also have young "guest journalists." A 28-year-old male said news coverage would improve if they would reach out on communication lines that Millennials use.

From the perspective of Millennials, journalists are not using "Best Practices" to cover their generation. Some "Best Practices" are more obvious, but a few of the recommendations are more subtle, and journalists may not be aware that this is how they are perceived. These recommendations echoed complaints in Chapter 3 that journalists looked down on them. A 25-year-old male emphasized: "Instead of judging them by your standards, get to know them and understand them.…" A female who was 24 said: "…ease up on the pity and condemnation." A male with some graduate school thought news coverage of Millennials would improve if the news media would "stop treating us like we all read at a middle school level."

Legacy News Media Must Get Engaged

If news consumers become extinct, legacy news media will be blamed and rightly so. It's not as if legacy news media did not have decades of evidence and warnings. It is, therefore, hoped that the call for legacy news media, a key stakeholder, to get engaged will underscore the importance of making the upcoming generation a priority if there are to be news consumers in the future.

The decision by the newspaper industry, in particular, to ignore the evidence and warnings that they were in danger of losing their news audience, has been particularly puzzling because non-news businesses, which traditionally advertise in the news media, understand that their success is not tied to their current market alone; their success is the relationship they build with their future market, which is the generation growing up. Coca-Cola, for example, which is launching a plan to double revenues to $200 billion by 2020, emphasized that for them to achieve their growth objectives, they cannot afford to ignore teens. As the senior vice president of sparkling brands said: "You can't think teens already know us and skip a couple of years. Every six years there's a new population of teens in the world" (Zmuda, 2011). If the news industry followed Coca-Cola's strategy, it would be directing its effort toward cultivating future news consumers by starting with Wave II Millennials, who are currently in middle and high school.

While companies such as Coca-Cola may have been motivated by building future brand loyalty and increasing future sales, legacy news media, especially newspapers, have too often believed the myth that it was okay to ignore the youth since once they grew up and established roots in a community, they would automatically become subscribers and viewers. Perhaps that was true a half century ago. Reality today is that creating a profile on Facebook may be an automatic rite of passage for Millennials, but engaging with news is not. Until legacy news media develops a strategy and implements a plan to cultivate news consumers among Millennials, news consumption in this generation will continue to decline until no hope is left that Millennials can be removed from the list of endangered news consumers. That's why engagement by legacy news media is so critical.

Commitment from the top of the legacy news organization and the chief news executive is a prerequisite to legacy news media engagement. Without this commitment, developing and implementing a strategic plan to engage Millennials with news will be impossible to achieve. While the top of the news organization—publisher, president, general manager, etc.—controls the overall budget and determines the allocation of resources, the person in charge of the newsroom, also known as the gatekeeper, whether editor, news director, etc., is the most powerful person in the newsroom because he or she ultimately determines what news is published, posted, or broadcast. The gatekeeper's decision-making was first studied in 1950, before the first Baby Boomers had even started first grade (White, 1950). While in this famous study there was not always a logical reason for what the editor, who was called "Mr. Gates," decided to publish or discard, he often referenced the audience as an explanation for his decision-making process. While the audience may have been one factor influencing the gatekeeper, over the past 60 years, many factors have been identified as influencing gatekeepers' decisions as to what gets published and how it is framed: journalism training, newsroom culture, supervisors and newsroom policies, professional norms, routines, staff make-up, unconscious assumptions about the subject, and even sources (Shoemaker & Reese, 1996; Weaver et al., 2007; Poindexter et al., 2008). In addition to the many forces and factors determining what news is available for us to read, watch, and listen to, we also have to keep in mind that there is not one gatekeeper. In the production of a news story, there are multiple gatekeepers, including reporters, photographers, videographers, section editors, managing editors, producers, news directors, and their deputies, to name a few.

Without a commitment from the top, any and all of these factors can undermine an effort to engage Millennials in news, especially if the first step to engagement requires not just including them in news coverage but also including their voices, and reporting news about them with some degree of respect. Basically, Millennials must be viewed by the newsroom as "newsworthy" subjects, too; until that happens little will change. The very fact that it is hard to find any news stories about Millennials underscores the problem that traditionally, journalists have not considered a young generation particularly worthy of being included in the news. That's not only how journalists have been trained, it's also what newsroom culture says.

If organizational theory is applied to newsrooms, newsroom culture would comprise, and be influenced by, visible, invisible, and embedded or unconscious factors (Daft, 2005, p. 557). It's the embedded or unconscious factors such as values, beliefs, and assumptions that are most difficult to change, especially because gatekeepers are not necessarily aware of unconscious factors that may be causing them to ignore best journalism practices when reporting news about and of interest to Millennials.

Whether in comments made during the Millennials and News Summit, the National Survey of News Engagement, or following the 60 *Minutes* Millennial story, Millennials have identified practices inconsistent with what the public, regardless of age, has a right to expect from journalism. These criticisms, combined with their recommendations for improving coverage, as well as a systematic look at published, posted, and broadcast Millennial news stories, make it possible to create a list of "Best Practices" when covering this young generation. If journalists made an effort to incorporate these "Best Practices" displayed in Figure 7.2, it would be a major step forward in living up to their journalistic responsibility of covering news in a balanced and representative way, and it would change the message that Millennials have been receiving from the news media. By not including Millennials in the news, or including them in limited or stereotyped ways, journalists have been communicating to Millennials that they are not valued. Clearly, that is the wrong approach if the news media is serious about engaging Millennials now and having an informed nation in the future.

FIGURE 7.2 Best Practices for Covering and Engaging the Millennial Generation

✓ Regularly include Millennial stories in news coverage.

✓ Include Millennials as sources in general news and trend stories that impact Millennials and are of interest to them.

✓ Stories about Millennials should include explicit references to this generation in the headline.

✓ Explicit Millennial stories should include Millennial sources, and these Millennial sources should be among the first quoted. Whether Millennial explicit or implicit, care must be taken to include direct Millennial quotes and not just paraphrased Millennial voices.

✓ Reduce stories about Millennial celebrities (entertainers, athletes, actors, reality show participants); increase stories about non-celebrity Millennials contributing to society and making a difference.

✓ Balance crime coverage with stories that are not about Millennial criminals.

✓ Include Millennial voters and issues in election stories.

✓ Not all Millennials are the same, so strive for diversity in stories and voices.

✓ For stories that are important for Millennials to know, include the reason the story matters, perhaps in a sidebar, but don't insult Millennials by "dumbing-down" the story.

✓ Use neutral tones in news coverage; avoid snide, disrespectful tones.

✓ Make headlines and photo captions explicit in stories about Millennials.

✓ Use multimedia strategically and effectively to showcase Millennial stories.

✓ Use linking effectively to provide context and facilitate engagement.

✓ Tag Millennial stories with key words: Millennial, young adults, 20-somethings, youth, Generation Y, Gen Y.

✓ Promote and archive stories about Millennials, stories of interest to Millennials, and stories Millennials should know.

✓ Generational rites of passage are a great source of Millennial story ideas. These rites-of-passage stories should be handled with sensitivity and from the Millennial point of view rather than journalists', parents', or

FIGURE 7.2 (*continued*)

employers' perspectives. Tag, promote, and tweet these stories so that Millennials can find them when they search for information to help them navigate these critical passages.

✓ Make improved Millennial news coverage a priority by making it the responsibility of an editor who reports directly to the newsroom's chief news executive.

✓ Regularly audit news content to assess Millennial inclusion; make sure that stories of interest to Millennials and stories that Millennials should know are written so Millennials can better relate to them.

✓ Integrate assessment of Millennial news coverage, with special attention paid to inclusion, story type, sources, and tone, into newsroom culture and routines.

✓ Make it a priority to assess how Millennials of color, women, and young voters are handled in the news. On an ongoing basis, assess if they are included or ignored, stereotyped, or treated as second tier. If coverage is consistent with concerns identified in Chapter 5, develop and implement a plan that will improve coverage of these three key groups.

✓ Appoint a Millennial advisory panel for consultation and regular feedback.

✓ Create an online Millennial style guide that is updated regularly for covering Millennials in general and Millennials of color, women, and voters in particular. Include examples of best and worst practices for stories, headlines, photos and videos, social media, placement, sentences, quotes, word choice, tone, etc.

✓ Enhance smartphone and tablet computer news and apps to engage Millennials.

✓ Connect with Millennials through social media.

✓ Add introductory comments or prompts to stories posted on Facebook that will encourage Millennial engagement with news.

✓ News organizations that have made charging for news on the Internet part of their business model should waive the subscription fee for Millennials at least through age 26.

For newsrooms that have a history of ignoring Millennials, Figure 7.2 will serve as a road map for evaluating and improving news coverage of Millennials. These "Best Practices" are an attempt to address Millennial criticisms and recommendations as well as the best and worst news coverage of this generation. These suggestions will get newsrooms started, but they will not transform the way the youngest generation is covered unless there is a commitment from the top and this commitment is integrated throughout newsroom culture and routines.

Since changing newsroom culture and routines is a daunting task, there needs to be independent and objective documentation that coverage of Millennials needs to be overhauled. That's why I recommend developing and implementing a system that audits news coverage on an ongoing basis. If designed correctly, this auditing system will provide data that will help newsrooms evaluate and improve their coverage of Millennials. With an eye toward improving news coverage over the long-term, results of these news audits should be discussed openly and often in the newsroom. In fact, open discussion is a necessary prerequisite for change when embedded and unconscious assumptions are involved (Valian, 1999; Poindexter et al., 2008).

A monitoring system that documents the presence, absence, and approach to stories about Millennials is not sufficient; insight from Millennials must also be part of any serious plan to improve coverage. That's why establishing a panel of Millennials is also recommended. This Millennial News panel can provide important and necessary feedback on stories that do a quality job covering Millennials, and on those that are deficient because they are examples of the type of news stories that Millennials complain about. For the Millennial News panel to be a credible source for feedback, it must have racial and ethnic diversity, which is of paramount importance for the most diverse generation ever. Plus, there should be representation in terms of gender, education, income, occupation, sexual orientation, and political identity as represented by party, ideology, and voting experience since turning 18.

Including voters and non-voters on the panel will provide insight about general and mid-term election coverage as well as news stories about young voters engaged in the political process and those who are not. Although the National Survey of News Engagement did not ask specific questions about news coverage of young voters, it's likely that if questions had been asked, young voter coverage would also have received low marks, especially because young voters are rarely included in election coverage, and if they are included, they are often criticized for their turnout. Even when young voters turned out in record numbers during the 2008 presidential election as discussed in Chapter 5, some journalists and cable news pundits still managed to criticize them. Journalists were also critical of young voters in 2004. In fact, journalism scholar Amy Zerba observed that in some of their coverage about young voter turnout, journalists were "downright wrong" (Zerba, 2008, p. 167).

As the 2012 presidential election season has gotten underway, Millennials have been the subject of some news stories framed around the theme of Millennial voter disaffection with the candidate they helped win the White House in 2008 (Nagourney, 2011; Gee, 2012). It's too early to know if this will be a recurring theme throughout the 2012 election season, but if it turns out that this is the only way the news media covers Millennial voters, it will be a missed opportunity. Not only are there so many more stories to write about the Millennial generation and the 2012 presidential election, this single-theme approach to covering young voters will do little to engage them with the news at a time when they will likely be paying attention.

Beyond the obvious demographic and political representation on the Millennial News panel, an effort should also be made to include Millennials with different interests such as environment, health, science, technology, business, economics, energy, politics, public policy, media, fine arts, culture, education, public service, and international. Mixing different interests on the panel will enhance the quality of feedback on stories about Millennials and stories that should include Millennials, but don't. Furthermore, a panel of Millennials with diverse interests could become a valuable resource for generating engaging story ideas to pursue.

This Millennial News panel could also be used to help answer the "So What?" that Amy Zerba, University of Florida journalism professor, emphasizes in her recommendations for improving how news stories are written and presented. As a former journalist and someone who researches young adults as well as the news products that target them, Zerba says veteran journalists and the stories they write would benefit from consulting with the young journalists in the newsroom because they know best what would make their age group relate to a news story.

> They [young journalists] know the pulse of this demographic better than anyone in the newsroom. Too often young journalists' ideas, and writing, become sterilized or even tossed aside by older, more experienced staff members, directors, or editors. And so the vicious cycle of not-relatable reporting continues. Being older and more seasoned does not always equate to being more knowledgeable about all stories, especially those regarding young adults. (Zerba, 2008, p. 168)

Whether young journalists in the newsroom or a panel of Millennials independent of the newsroom, the idea is the same: if the answer to the "So What?" question is to be credible, it can only be answered from the perspective of those who are puzzled as to why some of the news that is reported should matter to their lives.

Finally, this Millennial News panel could also be used as a reliable source for validating prospective entries into the recommended online Millennial News style guide. A convenient online reference available to everyone, from reporters to the most senior of editors, anytime, and from anywhere, the Millennial News style guide could include examples of best and worst practices when covering Millennials as well as stories in which Millennials should be included but are not. Additionally, because, as we learned in Chapter 5, African American Millennials are far more critical of news coverage and Millennial women are significantly less likely than their male counterparts to consume news, the style guide should devote special attention to coverage of these two groups so the news is a reflection of best and not worst practices. As noted in Chapter 5, some of the worst practices, in addition to exclusion, are stereotyping African Americans as criminals, athletes, celebrities, and poor. Women are also excluded from the news, or when they are included, their newsworthiness is treated as "second-tier," and they are less likely to be quoted in news stories (Poindexter, 2008b, p. 72). Additionally, issues that are important to women and directly impact them are often treated as less important subjects in the news. Women have also been treated as less important when they have run for the highest offices. Their clothes, how they style their hair, and their family life have received more attention than their stand on issues. What women candidates running for high office say on the campaign trail has been paraphrased rather than quoted directly. When compared to men, women have received more negative coverage, and their successes on the campaign trail have received less prominent attention (Carroll & Schreiber, 1997; Lueck, 2005; Poindexter, 2008; Cáceres, 2011).

Just as Millennials could be called the Facebook generation because they have overwhelmingly adopted this social networking site, they could also be labeled the "Mobile Device and App" generation because this cohort has taken to smartphones and apps (Survey: New U.S. Smartphone Growth, 2012). Plus, Millennials are poised to replace their laptops with tablets because of the competitive cost, small size, and cool features. What are the implications for the news industry if a generation is defined by mobile devices and apps? Enhancing smartphone news, tablet news, and news apps to engage Millennials must be of the highest priority, and the enhancements must be innovative, unlike how some of the largest newspapers have used Facebook as a platform for news. While the news media may think that it has been innovative in posting its news on Facebook, the National Survey of News Engagement found their Facebook pages are not resonating with Millennials. Only 6% of Millennials said they got news on the news media's Facebook page daily, and almost half (49%) said they never get news from a news organization's social media page. This lack of interest in the news media's Facebook page is not surprising given the observations of University of Texas at Austin Ph.D. student Melissa Suran while she was analyzing a week of the Facebook pages of the *Chicago Sun-Times, The New York Times, USA Today, The Washington Post,* and *The Wall Street Journal.* Suran said in an e-mail that "except for the *Wall Street Journal,* 85 to 100% of the items posted by the newspapers on their Facebook pages were introduced with a prompt that summarized the story" (M. Suran, personal communication, March 24, 2012).

Is introducing a news story with a summary the best way to engage Millennials with media Facebook pages? Is the news media even trying to engage the Millennial Generation on Facebook, or is it continuing its legacy of ignoring youth? Millennials and News editor Alexandra Wilson, who posts news stories for this generation on Facebook every morning, said that when news organizations do a poor job with their Facebook pages, it looks "like they don't know how to engage with young people or they don't care about young people." She added that this is "very irritating" to her generation, perhaps because this generation feels Facebook belongs to them since Facebook was started by someone of their generation, exclusively for their generation.

When asked for "Best Practices" for media Facebook pages, Wilson said introductory comments or prompts to news stories posted on Facebook should be short and to the point. Additionally, she said that if the story is explicitly about Millennials, the accompanying photograph should be of a Millennial.

The difference between the Millennial and legacy news media approach to posting news on a Facebook page is evident in a story about the Millennial Generation's lack of interest in purchasing a new car. Both *The New York Times* and the Millennials and News editor posted the story on Facebook. *The New York Times* used 60 words to introduce the story while the Millennial editor used 21 fewer words. *The New York Times* prompt or introduction to the story was a summary of the story plus a stroll down memory lane for older generations:

> Many young consumers today just do not seem to care that much about cars. That is a major shift from the days when the car served as the ultimate gateway to freedom and independence. When did you first put your foot to the pedal? What was the first car you drove? Submit a photo of your first car here: http://nytims/GW398S (Many young consumers, 2012)

In contrast to *The New York Times'* prompt, the Millennial editor introduced the story on the Millennials and News Facebook page with a comment
that showed a connection with both the story and her generation: "This story
rings true for me because I don't care about cars, and will not buy a new one
unless I have to. My Saturn Ion is seven, and if it lasts me another seven I will
be happy" (Wilson, 2012a).

The contrasting styles in the prompt that introduced the story is why the
Millennial editor recommended that if the news media has any intention of
connecting to Millennials through Facebook, they need to post stories and
prompts from a *real* Millennial perspective—not a journalism perspective. The
Millennial editor said without a real Millennial perspective, the news media will
"never get it right," that is, if their goal is to reach out and connect with the
generation that virtually lives on Facebook.

While many of the "Best Practices" to improve news coverage have focused
on older Millennials because they are already in their 20s and this time period may
be the last chance to get them engaged with news, it is important to keep in mind
that long-term thinking is required. As Wave I Millennials move into their 30s,
Wave II Millennials will move up and replace them as 20-somethings. Because
generations never remain the same age and do not have the same life experiences,
newsrooms must be alert to generational differences. Furthermore, just as
Generation X followed Baby Boomers, and Millennials are following Generation
X, there will be a new generation of teens and 20-somethings to replace today's
Millennials. What news organizations do now will play a major role in whether
younger Millennials and the generation that follows them will have news consumers among them, or whether news consumers will become extinct.

Ironically, editorial departments, especially at newspapers, have the best
opportunity to engage with Wave II Millennials because their news-in-the-
schools programs are in K-12 classrooms. But according to two national surveys,
editorial departments are barely engaged with the NIE programs that operate
in schools located in their own circulation areas. The Newspaper Association
of America (NAA) Foundation survey of the current state of NIE programs
found only 6% of NIE programs reported to the editorial department (NIE,
2010); furthermore, in my own national survey of NIE managers, only 16% said
the newspaper's editorial department was directly involved with NIE "a lot."

Editorial's low involvement in NIE is no longer acceptable if there is to be
a turnabout in Millennial engagement with news. In fact, concerning educating young people about the role of the press in society, including its purpose,
principles, and process, there's no one better to handle this task than editors

and reporters who practice journalism every day. Educating the youth about journalism's purpose, principles, and practices is the premise of the mynews@school program that I discussed in Chapter 6. I believe if the upcoming generation better understood the process of real journalism, they would better appreciate and respect news, know how to distinguish news from opinion and unverified information that passes for news, and be less likely to be candidates for the endangered list of news consumers.

Non-Legacy News Media Must Get Involved

To avoid a nation of news illiterates in the future requires programs like mynews@school and NIE and necessitates long-term, big-picture thinking and planning with full-board stakeholder participation. From journalism associations to educational, philanthropic, business, and political leaders, everyone must step up and do their part. Even non-legacy news media, including news portals such as Yahoo, and online non-profits such as *ProPublica, The Voice of San Diego,* and *The Texas Tribune,* must get involved. Although non-profit online-only news Web sites are being run by former journalists from legacy news media, it does not mean they have to carry on the legacy of excluding Millennials from news coverage. Since non-profits no longer have to worry about profits per se, they are free to cover Millennials in ways that respect and engage this young generation. Including the Millennial Generation will enhance these Web-based non-profits' mission of serving the "public interest, common good" or encouraging "civic participation or involvement" (Brown, 2011, p. 11).

In a study of non-profit news executives, presented at AEJMC's 2011 annual conference of journalism educators, Emily Donohue Brown, who is also the award-winning news director of KUT, the NPR radio station in Austin, Texas, found that many of the non-profit news executives she interviewed included in their mission doing "stories that no one else is doing," and "stories that aren't necessarily going anywhere else" (Brown, 2011, p. 11).

Ironically and sadly, "none of the executives interviewed viewed engaging young people as an integral part of current mission" (Brown, 2011, p. 16). Furthermore, these new additions to the news media landscape didn't sound very new in their thinking since "many executives assumed young people simply weren't interested in news" (Brown, 2011, p. 16). ProPublica's editor in chief, president, and CEO Paul Steiger, who was formerly the managing editor of *The Wall Street Journal,* perhaps best articulated this thinking when he said: "we're not going to kid ourselves and say we can get a huge percent of that demographic." In other words, serving the "public interest, common good," or encouraging "civic participation or involvement" as these non-profits claim is their mission (Brown, 2011, p. 11), appears not to apply when it comes to involving young people.

Social Media and Search Engines Must Become Active Players

There is also a pro-active role for potential gateways to and diversions from news that Facebook, Twitter, Google, Yahoo, and YouTube can play to help ensure that we don't become a nation of news illiterates. Social media, search engines, and the video Web site YouTube currently include a platform for news, but in many ways the platform is passive—Millennials have to find the news rather than the news from these platforms finding Millennials. These times, though, demand that Facebook, Twitter, Google, Yahoo, and YouTube play a more active role to facilitate and reinforce Millennial news engagement. One place that they can become more active is during a presidential election season, when Millennials are more likely to pay attention to news. It's great, for example, that Facebook, Google, Yahoo, and YouTube co-sponsored debates during the 2012 presidential primary season, but what if part of that co-sponsorship required the networks and cable news channels to share moderator responsibilities with an editor of a college paper who would ask candidates questions from the youth perspective. The answers could be posted on YouTube, promoted by social media, and reported on by legacy media.

With over 900 million Facebook users worldwide, Twitter and YouTube expanding their roles on the news media stage, the arrival of Google+ (Efrati, 2012) and the emergence of social media sensation Pinterest (Pogue, 2012), perhaps the most important contribution these sites can make to the effort to engage the Millennial Generation with news is to answer this very important question: What social media attributes can be duplicated in the news media terrain to get Millennials as excited about news as they are about social media? If the news media could incorporate some of these appealing attributes in their platforms and reports, it would be a major step forward on the path to engaging this generation with news.

Fake News Has an Important Role

Fake news, including *The Daily Show*, *The Colbert Report*, *SNL*'s news desk, and *The Onion*, also have to show up and get involved in encouraging the Millennial Generation's engagement with news, especially because they are often viewed by Millennials as trusted truth tellers about what's really going on with news-makers and how the news media covers them.

Civic, Education, Business, Foundation, and Political Leaders Must Step Up

The need for young people to acquire media and news literacy skills is high on the agenda of civic, education, business, foundation, and political leaders, but the lack of a defined national goal and agreed-upon approach for achieving that goal make it harder if not impossible to attain. Despite the fact that in the media and news literacy arena, non-profits have been established, programs have been funded, U.S. senators have authored a bill, think tanks have written white papers, universities are offering courses, and media and news literacy requirements are now incorporated into state education curricula (Waldman, 2011), news consumers in the Millennial Generation are endangered and may never engage with news.

Therefore, it's time for civic, education, business, foundation, and political leaders to wake up to the fact that the clock is running out, and a course correction is needed if we are to once again become a nation where being informed is valued. Correcting course can begin with three simple but important ideas:

1. Simplify the goal to focus on news literacy which encompasses becoming a savvy consumer of news and understanding the purpose, principles, and process of journalism that produces news. A clear focus on news literacy avoids the problem of getting lost under the digital and media literacy umbrella.

2. Support teachers' efforts to incorporate news and news literacy in the classroom. As discussed in Chapter 6, with the declining presence of news in the home, there is no one more influential in developing future news consumers than elementary, middle school, and high school teachers.

3. Support a national "Engage with News" Day to be held the first Tuesday of October. Teachers would bring news into the classroom; families would read, watch, and discuss news at home together. Journalists, representing their news organizations and journalism associations, would visit classrooms to emphasize the purpose, principles, and process of journalism. The news media and

journalism classes would cover the "Engage with News" Day event
and these stories with accompanying multimedia and lots of quotes
from Millennials could be posted and shared on social media.

With an annual day set aside to revitalize the public's engagement with
news, regardless of generation, we would be reminded that being informed of
news is empowering and even enjoyable. More importantly, as civic, education,
business, foundation, and political leaders know all too well, engaging with news
and becoming informed is essential to our democratic nation's future vitality.
Furthermore, an event such as "Engage with News" Day would be an opportunity for leaders of professional journalism associations, journalism education
associations, and continuing journalism education foundations to step off the
sidelines and get involved in this 21st-century issue that speaks to the future
of journalism and safeguards a free press.

What About Journalism Schools?

Journalism schools are a particularly important stakeholder because they also
represent the future. Interestingly, when former executive editor of *The New
York Times* Bill Keller spoke to journalism students and faculty at the University
of Texas at Austin, he admitted that he hadn't always respected the role of
journalism schools. But now Keller says that he appreciates the role that journalism schools are playing in producing future journalists. Evidence of the
important role of journalism schools can also be found in the national survey
of American journalists conducted by Indiana University journalism scholars
(Weaver et al., 2003). Journalism schools, more than any other place, teach
future journalists how to be journalists. But while journalism schools are
teaching journalists how to cover the nation, the world, the local community,
including courts, city hall, and the school board, they are neglecting teaching future journalists how to cover their own generation. This must change.
Journalism schools must incorporate "Best Practices" for covering Millennials
in the curriculum right along with the curriculum changes on how to report
with the digital reporting tools that are sweeping across the journalism education landscape. For journalism professors who think the curriculum is already
crammed with teaching future journalists how to use the new digital reporting tools, they should keep in mind that if they continue their legacy of poor
reporting on youth, it won't matter what new digital reporting tools they
teach in the curriculum, because in the future there won't be an audience to
read, watch, listen to, or engage with their news in any form or fashion. As

Glenn Frankel, director of the School of Journalism at the University of Texas at Austin, who won a Pulitzer Prize while at *The Washington Post*, said in his welcoming remarks at the Millennials and News Summit, journalism educators also have a responsibility to "help create the next generation of consumers of journalism."

Because journalism schools are now populating the news media landscape with non-profit Web-only news sites, it's hoped that they don't follow the lead of the professional non-profits that don't see young adults in their mission. That, of course, would be the ultimate irony, since stories posted on these J-School-based news sites are written by young people, even though they are overseen by editors who have moved from legacy newsrooms to university classrooms. These new J-School Web sites have a unique opportunity to be role models for both legacy media and non-profit Web-only news sites on how to cover and include Millennials in the news. It is hoped that they take that on as part of their mission, especially because news being reported from these journalism school-based news Web sites is being picked up and published in legacy news outlets (Downie Jr., 2011).

Parents and Teachers Have to Shoulder More Responsibility

Table 7.2 reminds us why everyone is responsible for ensuring a news literate population in the future, but some have more responsibility than others, especially because when asked to agree or disagree with three statements at the heart of a news literate nation, Millennials made it clear they don't necessarily embrace what they were taught about being informed while growing up. For this generation, there's no great sense of duty to keep informed. In fact, Millennials do not overwhelmingly value being informed, and neither do those important to them. Just a little more than half (54%) of Millennials agreed or strongly agreed that they had a duty to keep informed, and only 44% agreed or strongly agreed that being informed is important. Even fewer Millennials (31%) said people important to them value being informed of news.

If this young generation feels no responsibility to be informed, and those around them do not value news, is it too late to change their minds? Or will the value of being informed further erode in the generation that follows Millennials? Further erosion will occur only if parents and teachers shrug their socialization agent shoulders and don't continue to pass on and reinforce the importance of being informed to the next generation. Since these beliefs about the value of being informed are "learned in the formative years and come

TABLE 7.2 Where Millennials Stand on Being Informed and News % Saying Agree and Strongly Agree

Duty to keep informed	54%
Being informed is important	44%
People important to you value news	31%

about partly as a function of the milieu in which a person grows up and partly as a function of the basic personality of the individual" (Milbrath & Goel, 1977, p. 53), parents as the first teachers and role models are vital to passing on the importance of engaging with news and becoming informed. While there is no guarantee that believing it's important to be informed will actually lead to news engagement, it is likely that no engagement with news will take place if being informed is perceived as lacking value.

Passages in the News Engagement Socialization Process

Despite the lack of a one-size-fits-all blueprint for socializing a generation into future news consumers, with some planning it is possible to tailor news to the life stages young people will pass through as they grow up. Since studies have shown that home and school can contribute to news engagement, parents need to be conscious of a few things they can do as their child's first teacher and role model (Bogart, 1981; Grusin & Stone, 1993; B. Wilson, 2008).

With the availability of anytime, anywhere news, the days of families subscribing to newspapers may be behind us, but that doesn't preclude news from being part of the home environment, especially around the dinner hour. News can even be a part of the environment while taking a child to school or picking him or her up. There's nothing more engaging than NPR's *Morning Edition* and *All Things Considered* in the afternoon. Parents can also include news in the home environment by making a news portal such as Yahoo or AOL the home page for the home computer. That way, when the computer is signed on, news will automatically be encountered, whether accidentally or on purpose. (Unfortunately, when Google is the home page, news has to be clicked to be displayed.) The presence of news in the home environment and the car, coupled with parent encouragement, can have a positive life-long effect during the formative years (Lifelong readers, n.d.).

Just as the home environment is vital, what happens in the classroom is equally if not more important, especially because news is absent in so many homes. While the significance of news in the classroom cannot be underestimated, it should be recognized that news in the classroom also has the potential to turn students off. That's why teachers have to balance making news engaging for students and associating news with school and homework. If news is only viewed as school and homework, it will likely be harder to re-set that association in adulthood.

Fortunately, because of the availability of resources tailored to specific ages and grades, teachers aren't on their own when introducing kids to news. For elementary age children, resources include *Weekly Reader News*, *Time for Kids*, *Scholastic* news, and NIE programs, which include classroom newspapers, curriculum materials, and teacher training. NIE and programs such as mynews@school, discussed earlier, also have materials designed for Wave II Millennial middle school children. The mynews@school program is similar to other NIE programs because each student in the classroom has access to his or her own newspaper, but it's also different because it emphasizes the purpose, principles, and process of journalism so kids will know that real journalism is supposed to be guided by ethical standards, verification by reliable sources, and an effort to be fair and balanced, unlike some of the stuff that passes itself off as news. Although journalism doesn't consistently achieve this goal, especially in its coverage of Millennials, having this knowledge will help Millennials hold journalism accountable.

Additionally, mynews@school uses an electronic edition of the newspaper, directed activities that emphasize independent news exploration, and small-group discussions that are more like how news engagement happens in the real world. Modeling real world news engagement in the classroom is particularly important if what happens in the classroom is to carry over in real life.

While the e-replica edition of the newspaper is appropriate for middle school because it looks like a newspaper and does not change like a news Web site, as children age out of middle school and move into high school, their experience with news should expand to include the vast legitimate news possibilities available on the Internet. In some areas, there are also teen sections published in the newspaper to entice them into becoming future readers.

By the time Millennials reach college age, they are on their own, unless they get some direction from professors who incorporate news in class discussions and assignments, or free national and local newspapers are available on their campus through the Collegiate Readership Program developed by *USA Today Education*, or they are exposed to young adult-targeted products produced by the mainstream paper. One such example is the Chicago Tribune's *RedEye*, which was described as a "free commuter tabloid newspaper" designed to reach the "young and time-pressed" (Rosenthal, 2009). Additionally, *RedEye*, which is celebrating its 10th anniversary, serves as an advertising vehicle to "reach a larger portion of the younger, urban demographic" (Rosenthal, 2009). The *San Antonio Express* and *Dallas Morning News* also published young adult-targeted newspapers, but they have now been shut down.

Are youth-targeted publications gateways or barriers to engaging the Millennial Generation with news? University of Florida journalism scholar Amy Zerba conducted focus groups and found some young adults liked the youth-oriented papers, some disliked them, and some had mixed feelings. A 20-something male dismissed San Antonio's young adult paper as "ad paper," and a 22-year-old female said if the newspaper was for her age group, she was "kind of offended" (Zerba, 2009, p. 178). The young woman added that she cared about "what's going on in the world," but the young adult newspaper did not include news about what was going on in the world (Zerba, 2009, p. 178).

Whether or not these publications become stepping stones or impediments to future news engagement will likely be determined by the balance of advertising and news. If an ad-heavy, news-light publication reinforces the notion that news isn't very important, the news media will have missed another opportunity, which it cannot afford, to "help create a new generation interested in news" (Kovach & Rosenstiel, 2007, p. 211).

Will Charging for News on the Internet Become News Media's Self-Inflicted Wound?

It's understandable that some news organizations have tried to recoup lost revenues by charging for news on the Internet after the old business model collapsed. But the decision to charge for news doesn't seem very smart if short-term revenue gains are compared against a future in which news consumers in the Millennial generation no longer exist.

Because the vast majority of Millennials believe news on the Internet should be free, requiring them to pay for news, something that isn't even highly valued, will deter rather than encourage their engagement with news.

Not only are Millennials philosophically opposed to charging for news on the Internet, considering the financial burden this generation has endured thanks to the drying up of jobs during the Great Recession of 2008, and high debt, courtesy of college student loans, paying for news when so much on the Internet is free or virtually free doesn't seem like something this generation will be eager to do.

That's why I recommend all news organizations should make news on the Internet free through age 26, one year after Millennials can no longer be carried on their parents' health insurance. News organizations can get "credit" for these free subscriptions by requiring Millennials to register at the news site with their first and last name, city, state, and zip code, e-mail address, and date of birth. If free access to news on the Internet helps keep Millennials off the list of endangered news consumers, the long-term benefits for Millennials, the news media, and our democracy will overshadow the short-term revenue gains from charging for news that Millennials as well as many others believe should be free.

Millennials Have a Responsibility, Too!

Millennials have a choice. They can turn away from news for good and become lifelong news illiterates, or they can engage with news and become empowered by being informed, like Alex, whom you met in Chapter 1. Alex not only engages with news by following it through social media and the convenience of news apps on her smartphone, she also encourages other Millennials to do the same as the co-founder and editor of an aggregator of news stories for the Millennial Generation. Currently posted on Facebook, this digital collection of news stories, selected every morning from credible news organizations, includes stories about Millennials, stories of interest to Millennials, and important stories Millennials should know. (For information about Millennials and News, see Appendix D.) Alex's enthusiasm for news took a while to develop. Despite the fact that she grew up in a home in which her parents subscribed to two newspapers, she just wasn't that into news when she was younger. But Alex's attitude began to change when she went to a Midwestern university that participated in *USA Today*'s Collegiate Readership Program that allowed her to pick up a national paper such as *The New York Times* or *USA Today*, the nearest metropolitan paper, or the local paper, for free. By the time Alex was in graduate school, she perhaps began to experience some of the same attachments to news that her parents had.

Or maybe what happened to Alex is what Emily Donohue Brown, news director at KUT, the NPR station in Austin, Texas, said at the Millennials and News Summit held at the University of Texas at Austin. Thinking about her own experience with news, the award-winning news director said that she wasn't that into news growing up, but then one day "Something just clicked."

What is it that needs to happen for news to just click in the lives of Millennials? Journalism must have "meaning in people's lives, not only its traditional audience but the next generation as well" (Kovach & Rosenstiel, 2007, p. 223). If journalism were to incorporate "Best Practices" in covering Millennials, perhaps news would begin to have meaning in Millennials' lives and it would begin to click. In fact, Facebook and Twitter are poised to facilitate the process by which news clicks in the hearts and minds of Millennials. Whether it's Alex's aggregation of news stories that she currently posts on Facebook, or the Facebook News Feed that has yet to live up to its full potential for engaging Millennials with news, or Twitter, which makes it easy to follow news or the next big social media thing, social media is in the news media landscape to stay. And it's now the responsibility of all stakeholders to make sure that social media is not a diversion away from news but is a platform that Millennials and generations that have yet to be born can use to inform themselves of news so they, too, will be "free and self-governing" (Kovach & Rosenstiel, 2007, p. 5). That's the only way our democratic society can live up to the potential envisioned by not just the founders but all of us who have a stake in our country's future and the future of journalism.

But can we really live up to the full potential of our democracy and journalism if, as Pulitzer Prize-winning editorial writer Tod Robberson of *The Dallas Morning News* asserted at the Millennials and News Summit, that being uninformed is not the exclusive domain of the Millennial Generation? Furthermore, and equally disturbing, is that from Robberson's vantage point from the opinion page, a culture of being misinformed has taken root. Instead of just being illiterate of news, Robberson asserts that people are choosing to be illiterate of facts when they accept rather than reject outrageous claims passed along as facts. Add in the steep decline in press credibility, and we are reminded that although it's not impossible, all stakeholders have a lot of work to do before engaging with news is embraced and valued, not just among Millennials, but in our democratic society as a whole.

APPENDIX

Appendix A.1
National Survey of News
Engagement Questionnaire

Used with permission from Paula Poindexter

1. When you think about news, what words come to mind?

_____

2. Approximately how many days in an average week do you get news?
    1. 0 days—What is the main reason you do *not* get any news?
    2. 1 day (Skip to Q7)
    3. 2 days
    4. 3 days
    5. 4 days
    6. 5 days
    7. 6 days
    8. 7 days
2b. Do you primarily get news from:
    1. Hardcopy newspaper
    2. Hardcopy magazine
    3. TV
    4. Radio
    5. Online
    6. Other (Please specify)_____

3. If you get news at least one day per week, what is the main reason you get news?

_____

4. Please rank the two types of news that you pay most attention to. Please select a choice under "First Rank" for the news type that you rank first and select a choice under "Second Rank" for the news type you rank second.

First Rank:
1. International
2. National
3. State
4. Local
5. Your neighborhood and the area surrounding it
6. Other (Please specify)_____

Second Rank:
1. International
2. National
3. State
4. Local
5. Your neighborhood and the area surrounding it
6. Other (Please specify)_____

5. How often do you do the following? 1 = Often; 2 = Sometimes; 3 = Seldom; 4 = Never

A. Watch Jon Stewart's *The Daily Show*	1	2	3	4
B. Read journalists' blogs	1	2	3	4
C. Read blogs written by non-journalists who blog about the news	1	2	3	4
D. Watch *The Colbert Report*	1	2	3	4
E. Watch a video on a news Web site	1	2	3	4
F. Comment on a news story you read online	1	2	3	4
G. Upload a photograph you've taken to a news Web site	1	2	3	4
H. Upload a video you've produced to a news Web site	1	2	3	4
I. Watch a slide show posted on a news Web site	1	2	3	4
I. Read readers' comments on news stories	1	2	3	4

6. If you read readers' comments at least seldom, what is the main reason you read readers' comments?

_____

7. Do you read magazines?
   1. Yes
   2. No

7a. Approximately how many magazines do you read a month? (If you don't read magazines, skip to Q9)_____

8. What type of magazines do you read most often?

_____

9. If you get news online, how do you usually access it?
   1. Cell or smartphone with apps
   2. Cell with Internet access but no apps
   3. iPad or other tablet computer
   4. Laptop computer
   5. Desk computer
   6. Other (Please specify)_____
   7. Don't get news online (Skip to Q40)

10. Typically when you read news online, are you purposely searching for news or are you reading news because you saw it while online doing something else?
    1. Purposely searching for news
    2. Saw news while online doing something else
    3. Other (Please specify) _____

11. When you're online getting news, from what source do you usually get news? (Please be as specific as possible)

_____

12. Do you usually click on most, some, or none of the hyperlinks you come across while reading a news story online?
    1. Most
    2. Some
    3. None (Skip to Q14)

13. If you click most or some hyperlinks, what is the main reason you click on a link while reading a news story?

_____

14. How often does someone you know e-mail a news story to you?
    1. Often
    2. Sometimes
    3. Seldom
    4. Never (Skip to Q16)

15. How often do you read the news story e-mailed to you by someone you know?
    1. Often
    2. Sometimes
    3. Seldom
    4. Never

16. How often do you e-mail a news story to someone you know?
    1. Often
    2. Sometimes
    3. Seldom
    4. Never

Now I have some questions about social media such as Facebook and Twitter

17. Are you currently on Facebook?
    1. Yes
    2. No → Have you ever been on Facebook?
              1. Yes → Why are you no longer on Facebook?

                        _____

                        (Skip to Q26)
              2. No
              (Skip to Q26)

18. What year did you first get on Facebook?

_____

19. On average, how many days a week do you go on Facebook?
    1. 0 days
    2. 1 day
    3. 2 days
    4. 3 days
    5. 4 days
    6. 5 days
    7. 6 days
    8. 7 days

20. Approximately, how many hours do you spend on Facebook per day?

    _____

21. Approximately, what per cent of your time on Facebook do you spend getting news?

    _____

22. How often do you see news stories posted on a friend's Facebook page?
    1. Often
    2. Sometimes
    3. Seldom
    4. Never (Skip to Q24)

23. How often have you read a news story posted on a friend's Facebook page?
    1. Often
    2. Sometimes
    3. Seldom
    4. Never

24. How often do you post a news story on your Facebook page?
    1. Often
    2. Sometimes
    3. Seldom
    4. Never

25. Most media now have a Facebook page. How many days a week do you get news from a Facebook page produced by the news media?
    1. 0 days
    2. 1 day
    3. 2 days
    4. 3 days
    5. 4 days
    6. 5 days
    7. 6 days
    8. 7 days

26. Are you currently on Twitter?
    1. Yes
    2. No (Skip to Q30)

27. How many days a week do you read news on Twitter?
    1. 0 days
    2. 1 day
    3. 2 days
    4. 3 days
    5. 4 days
    6. 5 days
    7. 6 days
    8. 7 days

28. What is the main reason you get news from Twitter?

    _____

29. How often do you tweet a news story?
    1. Often
    2. Sometimes
    3. Seldom
    4. Never

Now I have some questions about smartphones, apps, and iPads

30. How often do you send a text message about something in the news?
    1. Often
    2. Sometimes
    3. Seldom
    4. Never

31. Some people have software applications or apps on their cell phones; others don't. Do you have apps on your cell phone which enable you to access news?
    1. Yes
    2. No

31a. Approximately, how many apps on your cell phone enable you to access news?

_____

(If you don't have apps, skip to Q34)

32. Which news apps do you have?

_____

33. How often do you use news apps to access news?
    1. Often
    2. Sometimes
    3. Seldom
    4. Never

34. How many days a week do you read the news on your cell phone?
    1. 0 days
    2. 1 day
    3. 2 days
    4. 3 days
    5. 4 days
    6. 5 days
    7. 6 days
    8. 7 days

35. What is the main reason you get the news on your cell phone?

_____

36. Do you have an iPad or other tablet computer?
    1. Yes
    2. No (Skip to Q40)

37. Do you have any apps on your iPad or tablet computer that enable you to access news?
    1. Yes
    2. No

37a. Approximately, how many apps on your iPad enable you to access news?

_____

38. Which news apps do you have on your iPad or tablet computer?

_____

39. How many days a week do you read the news on your iPad or tablet computer?
    1. 0 days
    2. 1 day
    3. 2 days
    4. 3 days
    5. 4 days
    6. 5 days
    7. 6 days
    8. 7 days

Now I have a few questions about growing up with news

40. Was news around you all of the time, most of the time, some of the time, seldom, or never in the home you grew up in?
    1. All of the time
    2. Most of the time
    3. Some of the time
    4. Seldom
    5. Never
    6. Can't remember

41. Growing up, how often was the TV tuned to news around dinner time?
    1. All of the time
    2. Most of the time
    3. Some of the time
    4. Seldom
    5. Never
    6. Can't remember

42. How often were newspapers around in the home you grew up in?
    1. All of the time
    2. Most of the time
    3. Some of the time
    4. Seldom
    5. Never
    6. Can't remember

43. How often were there discussions about something in the news in the home you grew up in?
    1. All of the time
    2. Most of the time
    3. Some of the time
    4. Seldom
    5. Never
    6. Can't remember

44. Can you recall anyone ever telling you explicitly or implicitly that being informed about news is important?
    1. Yes
    2. No (Skip to Q46)
    3. Can't remember (Skip to Q46)
    4. Other (Please specify) _____

45. Who was the person who said to you that being informed about the news is important?

    _____

46. Growing up, how often did you discuss news with your friends?
    1. All of the time
    2. Most of the time
    3. Some of the time
    4. Seldom
    5. Never
    6. Can't remember

47. Did you have a teacher who included news in your elementary, middle school, or high school classroom at least once a week?
    1. Yes
    2. No
    3. Can't remember

48. What words best describe your feelings about news while you were growing up?

_____

Attitudes About News and Journalism

49. Here are some things that have been said about the news and journalism. Please indicate your level of agreement or disagreement with the statement, with 1 being Strongly Disagree and 5 being Strongly Agree.

	Strongly Disagree				Strongly Agree
A. You enjoy keeping up with the news.	1	2	3	4	5
B. Most news is boring.	1	2	3	4	5
C. We all have a duty to keep ourselves informed about news and current events.	1	2	3	4	5
D. Keeping up with the news is a waste of time.	1	2	3	4	5
E. It's important for the news media to be a watchdog of powerful people and the government.	1	2	3	4	5
F. The news does a poor job of providing the context to understand a story.	1	2	3	4	5
G. You like to discuss news with others.	1	2	3	4	5

	Strongly Disagree				Strongly Agree
H. The press in America has too much freedom to do what it wants.	1	2	3	4	5
I. You were raised to believe being informed of the news is important.	1	2	3	4	5
J. Most news is biased.	1	2	3	4	5
K. Being informed of the news makes you feel empowered.	1	2	3	4	5
L. Most journalists lack high ethical standards.	1	2	3	4	5
M. The news media should act more like a good neighbor.	1	2	3	4	5
N. All news on the Internet should be free to the public.	1	2	3	4	5
O. The news media cares little about people like you.	1	2	3	4	5
P. Most of the people who are important to you value keeping up with the news.	1	2	3	4	5
Q. You depend on the news to help you with your daily life.	1	2	3	4	5

50. What grade from A to F would you give the news media for its coverage of young people in the age range of 18 to late 20s?
    1. A
    2. B
    3. C
    4. D
    5. F

51. What is the main reason for your grade?

_____

52. What specific recommendations do you have to improve the coverage of young people in the age range of 18 to late 20s?

_____

53. What is the most important problem facing this country today?

_____

54. How often do you keep up with news about the most important problem facing the country?
    1. Often
    2. Sometimes
    3. Seldom
    4. Never

55. Right now, is there an issue of particular importance to you personally?
    1. Yes→ 55A. What is that issue? _____
    2. No (Skip to Q57)

56. How often do you get news about the issue that is important to you personally?
    1. Often
    2. Sometimes
    3. Seldom
    4. Never

57. Did you vote in the 2008 U.S. Presidential Election?
    1. Yes
    2. No

58. Do you intend to vote in the 2012 U.S. Presidential Election?
    1. Definitely will vote
    2. Probably will vote
    3. Probably will not vote
    4. Definitely will not vote

59. Generally speaking, do you identify yourself as a?:
    1. Democrat
    2. Republican
    3. Independent
    4. Other (Please specify) _____

60. Do you consider yourself?:
    1. Conservative
    2. Middle of the road
    3. Liberal
    4. Other _____

61. What year were you born?

    _____

62. Are you?
    1. Male
    2. Female

63. Are you currently a full-time student?
    1. Yes
    2. No

64. What is the highest level of education that you've completed?
    1. Some High School or Less
    2. High School Degree
    3. Some College or Technical School Degree
    4. College Graduate
    5. Some Graduate or Professional School
    6. Master's, M.D., or Doctorate

65. What is your race or ethnic group?
    1. Caucasian or White
    2. African American or Black
    3. Hispanic or Latino
    4. Asian American
    5. Native American
    6. Other (Please specify) _____

66. Approximately, what is your household income?
    1. Under $20,000
    2. $20–$29,000
    3. $30–$39,000
    4. $40–$49,000

5. $50–$59,000
6. $60–$69,000
7. $70–$79,000
8. $80–$89,000
9. $90–$99,000
10. $100,000 or more

67. Are you?
    1. Employed full-time
    2. Employed part-time
    3. Self-employed
    4. Not employed

68. Is keeping up with the news?
    1. Required for your job
    2. Not required for work but beneficial
    3. Not required and *not* beneficial
    4. Other (Please specify)_____

69. Are you a parent?
    1. Yes
    2. No (Skip to Q71)

69a.   How many children do you have? _____

70. What are the specific ages of your children? (Check all that apply)
    1. 4 and under
    2. 5 to 10
    3. 11 to 13
    4. 14 to 17
    5. 18 to 22
    6. 23 to 29
    7. 30 to 49
    8. 50-plus

71. What is your zip code? (Please enter a valid 5-digit zip code)

_____

72. Participants between the ages of 18 and 29 will be asked to share their opinions about stories recently in the news. Participants selected to share their opinions will be eligible for a drawing for gifts and cash prizes. If you are willing to share your opinion about stories recently in the news, please enter your e-mail address:

Appendix A.2
National Survey of News
Engagement Methodology

The National Survey of News Engagement, which was approved by the University of Texas at Austin's Institutional Review Board (IRB), was conducted online May 22 through June 10, 2011. I wrote the survey questionnaire and commissioned the Office of Survey Research (OSR) at the University of Texas at Austin to handle the fieldwork. The survey questionnaire, which took 10 to 15 minutes to answer, was completed by 1,011 respondents. The sample of online respondents was acquired through Survey Sampling International, an internationally respected survey sampling firm. The source of the online sample was an actively managed panel. Since the panel sample was non-probability rather than random, it was requested that the sample match U.S. demographic statistics. A total of 64,400 e-mail invitations were sent to panel participants; a total of 1,212 clicked the survey link to access the survey and 1,011 or 83% completed the survey. For information on online panels and evaluating non-probability Internet panels, see Callegaro & Disogra (2008) and AAPOR's Standard Definitions (2011, p. 38).

Fifty-two percent of the total sample was female, and the 18% who were 18 to 29 were classified as the Millennial Generation. Millennials under the age of 18 were not interviewed for the survey. Baby Boomers were represented by 343 sample respondents. Eighty-four percent of the sample respondents were white, 10% were African American, 7% were Hispanic or Latino, and 6% were Asian American. Since Hispanics may have selected white rather than the ethnic group of Hispanic or Latino, there may have actually been more Latinos in the sample than indicated by the question on race and ethnicity.

Appendix B.1
Invitation to Participate in mynews@school Program and Screening Questionnaire

Used with permission from Paula Poindexter

As part of its NIE program, the *Austin American-Statesman* is collaborating with the School of Journalism at the University of Texas at Austin in a 10-week, news-in-the-schools program. UT's School of Journalism is looking for middle school teachers who would like for their classrooms to participate. This year, students will have access to the eEdition of the *Statesman* as well as hard copies of the paper, so classrooms must have computers and Internet access. To be considered for the program, teachers will need to agree to the mynews@school activities below, including completing and returning the questionnaire by the deadline.

Activities

1. Receive and use free eEdition of the *Statesman* plus weekly class-room-tested, news-based activities for 10 weeks beginning the week of October 3 and ending the week of December 5. *Please note, if you currently receive only print newspapers, you will also receive eEdition access during this period. If you currently only receive eEdition, we will also send print copies during this period. And if you are not currently receiving newspapers at your school, eEdition access and print copies will be provided on or before October 3 and through the final week of the program.*

2. Complete one evaluation questionnaire from students and teacher.

3. If your classroom is selected, devote one class period to guest speaker from the UT School of Journalism.

4. Provide teacher and student feedback on weekly classroom activities and stories that may interest kids of their age.

5. If your classroom is selected, give permission to video newspaper-related activities in the classroom during one class period.

6. Classrooms participating in all weekly activities will be eligible for a drawing for a class pizza party.

Teachers completing all weekly activities during the duration of the program will receive $50.00 at conclusion of program. Additionally, participation certificates will be given to teachers and students completing all program activities.

The questionnaire is attached. If you would like to participate, please return by September 12.

Appendix B.2
Teacher Screening Questionnaire
to Participate in mynews@school Program

Used with permission from Paula Poindexter

Please answer the following questions about yourself, your class, and your school.

1. Name: _____
2. School: _____School District: _____
3. Principal's Name: _____
4. Your E-mail Address: _____
5. School Address:_____
   _____
6. School Phone Contact:_____ Cell Phone:_____
7. Grade Level for Primary Class That Will Participate in News-in-the-Schools Program: _____
8. Subject of Class? _____
9. Is This Class Gifted? _____
10. Number of Students in Class:_____
11. Approximate Gender Percentage of Class: Girls _____ Boys _____
12. Approximate racial and ethnic percentage of class:
    White____ African American/Black____ Latino/Hispanic____
    Asian American_____ Native American_____ Other____
13. Academic Performance Level of Class: Mostly Above Grade Level_____
    Mostly at Grade Level _____ Mostly Below Grade Level_____
14. Approximate percentage of class proficient in English:_____
15. Years using newspaper in your classroom:_____
16. Specify other news sources, if any, used in your classroom:
    _____
17. How many computers do you have in your classroom? ____

18. How many of the computers have Internet access? _____
19. What percentage of the students in your school are economically disadvantaged?_____
20. Number of years as a teacher:_____
21. If you were selected to participate, which day of the week would you want to receive the newspaper?_____

Appendix B.3a
mynews@school E-mail
to Teachers for Week 1

Used with permission from Paula Poindexter

Getting Acquainted with the E-edition of the Newspaper

Dear Teachers:

I'm thrilled that you are participating in the Fall 2011 mynews@school Program. This year, mynews@school, which is a collaboration with the *Austin American-Statesman* and the University of Texas at Austin School of Journalism, is funded with personal funds. The mynews@school program, which is now in its fourth year, complements a traditional newspaper-in-education program while emphasizing the purpose, principles, and process of journalism in an engaging and challenging way.

You should have already started receiving the e-edition of the *Austin American-Statesman* as well as two hard copies of the newspaper. The *Statesman* Educational Services and Development Manager started your subscription based on the day you specified in your screening questionnaire. By starting the subscriptions the week prior to the kick-off week, deliveries should run smoothly. If, however, you encounter problems, please contact the *Statesman*.

This first week is devoted to organizing your mynews@school groups, getting acquainted with the e-edition of the *Statesman* and the mynews@school activities. The activities are very important to the success of the program. It's also very important that you e-mail feedback when it's requested. To facilitate e-mailing feedback, each week you might assign one of your mynews@school groups the responsibility of collecting, organizing, synthesizing, and typing up the most popular answers to the questions. Once you have the answers, you can copy and paste them in an e-mail to me. This year you do have a choice in communicating your classroom's activities to me. Instead of an e-mail, you can also create a mynews@school blog or Facebook page. If you choose the blog or Facebook route, you can post the activities from your classroom and e-mail me the link for the blog or your Facebook page name so that I'll know you have completed the activities for that week.

For your convenience, I am also sending this week's activities in PowerPoint slides. Also, please do not forget that you will receive two copies of the hard copy paper. One teacher would let her students check out sections of the newspaper to take home and share with their parents. You might consider using your hard copy paper in a similar fashion.

It's very exciting that so many different districts and communities are participating. Most of the participants are middle school English Language and Social Studies classrooms. In some cases teachers are including more than one class. This year over 300 school children will be participating.

Please remember that classrooms participating in all weekly activities will be eligible for a drawing for a class pizza party. Additionally, teachers completing all weekly activities during the duration of the program will receive a $50.00 cash gift at the conclusion of the program. Participation certificates will also be given to teachers and students completing all program activities.

Please e-mail me to confirm that you have received this e-mail, and if you have questions about the delivery of your e-edition and hard copy papers, please contact the *Statesman*.

Thank you for participating in the 2011 mynews@school program. If there are any other questions, feel free to call me on my cell phone number.

Best regards,

Paula M. Poindexter, Ph.D.

10 Weeks of mynews@school Activities:
Week of October 3–Week of December 5

Week 1:	Getting acquainted with the e-edition of the newspaper
Week 2:	What is news? What is the process of journalism?
Week 3:	The front page
Week 4:	News story formats and writing styles
Week 5:	News story ideas and quotes

Week 6:	Visuals in the newspaper
Week 7:	Datelines and Geography
Week 8:	Holidays, commemorations, and history in the news
Week 9:	Exploring news Web sites
Week 10:	Teachers and students complete end-of-program questionnaires

Organizing Your Class and Getting Started with the e-Edition of the Statesman

1. Organize students into mynews@school groups—4 to 5 students per group.

2. Provide each student with password to access e-edition of the *Statesman*. I encourage you to write the password on the board and let students copy it down so they can also use it at home and show their parents, siblings, and friends what they're doing with the e-edition of the *Statesman*.

3. Once students have the password and are organized into their groups, please give them 5 to 10 minutes of free reading of the e-edition of the *Statesman*. Encourage your students to look through all sections of the paper. Once they have familiarized themselves with the e-edition, tell them to find and read a story that interests them. As they read the story, encourage them to think about the five Ws and H that journalists use as a foundation for reporting a story: Who, What, When, Where, Why, and How.

4. After your students have explored the e-edition on their own, allow them 5 to 10 minutes in their groups to discuss stories and photos they found engaging and the reasons why.

5. Following the group discussion, have a student-led class discussion on the following questions:

   (a) How is the e-edition similar and how is it different from reading a print newspaper?

   (b) How is the e-edition similar and how is it different from news Web sites?

   (c) What is the best thing about the e-edition of the *Statesman*?

    (d)   What are some suggestions for improving the experience of using the e-edition of the newspaper?

6.   Before the end of the day that you use the newspaper, please send me an e-mail that includes:

- Most popular answers to questions 5a, 5b, and 5c.

- Your observations (a couple of paragraphs) about your students' experience with using the e-edition of the *Statesman*.

- Your recommendations for making the experience of using the newspaper more educational and engaging.

If you decide to create a blog or a Facebook page, you may e-mail the link to me after you post the week's material. Please use a version of mynews@school in your blog title or Facebook page. For example, you might title it mynews@MillennialSchool. Or you might use a title that incorporates your name and the school name, which would be mynews_in_MsTillmon's class@MillennialSchool.

Appendix B.3b
mynews@school E-mail
to Teachers for Week 2

Used with permission from Paula Poindexter

What is News? What is the Process of Journalism?

Dear Teachers:

Now that your students have compared reading an electronic edition of the *Statesman* and the print edition, the focus this second week of the mynews@school program is on news and the purpose and process of journalism. At the bottom of this e-mail, I have provided information about the definition of news, why people get news, the purpose of journalism, the expectations of journalists, and the principles of verification. Before providing some of the information, you might find out what your students think, especially, what is news, where people get news from and why. The main points of this week's activities are in the attached PowerPoint.

Once you have discussed news and journalism, please allow your students time for free reading the e-edition of the *Statesman*. Ask your students to find a story of interest and answer the following questions:

1. What is the date of the paper and where is the story located? (Section? Page number?)

2. What is the headline (title) and who is the author (byline)?

3. What is the story about?

4. What is the main reason this story is of interest?

5. Thinking about the purpose of journalism and the responsibilities of journalists, what grade would you give the reporter in fulfilling his/her journalistic responsibility? What is the main reason for your grade?

6. Who were some of the sources used to report the story and why did the reporter select these sources? What other sources might you have selected?

After students have answered the questions on the stories of interest, please allow time for group discussion with special attention paid to questions 4 and 5.

In the follow-up class discussion, please have students write the headline, byline, date, section, and page of the stories of interest on the board. Ask your students to review the stories of interest and identify the characteristics of the stories that make them of interest.

Please e-mail the headlines, date, and locations of three to five stories of interest to your students. In your e-mail, please include the characteristics of the stories that made them interesting. If you are posting your answers to a mynews@school blog, please e-mail me the link.

If you have questions or problems, please don't hesitate to e-mail me. If you had delivery problems with the e-edition or paper edition of the *Statesman*, please e-mail the *Statesman*. The quickest and most efficient way for students to access the e-edition is to give them the password. If they have the password, they can also access the paper at home or in the library and share articles with their parents.

Have a great week!

Paula Poindexter

News and Journalism

1. What is news?

News has been defined as "new information about a subject of some public interest that is shared with some portion of the public" (Stephens, 1997, p. 4). A different definition of news sounds more like journalism: the "process of gathering information and making narrative reports," which help the "public make sense of prominent people, important events, and unusual happenings in everyday life" (Campbell, 1998, p. 388).

2. From where do people get news?

People get news from a variety of sources. They read the news in a newspaper. They use a computer to get news from the e-edition of a newspaper, a news Web site or blog. They get news from TV, radio, and cable. They also get news through e-mail, a cell phone, Facebook, YouTube, Twitter, or iPad. Other sources of news include parents, teachers, brothers and sisters, friends, neighbors, acquaintances, and sometimes even strangers.

3. Why do people get news?

Just as there are many sources of news, there are many reasons for getting news. Here are some reasons why people pay attention to news:

1. To be informed.
2. To have something to talk about.
3. To pass the time.
4. To be entertained.
5. To know about threats in the environment.

4. What is the purpose of journalism?

Although there are many sources to get news and the reasons for getting news vary, journalism has one primary purpose according to the authors of *The Elements of Journalism: What Newspeople Should Know and the Public Should Expect*: "to provide citizens with the information they need to be free and self-governing" (Kovach & Rosenstiel, 2007, p. 12). The Hutchins Report said citizens have a right to expect five requirements of the press; the first requirement speaks to what journalism should be providing: "A truthful, comprehensive, and intelligent account of the day's events in a context which gives them meaning" (Commission on Freedom of the Press, 1947, p. 21).

5. What are the responsibilities of journalists who report the news?

✓ Journalists are expected to provide a truthful account of the news in order for people to understand their community, their country, and the world.

✓ Journalists are expected to report news that is comprehensive, in proportion, and a balance of the significant and interesting.

✓ Journalists are expected to make sense of what happened.

✓ Journalists are expected to separate fact from opinion and verify the accuracy of facts and what happened from multiple reliable sources.

✓ Journalists are expected to concentrate on what is verified and important and exclude rumor, innuendo, unverified allegations, the trivial, and opinion.

✓ Journalists are expected to project a fair and balanced representation of society's constituent groups.

✓ Journalists are expected to include identifiable sources when reporting what happened.

✓ Journalists are expected to maintain an independence from those they cover.

✓ Journalists are expected to serve as an independent monitor of power and watchdog of the powerful.

Note: Journalists' responsibilities above represent a variety of perspectives on journalism, including ideas from *The Elements of Journalism* (Kovach & Rosenstiel, 2007) and the report of the Commission on Freedom of the Press (1947).

6. What is the significance of verification in journalism and what are its principles?

According to the authors of *The Elements of Journalism*, "the essence of journalism is a discipline of verification" and it's the verification aspect of journalism that "separates journalism from entertainment, propaganda, fiction, or art" (Kovach & Rosenstiel, 2007, p. 79). The principles of verification in journalism include:

1. Never add anything that was not there.

2. Never deceive the audience.

3. Be as transparent as possible about methods and motives.

4. Rely on own original reporting.

5. Exercise humility. (Kovach & Rosenstiel, 2007, p. 89)

Appendix B.3c
mynews@school E-mail
to Teachers for Week 3

Used with permission from Paula Poindexter

The Front Page

Dear Teachers:

Thank you to the teachers who e-mailed me their students' deliberations on Week 2's mynews@school activities. If you're having problems with the activities or delivery of the e-edition or hard copy newspaper, please let me know so we can help you. Now is the time for those who are behind to catch up.

Now that we're in Week 3, I'd like to bring in the editor's perspective on journalism, as it relates to deciding what actually gets published in the paper. One of the most important decisions that editors make is which stories to publish in the newspaper, which stories to publish on the front page, and even where to place stories on the front page. Placement is not accidental—where a story is located has meaning. For example, stories on the front page are considered by editors to be the most important stories of the day.

Stories that begin at the top of the page or above the fold for print newspapers are generally considered more important than other stories on the front page. The size of the headline or title will also signal a story's importance. The bigger the headline, the more important the story. The most important story is also called the lead story and it is usually located at the top of the page on the right.

When you look closely at a story, you can find out other information: the headline or title of a story; the date and place from where the story was reported, which is called a dateline; the author's name, also called the byline, and the newspaper the writer works for.

Many stories are accompanied by a photo, which has a caption, also called a cutline. Sometimes stories have a photo; sometimes the photograph stands alone. When a photograph is published by itself with only a caption, it's called "wild art." These stand-alone photographs are to capture a slice of everyday life. Other information in the story might be a link to another story or information about multimedia. Finally, the front page includes other information useful for the reader.

While Fred Zipp was editor of the *Austin American-Statesman*, he answered my questions about the importance of the front page. After your students have spent five minutes free reading today's paper, please have them discuss the questions, then e-mail me the most popular answers to questions # 2 and 3. For your convenience, I have also attached a PowerPoint presentation on the newspaper front page and the student activities.

1. Which story did the editor pick as most important? Why do you think that story was picked as most important? Do you agree with the editor?

2. Look through the newspaper and see if you can find a story that as editor you would have placed on the front page. Why do you think that article should have been published on the front page?

3. The editor talks about a "reader" on the front page. Which story do you think is a reader? Do you agree or disagree with the editor that story "fascinates" or "charms?" Why? Is there another story that if you were editor, you would have made today's reader? What is it? Explain why you would have selected that story as today's reader.

mynews@school Q&A with Newspaper Editor

mynews@school: What is the front page and why is this section of the newspaper treated with such high regard?

Editor: The front page is the first page of the newspaper, and it's the face that we show the world every morning. As such, it reflects our values and judgments about the most important and most interesting news of the day. It also serves a marketing function; it allows us to promote stories inside the newspaper.

mynews@school: Is the front page unique to newspapers or is there an equivalent in other news media (TV news, online news, cable news, news magazines, radio news)?

Editor: Print and online publications have covers and home pages that serve the same functions.

mynews@school: In general, what are you trying to accomplish with the front page in terms of what's important and the mix of stories?

Editor: We're a local news organization in an environment where most non-local news is widely available from many different sources. So we focus on local stories on the front page as a way of making clear to readers the difference we bring to the competitive scene. We define local broadly; it can mean a story about an Austin person doing something important or interesting elsewhere just as well as an Austin city government story. We also try to include a "reader," or a story that's notable primarily for its ability to fascinate or charm.

mynews@school: What specific criteria, if any, do you use to determine what stories make it to the front page?

Editor: We do not have a checklist of specific criteria.

mynews@school: Are there certain types of stories or story formats that would never be published on the front page?

Editor: There are not.

mynews@school: How do you use the layout of the front page to tell readers which stories are important?

Editor: Typography is our most important cue; we signal hierarchy by the visual weight of the headlines on the page. Generally, we use placement on the page as well; the higher on the page a story appears, the more important we think it is.

mynews@school: How important are photographs on the front page? Why?

Editor: Photos are critical. Studies show that most readers tend to look at photos first as their eyes sweep around the page in a clockwise direction from top right. Photos also help establish a dynamic, energetic quality that we seek. They also give readers a feeling for how we view, literally, the area we cover.

mynews@school: Who decides the lead story and what criteria do you use to make that decision?

Editor: The slot, or person running the production operation, makes the decision in collaboration with the managing editor and other top editors. The lead story is the one we deem most significant. Usually, we're looking for either the most important event or the most revealing piece of reporting available.

mynews@school: At what time of day is that decision made and why is the decision made then?

Editor: The decision is made about 4 p.m. so that we can proceed with putting the paper together. We can change our plan up to about the middle of the press run, which generally means about 1 a.m.

mynews@school: What does the editor do and what path did you take to become editor?

Editor: The editor is responsible for all facets of newsroom operation at the policy-making, goal-setting level and then works with colleagues to translate various plans into action. I started as a reporter, working a variety of assignments, then progressed through assigning editor jobs working with reporters. Along the way, I did a couple of stints as a copy/production editor. Since about 1991, I have worked as a department head, assistant managing editor and managing editor.

mynews@school: What principles guide you as editor?

Editor: We need to be the most trusted news source in Central Texas. That requires speed, accuracy and, most of all, credibility. We build credibility by demonstrating daily that we understand our community and report on it fairly, celebrating its successes and probing failures.

mynews@school: What do you most love about newspapers?

Editor: The variety of experiences the work offers.

Appendix B.3d
mynews@school E-mail
to Teachers for Week 4

Used with permission from Paula Poindexter

News Story Formats and Writing Styles

Dear Teachers:

Thank you to the teachers who have been sending weekly feedback on mynews@school activities in your classroom. To the teachers I have not heard from, please let me know what I can do to help you. We are now in the fourth week of the program and it's important for your students to catch up.

This week is one of my favorites because the focus is on good writing and the types of news and the formats typically used to write news stories. Many of the stories on the Front Page which you learned about last week are Hard News, which is one type of news that my colleague Bill Minutaglio talks about in the attached Q&A on News Story Formats and Good Writing. Bill's answers to my questions will not only provide insight into how news stories are written, his comments will help make your students better writers. I think this Q&A should be required reading for anyone who loves to write or aspires to be a better writer.

This week, after you've discussed news story formats and good writing, please allow your students time for free reading and a Scavenger Hunt on story formats and writing styles. This Scavenger Hunt, which was inspired by one of the mynews@school teachers, will encourage students to look closely at the various story formats and writing styles. Your students may not find all of the story formats and styles of writing in that day's paper but it should be fun to try.

For the Scavenger Hunt, please have your students look through the newspaper and find a story that fits one of the following news formats and styles of writing.

- ✓ Hard News
- ✓ Soft News
- ✓ Inverted Pyramid
- ✓ Features (First Person Story, Delay Introduction, Narrative)
- ✓ Column/Essay
- ✓ Side Bar
- ✓ Q&A
- ✓ Analysis

For the stories they find, have them write the date, headline, section, and page the news story was published. In small group discussions, please encourage your students to share and compare their Scavenger Hunt treasures. In the class discussion, please have your students pick the top three formats and/or writing styles and the reasons they like these story formats/styles best. Please e-mail me their top formats/styles and reasons behind their selections.

For your convenience, I've also attached a PowerPoint with highlights from Bill Minutaglio's Q&A and the Scavenger Hunt.

Best regards,

Paula Poindexter

mynews@school Q&A with Bill Minutaglio on News Story Formats and Good Writing

Bill Minutaglio is the author of *In Search of the Blues: Journey to the Soul of Black Texas, First Son: George W. Bush & the Bush Family Dynasty, City on Fire: The Forgotten Disaster That Devastated a Town and Ignited a Landmark Legal Battle, The President's Counselor: The Rise to Power of Alberto Gonzales,* and co-author of *Molly Ivins: A Rebel Life.* The book on former President George W. Bush influenced the director and screenwriter of the 2008 film, *W.*

A UT School of Journalism professor, Minutaglio created and teaches the course Narrative Nonfiction Book Writing, oversees the Journalism School's investigative journalism class, and teaches the first news-reporting class that graduate students on the professional track take. Minutaglio has been a writer or editor for the *Dallas Morning News,* the *Houston Chronicle,* the *San Antonio Express-News,* and *People* magazine. Called "one of the great writers in Texas journalism" by the *Austin American-Statesman,* Bill Minutaglio answers questions about different types of news stories and writing that can be found in a newspaper.

mynews@school:	Newspapers publish stories that vary in format and style. What are the different story formats that can be found in a newspaper and what are their key elements?
Minutaglio:	Broadly speaking, many editors break down their stories into two large categories: Hard News & Soft News.
	Hard News is often the news that is breaking, fresh, timely, and needs to be relayed right away to the reader in a clear, straight, way—often emphasizing the most important news in the very first sentences of the story. New news about war, crime, elections, the economy, often fall into the Hard News format.
	Soft News is often the news that is not pegged to rapidly breaking events, that sometimes does not have to run immediately, that can "entertain" rather than "inform," that can lend itself to different writing styles, including introducing the "essential news value"

of the story later in the story—not in the first sentences of the story.

More specifically, when editors talk about formats they begin to think of these types:

- Inverted Pyramid format: Where you have your most "newsy," most important, information in the first sentence and paragraph. The story diminishes in "news value" in each subsequent paragraph. Often used with Hard News stories.

- Features format: Where you abandon the Inverted Pyramid, you "delay" the specific introduction of the "hard news" in the story.

- Column/Essay format: Where you sometimes espouse an opinion.

- Sidebar format: A companion piece that runs alongside another story, that serves to "add" information to that other story.

- A Q&A format: Where you simply print questions and answers (perhaps introduced by a short paragraph that explains what the Q&A is generally about).

- Analysis format: Where you take a Big Picture look at an issue, theme, person, and use some history, context, sweep, even statistics.

mynews@school: In general, how do you decide what format to use when writing a news story?

Minutaglio: First decide whether it is Hard News or Soft News: With your editor, you need to decide what the "news value" of your story is and when and where your story needs to run. If you and your editors say "hey, this is a story that everyone needs to know about Right Now," then you probably will use the Hard News/Inverted Pyramid formats and the piece will go on Page One.

On the other hand, editors may see the story as an "evergreen"— a story that can run any day of the week. Then it is probably in the Soft News category—and you will choose from a feature, column, essay, analysis, or sidebar format.

mynews@school: Are certain story formats more likely to be found in certain sections of the newspaper? If yes, which sections generally have what types of formats?

Minutaglio: The front page of your paper is often home to the Hard News/Inverted Pyramid format—the breaking news, the latest news, the most "newsy" material that readers need/want to know about as soon as possible. Those stories, of course, can also run on the Sports, Metro, and Business sections. There could be a "big game" that is covered on the front page of Sports. A big corporate story on the front of the Business section. A big to-do at City Hall that needs to be mentioned on the Metro front page. Many times, stories referenced on the front page of the newspaper will be explored in other stories on the front pages of the inside sections.

Most newspapers also have "feature sections"—they are sections of the paper that often run Soft News, "evergreen" stories, stories that can run almost any day of the week, that are not exclusively tied to an immediate news event. You can find Arts sections, Food sections, Travel sections, etc. They will have feature formats, columns, essays, etc.

mynews@school: How is *style* of writing different from story format?

Minutaglio: Writing style refers to how you compose the story, how you write each piece. It has to do with tone, presentation, composition. There are many writing styles: Some writers often use a "straight" or "hard" news style. It is usually not invested with "colorful writing"—it is often hard facts presented in a clear order (Who, What, When, Where, and Why). You put the most important information in the first paragraph, the second most important information in the second paragraph, and so on, as the story diminishes in "news value."

There are also several "feature writing" styles you can choose from: You "delay" the introduction of the most important news (in order to draw the reader in, in order to make them "want" to "find out" what happens in the story). You do a first-person story, where you, the writer, are in the story. You can do a "narrative"—where you begin a story in a moment in time and watch events unfold over time (like a plot in a book or movie).

mynews@school: Once you've finished writing a story, who else is involved in the writing and what role do they play in the story that you've written?

Minutaglio: At good publications, you should have a copy editor looking at your work—someone who will go over each word, sentence, paragraph in your story and make sure grammar, language, punctuation are all in good order. You will have other editors who will take a Big Picture look at your story—suggesting ways to change the beginning, middle, and end of your story. Suggesting additional reporting. Suggesting structural changes, changes in tone. If you are lucky to work with a photographer, they will have input on your story.

mynews@school: What are the major differences in writing for newspapers vs. magazines vs. online vs. blogs vs. books?

Minutaglio: Every publication is different. As a broad, broad rule, deadlines for newspapers and online publications are often a bit more intense.

Newspapers don't usually run stories that are as long as the ones you will find in magazines. Magazine editors sometimes have more time to work with you on stories. Online publications sometimes move briskly, quickly and ask for you to turn your material in sooner than later. Online publications sometimes lean a lot on multimedia components—that you provide links, audio, video. Again, every publication is unique. Some magazines will allow you to write 10,000-word stories. Some newspapers have their own magazines. Books and blogs are probably more varied. Obviously blogs lend themselves to essays, opinions, personal pieces. Books can be the "ultimate long story"—what I tell people is that books are very long feature stories. They have to have great reporting and an attempt at great writing. They require outlines, some sense of structure.

mynews@school: What role, if any, does your audience play when you're writing a news story?

Minutaglio: It's key. You have to understand your audience. You have to understand the readership for your particular publication. If you are writing for a sports publication, or a sports section in a newspaper, you should think about your audience. Ditto music magazines, etc. Most book publishers will ask you to really think hard about who will buy your book, who will read it, who you are writing for. These days, most editors want to know this: WHAT VALUE WILL YOUR WORK BRING TO MY PUBLICATION? In other words, how will your story reach my readers—and get me more readers.

mynews@school: When did you first discover that you were good at writing and how did you know?

Minutaglio: Not sure I'm good at it. (I've had plenty of critics tell me I'm not!) I like it, and I always wanted to write for newspapers, magazines, and books. One of my favorite writers when I was young was a newspaper columnist named Jimmy Breslin. I liked the way he would visit "ordinary people"—not famous people—and just hang out with them and write their stories. Those are called slice-of-life pieces— little windows into the worlds of real people. It was what I wanted to do. I was very, very lucky to have some editors who indulged me and who worked hard with me. A friend of mine once said that if you are insecure about your writing, it means you are doing it the right way—you care enough to worry about it. You can decide if you are good at writing in two ways: You tell yourself you are good . . . or other people tell you that your work is good.

mynews@school: What are the elements of good writing?

Minutaglio: There are a lot of them—and each story is different. But generally, I would say that you need to have vivid writing (no clichés, no overheated writing), colorful writing, dialogue, a sense of events unfolding—you need some action in your stories. You need details, specifics, what I call "intimate details"—about the people you write about, about the places you write about. You have to "show the reader, don't tell the reader"—show action unfolding, don't tell readers that action is unfolding. Think of your stories as movies—with plot, color, mood, dialogue, action. I love writing that has very specific details—and then can weave in Big Picture issues, thoughts, beliefs. I call it the marriage of the Micro and the Macro in your writing. You have details—and you have a sweep.

mynews@school: What are your recommendations for becoming a great writer?

Minutaglio: Writing is like riding a bike—you get better by doing it over and over again. Your writing improves by reading. Study the publications where you want your work to appear and study how the writers did their stories. Think, hard, about creating an outline of how you would structure your story. One simple thing is to gather as many "intimate details" as you can when you are doing your reporting: Look for specifics, look for dialogue, make sure you really bring people to life—and that you really draw a picture of where events take place. And, as always, ask a friend to read your work—see what they recommend. Finally, think outside the box—say to yourself, how do I make this story as fresh as possible, how do I do it in a new way, an interesting way, a way that will keep people reading? Stephen King says the scariest part of writing is just before you begin. Gay Talese says the pursuit of good writing is like driving with the lights turned off. Norman Mailer and others have said the secret to being a writer is . . . to go to your desk and begin writing. H. L. Mencken says it is a very, very lonely profession.

Appendix B.3e
mynews@school E-mail
to Teachers for Week 8

Used with permission from Paula Poindexter

Datelines and Geography

Dear Teachers:

This week your students will learn a new vocabulary word—dateline—and focus on world geography. Additionally, your students will become familiar with the weather page on the back of the Metro & State section. In newspaper jargon, the place (city, state, and/or country) from where a story is reported is called a "dateline."

Datelines, which in the *Austin America-Statesman* are in all caps, are only used in non-local stories since the Austin metropolitan area would be considered local. Some of the datelines in the Monday, November 14, 2011 edition include RIO DE JANEIRO, CAIRO, MEXICO CITY, GENEVA, PORTLAND, Ore., and KAPOLEI, Hawaii.

As is always the case, please allow your students time for free reading. In their small group discussions, they might talk about a story they found engaging and its dateline.

Since the dateline is a wonderful opportunity to learn about the world and practice research skills, this week's activity is: "Where in the world is the dateline?"

Working in their small groups, please have your students count the large and small stories in Section 1 of the *Statesman, excluding* the editorial and op-ed pages. Since it's likely that the total number of stories in Section 1 will vary slightly after everyone's count, please have your students take the average and use that number as the base. Now have them write down each international dateline for large and small stories. Again, since the number may vary slightly, just have them take an average. After your students have compiled a complete list of the international datelines in Section 1 of the paper, they can begin the activity, after first selecting one *unfamiliar* international dateline to answer the following questions:

1. What is the phonetic spelling and how is the dateline pronounced?

2. Where in the world is the dateline? (Continent? Adjacent country or closest well-known city?)

3. What is the population? What city or town in the United States has a similar population size?

4. What is the primary language?

5. What is the primary religion?

6. What type of government does the country have?

7. What is the largest newspaper?

8. What is the weather today? (Look on the weather page in the Metro & State section and find high and low temperature as well as sky, such as "r, ts, c, pc, fg, sn." The key under the U.S. map inter-

prets this alphabet soup. If the specific city is not listed, find weather of closest city.)

9. What resource(s) did you use to answer questions 1 through 7?

10. Time permitting, other questions to answer:

   a. What percent of the stories in Section 1 are international?

   b. Should there be more or fewer international stories? Why?

   c. What are the 5-Ws (Who, What, When, Where, and Why) of a story with an international dateline?

   d. What story format was used to write the story?

   e. What context is missing that could better help you understand the story?

Once the groups have completed their research, please discuss some of the interesting datelines as a class. Please e-mail answers to questions 1–9 for one of the international deadlines discussed. For your convenience, I have included PowerPoint slides.

Thank you to the teachers who have e-mailed their students' feedback. Have a great week!

Best regards,

Paula Poindexter

Appendix B.3f
mynews@school E-mail
to Teachers for Week 9

Used with permission from Paula Poindexter

Exploring News Web Sites

Dear Teachers:

I hope you had a great Thanksgiving holiday. Now that your students are "experts" on the news, the newspaper (e-replica and print), and journalism, it's important to help them make the transition to getting news on the Internet since that's the future of consuming news. That's why this week is devoted to news Web sites on the Internet.

As you know, the most popular ways of getting news on the Internet include:

- Going directly to a news Web site such as Statesman.com, msnbc.msn.com, huffingtonpost.com, or cnn.com.

- Going to a news aggregator such as news.yahoo.com, huffingtonpost.com, or news.google.com.

With more and more people acquiring smartphones and iPads and downloading news apps, accessing news on the Internet is as easy and fast as one click.

This week, I hope your students can explore the news Web sites and have small group discussions about the news, its format, and some of the extras that can't be found in the newspaper's e-edition or hard copy. We'll explore:

1. Google News

2. Statesman.com

3. Other news Web sites

To explore Google news:

1. Go to Google's Home Page

2. Click on News, and you'll see headlines representing stories from around the world, the nation, Austin-Round Rock, etc. You'll also see news categories.

3. On the left of the screen, click on Austin-Round Rock stories.

4. What are some of the top stories in the Austin-Round Rock area? Who produced the stories?

5. Find a story of interest on Google news; click it, and read it.

6. What story did you click and read?

To explore Statesman.com:

1. Go to Statesman.com on the Internet.

2. Scan the headlines on the screen.

3. Click on a story of interest and read it.

4. At the top of the screen, find the multimedia tab and click on it.

5. What did you find under the multimedia tab?

6. Explore some of the multimedia choices.

7. Share the multimedia you like best.

Explore other news Web sites (cnn.com, usatoday.com, nytimes.com, npr.com, time.com, or others of your choice).

Now that your students have explored news Web sites, please have them answer the following questions and e-mail their answers to me:

1. What do you like most about news Web sites?

2. What do you like least about news Web sites?

3. If you were the editor of a news Web site, what, if anything, would you add for kids so they would find it more appealing?

This is the first time that I've done this activity so I'm anxious to hear what you and your students have to say about it. This activity was inspired by discussions I had with participants at the Millennials and News Summit sponsored by the School of Journalism. Originally, I thought I would focus more of this activity on researching on the Web but because news Web sites are fast becoming the preferred way of getting news, I decided helping your middle school students make the transition from the e-replica edition to news Web sites should be the priority. I hope you agree. As usual for your convenience, I've included a PowerPoint of this week's activity.

Next week is the 10th and final week of mynews@school. I'll be sending questionnaires for you and your students to complete and return to me. Even if you did not complete the activities each week, it's very important for you and your students to complete the questionnaires so I can improve the program for teachers and students who will participate next year.

Best regards,

Paula Poindexter

Appendix B.4
End of Program mynews@school E-mail
with Teacher and Student Questionnaires

Used with permission from Paula Poindexter

Dear Teachers:

This week marks the final week of mynews@school for Fall 2011. Thank you to the teachers who were able to participate in the program every week. For teachers who were not able to participate every week, I appreciate your trying to bring this program to your students. For this final week, I have attached a teacher questionnaire and a student questionnaire.

The questionnaires are very important to the evaluation of mynews@school. As I reminded everyone in the teacher screening question- naire at the beginning of the program, teachers who completed the weekly activities, including e-mailing activities to me, are eligible for a $50 cash gift, a classroom pizza party, and participation certificates for their students.

If you were unable to complete at least most of the weekly activities, it is not necessary for you to have your students complete the questionnaires but I would greatly appreciate it if you would complete the teacher questionnaire so I can improve the program for future participants. If you are *only* completing the teacher questionnaire, you may e-mail it to me.

For teachers who completed the activities, I will mail or deliver the $50 cash teacher gift, participation certificates for your students, and money for a class pizza party upon receipt of completed teacher and student questionnaires. Please mail the completed questionnaires (teacher and students) no later than December 9 to me.

If you have any questions, please don't hesitate to e-mail me.

Again, thank you for your participation in the Fall 2011 mynews@school program and have a wonderful holiday.

Best regards,

Paula Poindexter, Ph.D.

End of ProgramQuestionnaire for Teachers Participating in Fall 2011 mynews@school Program

Used with permission from Paula Poindexter

Name and School: _____

Date: _____

1. Each week focused on a different activity. How many of the weekly activities were you able to do with your class?
    1. All (Please skip to Q3)
    2. Most (Please skip to Q3)
    3. Some (Please skip to Q3)
    4. A few
    5. None

2. If you answered a few or none, what was the primary reason you were unable to do more activities with your class and what recommendations do you have for getting teachers to do more activities?

    _____

    _____

    _____

    (Please skip to Q7)

3. Please rate the value of the different components of the mynews@school program:

	Valuable	Somewhat Valuable	Not Valuable
A. Free reading of the e-edition of the newspaper.	1	2	3
B. Small group discussion of the news	1	2	3
C. Class discussion of the news	1	2	3
D. Weekly activities	1	2	3
E. e-edition of the newspaper	1	2	3
F. Print copy of the newspaper	1	2	3

4. What is the primary benefit of participating in this news-in-the-school pro-gram?

   _____

   _____

5. As a result of using the *Statesman* and doing the weekly activities during the past two months, do you feel your students know more, the same, or less about the purpose, principles, and process of journalism?
   1. More
   2. Same
   3. Less

6. What specific recommendations, if any, do you have for improving the pro-gram in the future?

   _____

   _____

   _____

7. What specific suggestions do you have for making news more appealing to middle school children?

   _____

   _____

Questionnaire for Students Participating in Fall 2011 mynews@school Program

1. Date:_____
2. Name:_____
3. Teacher for this class: _____
4. School:_____
5. School District:_____

6. Some kids are interested in news; others are not that interested in news. How interested are you in news?
   1. Very interested
   2. Interested
   3. Somewhat interested
   4. Interested just a little
   5. Not interested

7. Some kids read news in newspapers or online; others watch news on TV or listen to news on the radio. Approximately how many days a week do you pay attention to news?_____

8. If you pay attention to news at least one day a week, from what source do you usually get your news? _____

9. On average, how many days a week do you discuss news? _____

10. With whom do you usually discuss news?
    1. Classmates
    2. Friends
    3. Parents
    4. Teachers
    5. Other _____

11. Some kids enjoy keeping up with the news; others do not. How much do you enjoy keeping up with the news?
    1. A lot
    2. Some
    3. A little
    4. None

12. What is the main reason for your answer?

    _____

    _____

13. Some kids feel it is important to keep informed of news and current events; others feel it's not that important. What do you think? How important is it to keep informed of news and current events?
    1. Very important
    2. Important
    3. Somewhat important
    4. Slightly important
    5. Not important

14. What is the main reason for your answer?

    _____

    _____

Now I have some final questions about you and your activities

15. What grade are you in? ____

16. How old are you? _____

17. Are you:
    1. Female
    2. Male

18. What is your race or ethnicity?
    1. White
    2. Latino/Hispanic
    3. African American/Black
    4. Asian
    5. Native American
    6. Other: _____

19. Do you plan to go to a 4-year college after high school?
    1. Definitely Yes
    2. Probably Yes
    3. Probably No
    4. Definitely No

20. Which of the following apply to you:

	Yes	No
A. You have your own cell phone	1	2
B. You've taken a picture with a cell phone	1	2
C. You've sent a text message with a cell phone	1	2
D. You've accessed news on a cell phone	1	2
E. You have a computer at home	1	2
F. You have access to the Internet at home	1	2
G. You're on Facebook	1	2
H. You've read news on Facebook	1	2

	Yes	No
I. You've posted a video on YouTube	1	2
J. On your own, you've read news on a news Web site	1	2
K. On your own, you've done a Google search	1	2
L. You have an iPad	1	2
M. You're on Twitter	1	2
N. You've followed news on Twitter	1	2
O. On your own, you've read a print newspaper	1	2
P. On your own, you've watched news on TV	1	2

21. Some kids will pay attention to the news when they grow up; others will not. What about you? Do you think you'll pay attention to the news when you grow up?
    1. Definitely
    2. Probably
    3. Unsure
    4. Probably not
    5. Definitely not
22. What is the main reason for your answer?

    _____

    _____

23. What, if anything, did you like *most* about devoting time in your class to reading and discussing news and doing the activities?

    _____

    _____

24. What, if anything, did you like *least* about devoting time in your class to reading and discussing news and doing the activities?

    _____

    _____

25. Every week, what part of the paper did you turn to first?

    _____

26. As a result of reading the *Statesman* and doing the weekly activities during the past two-and-a-half months, do you feel you know more, the same, or less about the purpose, principles, and process of journalism?
    1. More
    2. Same
    3. Less

Appendix C
National Survey of
NIE Managers Questionnaire

Used with permission from Paula Poindexter

1. Which of the following versions of the newspaper do you offer schools as part of your newspapers in education (NIE) program?
   1. Print copy of newspaper only
   2. E-edition that is a replica of the print newspaper only
   3. Both print copy and e-Edition
   4. Other _____

2. Which format of the newspaper—print or e-Edition—is being requested most by teachers?
   1. Print copy
   2. E-edition
   3. Other

3. During the past three years, how much direct involvement has your newspaper's editorial department had with your NIE program?
   1. A lot
   2. Some
   3. None (Skip to Q 5)

4. What has been the primary direct involvement of the editorial department in your NIE program?

   _____

5. During the past three years, how much have you worked directly with the journalism department at a nearby university?
   1. A lot

2. Some
3. None (Skip to Q 7)

6. Briefly describe how you have worked with the journalism department.

_____

7. Do you have NIE programs targeted to any of the following groups?

		Yes	No
A.	Disadvantaged Students	1	2
B.	Gifted Students	1	2
C.	Middle School Girls	1	2
D.	High School Girls	1	2
E.	Latinos/Latinas	1	2
E1.	(If yes, please specify gender and grade level)_____		
F.	African Americans	1	2
F1.	(If yes, please specify gender and grade level) _____		
G.	Asian Americans	1	2
G1.	(If yes, please specify gender and grade level) _____		
H.	College students	1	2
I.	English language learners	1	2
J.	Elementary students	1	2
K.	After school programs/clubs	1	2
L.	Other	1	2
L1.	(If yes, please specify)_____		

8. Have you incorporated any of the following digital platforms into your NIE program?

	Yes	No
A. MySpace or Facebook or other social networking site	1	2
B. Video	1	2
C. YouTube	1	2
D. Audio Slideshows	1	2
F. Podcasts	1	2
G. Blogs	1	2
H. Twitter	1	2
I. Other multimedia platforms	1	2

9. If you have answered yes to any of the above, please briefly describe how you're using these digital platforms:

    _____

10. Do you have any program activities that involve direct contact with students?
    1. Yes
    2. No (Skip to Q 12)

11. If yes, please describe: _____

12. What digital content, if any, have you asked students to produce?

    _____

13. Do you have any program activities that involve direct contact with parents?
    1. Yes
    2. No

14. If yes, please describe: _____

15. Please indicate if you have programs or curricula that emphasize the following:

	Yes	No
A. Purpose and principles of journalism in society	1	2
B. Being an informed citizen	1	2
C. Connecting global news to the local community	1	2
D. Analyzing news coverage for bias	1	2
E. Analyzing news coverage for diversity	1	2
F. Providing the context for news	1	2
G. Leadership development	1	2
H. Navigating rites of passage that young people experience growing up	1	2
I. Meeting state educational requirements	1	2
I1. If yes, please describe: _____		
J. Meeting national education requirements for No Child Left Behind (NCLB)	1	2
J1. If yes, please describe: _____		
K. Health	1	2
L. Sports	1	2

	Yes	No
M. Public or community service	1	2
N. Being a good citizen	1	2
O. First Amendment	1	2
P. Twenty-first century skills	1	2
Q. Reading comprehension skills	1	2
R. Character education	1	2
S. Connecting course work with the "real" world	1	2
T. Other (Please specify)_____	1	2

16. In addition to curriculum materials, do you make the following available to your NIE teachers?

	Yes	No
A. News quiz	1	2
B. Videos on journalism	1	2
C. Videos on the First Amendment	1	2
D. Speakers from the editorial department	1	2
E. Other (Please specify):_____	1	2

17. How much do you promote going directly to your newspaper's Web site?
    1. A lot
    2. Some
    3. None

18. Does your newspaper participate in a college or university Collegiate Readership Program in which any student with a current University ID card can pick up a newspaper from a designated newspaper rack in the Student Union or other public place on campus?
    1. Yes
    2. No
    3. Don't know.
    4. Other _____

19. During the past three years, approximately how many times have you surveyed the following groups to compile their opinions about the newspaper in the classroom?
A. Teachers/Professors _____
B. Students _____
C. Parents_____

20. Does your newspaper produce a separate newspaper or special section for?

	Yes	No
A. Kids	1	2
B. Teens	1	2
C. Young Adults (18 to 29)	1	2
C1. (Specify frequency and purpose)_____		
D. Parents	1	2

21. For each yes answer, please specify name of separate newspaper or special section and frequency of publication:

_____

_____

22. Does your editorial department produce the separate newspaper or special section?
1. Yes
2. No
3. Other (Please specify: _____)

23. How effective is this section in engaging its target audience?
1. Effective
2. Somewhat effective
3. Not effective

24. What is the main reason for your answer?

_____

25. How concerned are you about the future of NIE?
1. Very concerned
2. Concerned
3. Somewhat concerned

4. Not concerned

26. What is the main reason for your answer?

   _____

27. If money, time, and staff were not limiting factors, what one thing, if any, would you do to increase the potential of life-long newspaper readers through NIE?

   _____

28. In what ways, if any, do you think newspapers in classrooms contribute to the public good?

   _____

29. What is the URL for your NIE program?

   _____

30. Please specify the number of years of experience that you have as a:
   A. Teacher/Professor _____
   B. Journalist _____
   C. Other (Please specify) _____
   D. Manager of NIE _____

31. What department are you located in at the newspaper?

   _____

32. How many full-time NIE staff members are at your newspaper?

   _____

33. Are you the manager/director of the NIE program?
   1. Yes
   2. No

34. If no, what is the name and e-email address of the NIE manager/director?

   _____

35. What is the title of the person to whom you directly report?

   _____

36. Circulation size of your newspaper: _____

37. Approximate number of the following participating in your NIE program:
    A. School Districts _____
    B. Schools _____
    C. Teachers _____
    D. Students _____

38. Average number of weeks per school year newspapers delivered to class-rooms/campuses: _____

39. If you would like to receive results of this survey, please write in your e-mail address:

    _____

40. Are you interested in participating in a future pilot study that emphasizes the purpose and principles of journalism and includes complimentary class-room sets of your newspaper that are paid for by my grant?
    1. Definitely Yes
    2. Probably Yes
    3. Probably No (Skip to Q 42)
    4. Definitely No (Skip to Q42)

41. This program requires working with your newspaper's editorial department and the nearest journalism school. If you are interested in participating, please supply the following information:
    A. Name of editor of your newspaper:

        _____

    B. E-mail address of editor of your newspaper:

        _____

    C. Name of journalism school: _____
    D. Director of journalism school: _____
    E. E-mail address of director of journalism school: _____

42. Please add other ideas or comments you may have about NIE and its future:

    _____
    _____
    _____

Appendix D
Engaging Millennials in News by
Aggregating News Stories for Them Online

Millennials and News is a digital collection of news stories for and about Millennials that Alexandra Wilson, a Millennial, and I, a journalism professor, created to encourage engagement with news by this young generation that is more devoted to Facebook than news. Started online in 2011, *Millennials and News*, which is updated every morning, seven days a week, is a one-digital stop for Millennials to scan, read, share, and comment on news stories about their generation, stories of interest to their age group, and news stories they should know.

Millennials and News is not your typical news aggregator—posted news stories are decided by human editors—not algorithms. The daily editorial cycle for *Millennials and News* begins the night before stories are posted; the Millennial editor follows news on Twitter, identifying possible stories. The Millennial editor also checks *USAToday College*. Before 5:30 a.m. on the morning of the posting, I use news apps on my smartphone and iPad to search NPR, *USA Today*, *The Washington Post*, CNN, *The Los Angeles Times*, *The New York Times*, *The Wall Street Journal*, the Associated Press, and sometimes the BBC. The stories I find about Millennials, that might be of interest to Millennials and stories that this age group should know are e-mailed to the Millennial editor. After stories have been e-mailed, I text the Millennial editor to confirm that stories have been sent. The Millennial editor selects which stories to post and which ones she'll introduce with a comment. Once stories are posted, the Millennial editor sends me a confirming text which is also my signal to check the stories and comments. In my final confirming text, I state that everything looks good or a correction in a comment is required. During the week, stories are posted by 8 a.m.; on weekends, stories are generally posted by 10:30 a.m. The evening following the morning posting, the editorial process starts up again. The Millennial editor follows news on Twitter and early the next morning I use news apps on my smartphone and iPad to search for news about Millennials, of interest to Millennials, and stories Millennials should know.

As the gatekeepers of stories posted on *Millennials and News*, we abide by agreed upon editorial standards. Our first standard addresses the type of story that qualifies for posting on *Millennials and News*; stories must be about Millennials, of interest to Millennials and stories Millennials should know. Our second standard specifies that stories must have been produced by credible news organizations that do original reporting and verify sources. Because we take to heart Millennial criticisms discussed in Chapter 3, our third standard is that Millennial celebrities and criminals are typically avoided. Of course, from time to time, there are exceptions. Millennial-bashing stories and stories with a disrespectful tone about this generation also do not qualify for posting on *Millennials and News*. Our final standard is that we post news stories and analyses; editorials and op-ed pieces are generally excluded.

Approximately five of the ten possible stories identified daily are posted. Typically, two of the five stories report news Millennials should know to be informed. During the 2012 presidential election season, election stories have been posted regularly. Unfortunately, few of those election stories have focused on or included Millennials.

All stories posted on *Millennials and News* are not serious; some are posted because they may elicit a "lol" response; others are posted because they have a "Wow, I didn't know that" factor. Following are examples of stories that have been posted on *Millennials and News*, including some with an introduction from the Millennial editor.

Examples of Stories Posted on Millennials and News

With Millennial editor introductory comment:

"How do high gas prices change your spending habits? Share your thoughts here." (Wilson, 2012b)

- "Surging gas prices threaten to derail economic recovery" (Lee & Stevens, 2012)

"Click 'like' if you are using Twitter to follow the campaign." (Wilson, 2012c)

- "Twitter is a critical tool in Republican campaigns" (Parker, 2012)

"What do you think about this story?" (Wilson, 2012d)

- "Addressing the political gender gap with Citizen Jane" (Rothfield, 2012)

"A feel good story for your Friday!" (Wilson, 2012e)

- "Over bowls of soup, donors find recipe for change" (Weeks & Sanders, 2012)

Without Millennial editor introductory comment:

- "A new ailment on the 2012 campaign trail: debate fatigue" (Horowitz, 2012)

- 'We the People' loses appeal with people around the world" (Liptak, 2012)

- "Study: Blacks are less segregated than ever before" (Nasser, 2012)

Millennials and News is not just an aggregator of all news Millennial; it's a regularly updated digital resource accessible through a Google search or on Facebook. As a resource, I use it in my news literacy course, Journalism, Society and the Citizen Journalist, to encourage discussions about news and gain more insight into how this generation evaluates news. Students read posted stories, and once a week some class time is devoted to discussing and critiquing the posted stories. Before beginning the discussion students complete a brief questionnaire on the stories they recall, what they did with the stories, and what they liked or disliked about the stories. Some weeks instead of completing a questionnaire, students post a comment directly on a story that interests them. Whether completing a questionnaire or posting a comment, both activities will help Millennials become discerning critics who can pinpoint the attributes in news stories that engage them and the aspects that turn them off. So far, my Millennial students find election stories boring and many of the poll stories pointless. Not surprisingly, they connect most with stories about their generation and stories on subjects they are interested in.

REFERENCES

About the Daily Show. (n.d.). Retrieved from http://www.thedailyshow.com/about

Alexovich, A. (2008, February 4). Obama supporters sing, 'Yes We Can.' Retrieved from http://thecaucus.blogs.nytimes.com/2008/02/04/obama-upporters-sing-yes-we-can/

Allison, J. (2010). #3 Obama girl. Retrieved from http://2010.newsweek.com/top-10/internet-memes/obama-girl.html

Barack Obama's New Hampshire primary speech. (2008, January 8). Retrieved from http://www.nytimes.com/2008/01/08/us/politics/08text-obama.html?pagewanted=all

Baracknophobia—Mongering. (2008, June 16). Retrieved from http://www.thedaily show.com/watch/mon-june-16–2008/headlines—baracknophobia

Berelson, B. (1949). What 'missing the newspaper' means. In P. F. Lazarsfeld & F. N. Stanton (Eds.), *Communications Research 1948–1949* (pp. 111–129). New York, NY: Harper and Brothers.

Berry, D., Barstow, D., Glater, J. D., Liptak, A., & Steinberg, J. (2003, May 11). Correcting the record; Times reporter who resigned leaves long trail of deception. Retrieved from http://www.nytimes.com/2003/05/11/us/correcting-the-record-times-reporter-who-resigned-leaves-long-trail-of-deception.html?pagewanted=all&src=pm

Bissinger, B. (1998, September). Shattered glass. Retrieved from http://www.vanity fair.com/magazine/archive/1998/09/bissinger199809

Blais, J., Memmott, C., & Minzesheimer, B. (2007). Book buzz: Dave Barry really rocks. Retrieved from http://www.usatoday.com/life/books/news/2007–05–16-book-buzz_N.htm

Bleske, G. L. (1991). Ms. Gates takes over: An updated version of a 1949 case study. *Newspaper Research Journal, 12*(4), 88–97.

Bogart, L. (1981). *Press and public: Who reads what, when, where, and why in American newspapers.* Hillsdale, NJ: Lawrence Erlbaum Associates.

Brisbane, A. S. (2011, September 10). Thoughts from Jill Abramson, Executive Editor. Retrieved from http://www.nytimes.com/2011/09/11/opinion/sunday/thoughts-from-jill-abramson-executive-editor.html

Brown, E. D. (2011, August). *For love or money?: The role of online non-profits in preserving journalism.* Paper presented at the AEJMC.

Cáceres, I. B. (2011). *Toward a theory on gender and emotional management in electoral politics: A comparative study of media discourses in Chile and the United States* (unpublished dissertation). University of Texas at Austin.

Callegaro, M., & Disogra, C. (2008). Computing response metrics for online panels. *Public Opinion Quarterly, 72*(5), 1008–1032.

Campbell, R. (1998). *Media and culture: An introduction to mass communication.* New York, NY: St. Martin's Press.

Carrns, A. (2011, June 15). College students don't view debt as burden. Retrieved from http://bucks.blogs.nytimes.com/2011/06/15/college-students-surprising-attitude-toward-debt/?smid=tw-nytimesbusiness&seid=auto

Carroll, S. J., & Schreiber, R. (1997). Media coverage of women in the 103rd Congress. In P. Norris (Ed.), *Women, media, and politics* (pp. 131–149). New York, NY: Oxford University Press.

Clarke, P. (1965). Parental socialization values and children's newspaper reading. *Journalism & Mass Communication Quarterly, 42,* 539–546.

Comments on music video has a "crush on Obama." (2007). Retrieved from http://abcnews.go.com/Politics/comments?type=story&id=3275802

Comments on the Millennials are coming. (2007). Retrieved from http://www.cbsnews.com/8601–18560_162–3475200–48.html?assetTypeId=30&blogId=&tag=contentBody;commentWrapper

Commission on Freedom of the Press, The. (1947). *A free and responsible press: A general report on mass communication: Newspapers, radio, motion pictures, magazines, and books.* Chicago, IL: University of Chicago Press.

Cooper, M. (2011, August 30). Hurricane cost seen as ranking among top ten. Retrieved from http://www.nytimes.com/2011/08/31/us/31floods.html?_r=2&hp=&pagewanted=all

Copeland, L. (2011, July 11). Distracted-driving programs show success. Retrieved from http://www.usatoday.com/news/nation/2011–07–11-programs-help-cut-distracted-driving_n.htm

Daft, R. L. (2005). *The leadership experience* (3rd. ed.). Mason: South-Western.

Dallas, M. E. (2011, July 1) Study: Even one glass of beer, wine boosts car crash risk. Retrieved from http://yourlife.usatoday.com/health/story/2011/07/Study-Even-one-glass-of-beer-wine-boosts-car-crash-risk/49022560/1

Davies, M. (2011, June 19). Oh, the places you'll go. *The New York Times* Week in Review, p. 2.

De Fleur, M. L., & Ball-Rokeach, S. (1982). *Theories of Mass Communication* (4th ed.). New York: Longman Inc.

Dennis, E. (1992). *The homestretch: New politics. new media. new voters?* The Freedom Forum Media Studies Center.

Desmond, R., & Danilewicz, A. (2010). Women are on, but not in the news: Gender roles in local television news. *Sex Roles, 62,* 822–829.

Dixon, T. L., & Linz, D. (2000). Overrepresentation and underrepresentation of African Americans and Latinos as lawbreakers on television news. *Journal of Communication, 50*(2), 131–154.

Downie Jr., L. (2011, Winter). Big journalism on campus. *American Journalism Review,* 36–41.

Efrati, A. (2012, February 28). The mounting minuses at Google: Playing catch-up to Facebook, Google's social network is a virtual ghost town. Retrieved from http://online.wsj.com/article/SB10001424052970204653604577249341403742390.html

Egyptian Revolution. (2011). Retrieved from http://en.wikipedia.org/wiki/Egyptian_Revolution_of_2011

Entman, R. M. (1994). Representation and reality in the portrayal of blacks on network television news. *Journalism & Mass Communication Quarterly, 71*(3), 509–520.

Facebook Newsroom. (n.d.). Retrieved from http://newsroom.fb.com/content/default.aspx?NewsAreaId=22

Farhi, P. (2011, Winter). Speak no evil. *American Journalism Review,* 22–27.

Following rules and best practices. (n.d.). Retrieved from https://support.twitter.com/articles/68916-following-rules-and-best-practices

Gee, R. (2012, January 3). In Iowa, young voters unenthusiastic about Obama. Retrieved from http://www.npr.org/2012/01/03/144626748/in-iowa-young-voters-unenthusiastic-about-obama?sc=17&f=1001

Generation Y. (n.d.). Retrieved from http://en.wikipedia.org/wiki/Generation_Y

Gibbs, A. (2011). A conversation among young African American males. Comments at the Evolving the image of the African American male in American media summit.

Gilens, M. (1996). Race and poverty in America: Public misperceptions and the American news media. *Public Opinion Quarterly, 60,* 515–541.

Gilliam, F. D., & Iyengar, S. (2000). Prime suspects: The influence of local television news on the viewing public. *American Journal of Political Science, 44*(3), 560–573.

Griffith, T. (1981, May 4, 1981). The Pulitzer Hoax—Who Can Be Believed? *Time*, *117*, 4.

Grossman, L. (2010, December 27). 2010 person of the year—Mark Zuckerberg. *Time*.

Grusin, E. K., & Stone, G. C. (October 1993). The newspaper in education and new readers: Hooking kids on newspapers through classroom experiences. *Journalism Monographs* (No. 141), 1–39.

Harris, C. (2008, November 5). Youth voter turnout up 2.2 Million From 2004 Election. Retrieved from http://www.mtv.com/news/articles/1598667/youth-voter-turnout-up-22-million-from-2004-election.jhtml

Headlines-gaffe-in. (2008, April 14). Retrieved from http://www.thedailyshow.com/watch/mon-april-14–2008/headlines—gaffe-in

Heider, D., McCombs, M., & Poindexter, P. M. (2005, Winter). What the public expects of local news: Views on public and traditional journalism. *Journalism & Mass Communication Quarterly*, *82*(4), 952–967.

The Heinz Endowments African American Men and Boys Task Force. (2011, November 1). *Portrayal and perception: Two audits of news media reporting on African American men and boys: A report from the Heinz Endowments African Americans Men and Boys Task Force*. Pittsburgh, Pennsylvania.

Hill, R. (2011, November 23). Black men in the media: They almost always show up in stories of crimes or sports, which does them an injustice and does not reflect reality. Retrieved from http://www.post-gazette.com/pg/11327/1191907–109–0.stm

History of NIE. (n.d.). Retrieved from http://www.naafoundation.org/About/Programs/NIE/History-Of-NIE.aspx

Horowitz, J. (2012, January 20). A new ailment on the 2012 campaign trail: Debate fatigue. Retrieved from http://www.washingtonpost.com/lifestyle/style/a-new-ailment-on-the-2012-campaign-trail-debate-fatigue/2012/01/20/gIQADrkuEQ_story.html?tid=wp_ipad

Howe, N., & Strauss, W. (2000). *Millennials rising: The next great generation*. New York, NY: Vintage Books.

Hurricane Irene death toll rises to at least 44. (2011, August 30). Retrieved from http://www.msnbc.msn.com/id/44314551/ns/weather/t/hurricane-irene-death-toll-rises-least/

Ifill, G. (1992, June 17). Clinton raps overtime with the MTV generation. *The New York Times*.

Iphigene Ochs Sulzberger is dead; Central figure in *Times*'s History. (1990, February 27). Retrieved from http://www.nytimes.com/1990/02/27/obituaries/iphigene-ochs-sulzberger-is-dead-central-figure-in-times-s-history.html?pagewanted=all&src=pm

Kaufhold, W. T. (2011). *Seriously social: Crafting opinion leaders to spur a two-step flow of news* (Unpublished dissertation). The University of Texas at Austin.

Kaufman, G. (2008, February 4). Will.I.Am gathers Common, Nick Cannon, Scarlett Johansson for Barack Obama video. Retrieved from http://www.mtv.com/news/

articles/1580884/william-yes-we-can-obama-video.jhtml

Kirkpatrick, D. (2010). *The Facebook effect: The inside story of the company that is connecting the world*. New York, NY: Simon & Schuster Paperbacks.

Kovach, B., & Rosenstiel, T. (2007). *The elements of journalism: What newspeople should know and the public should expect*. New York, NY: Three Rivers Press.

Larris, R. J. (2005). *The Daily Show effect: Humor, news, knowledge and viewers*. Georgetown University, Washington DC.

Lee, D., & Stevens, M. (2012, February 20). Surging gas prices threaten to derail economic recovery. Retrieved from http://www.latimes.com/business/autos/la-fi-gas-prices-20120221,0,2040833

Lifelong readers: The role of teen content. (n.d.). Retrieved from http://www.naa foundation.org/docs/Foundation/Research/LR_teencontent.pdf

Liptak, A. (2012, February 6). 'We the People' loses appeal with people around the world. Retrieved from http://www.nytimes.com/2012/02/07/us/we-the-people-loses-appeal-with-people-around-the-world.html

Lueck, T. L. (2005, August). *A woman's place in 2004 election coverage: Stereotypes and feminist inroads*. Paper presented at the Association for Education in Journalism and Mass Communication.

Many young consumers. (2012). Retrieved from http://www.facebook.com/#!/nytimes

McCombs, M., & Poindexter, P. (1983). The duty to keep informed: News exposure and civic obligation. *Journal of Communication, 33*(2), 88–96.

McCormick Foundation gives $330K to accelerate school of journalism expansion of news literacy (2011, September 23). Retrieved from https://journalism.cc.stony-brook.edu/?p=2145

McElroy, K. (2012, August). *Herding Reader Comments into Print: Gatekeeping Across Media Platform*. Paper presented at the Association for Education in Journalism and Mass Communication.

McQuail, D. (1983). *Mass communications theory: An introduction*. London, England: Sage.

Meraz, S. (2008). The blogosphere's gender gap: Differences in visibility, popularity, and authority. In P. Poindexter, S. Meraz, & A. S. Weiss (Eds.), *Women, men, and news: Divided and disconnected in the news media landscape* (pp. 129–151). New York, NY: Routledge.

Meyer, E. (2011, October 6). Steve Jobs remembered: 'He wanted to make a dent in the universe.' Retrieved from http://www.redeyechicago.com/news/chi-locals-react-to-so-sad-death-of-apple-cofounder-jobs-20111005,0,5297757.story

Milbrath, L. W., & Goel, M. L. (1977). *Political participation: How and why do people get involved in politics?* (2nd ed.). Chicago, IL: Rand McNally College Publishing Company.

Miller, J. (1992, October 11). MTV turns to news: But can you dance to it? *The New York Times Magazine*, 30–41.

Mindich, D. T. Z. (1998). *Just the facts: How "objectivity" came to define American journalism*. New York, NY: New York University Press.

Mindich, D. T. Z. (2005). *Tuned out: Why Americans under 40 don't follow the news*. New York, NY: Oxford University Press.

Morrison, B. (2004, March 19). Ex-USA Today reporter faked major stories. Retrieved from http://www.usatoday.com/news/2004–03–18–2004–03–18_kelleymain_x.htm

Music television. (n.d.). Retrieved from http://www.museum.tv/eotvsection.php?entrycode=musictelevis

Nagourney, A. (2011, November 15). Students lose zeal for aiding Obama again. *The New York Times*, p. A1+.

Nasser, H. E. (2012, January 31). Study: Blacks are less segregated than ever before. Retrieved from http://www.usatoday.com/news/nation/story/2012–01–30/racial-segregation-decline/52889370/1

Navigating news online: Facebook is becoming increasingly important. (2011, May 9). Retrieved from http://www.journalism.org/analysis_report/facebook_becoming_increasingly_important

Neighmond, P. (2011, July 11). An affliction of the cornea gets a closer look. Retrieved from http://www.npr.org/2011/07/11/137705081/an-affliction-of-the-cornea-gets-a-closer-look

News feed basics. (n.d.). Retrieved from http://www.facebook.com/help?page=408

News literacy expands to DC. (2011, September 6). Retrieved from http://www.cjr.org/the_kicker/news_literacy_expands_to_dc.php

NIE in 2010: Leaner +locally focused+digital (2010). Retrieved from http://www.naafoundation.org/docs/Foundation/Research/NIE2010Fullreport_v11.pdf

Nintendo company history. (n.d.). Retrieved from http://www.nintendo.com/corp/history.jsp

"Obama girl" may become Clinton's girl. (2007, August 23). Retrieved from http://politicalticker.blogs.cnn.com/2007/08/23/obama-girl-may-become-clintons-girl/

Osgerby, B. (2008). Understanding the 'jackpot market': Media, marketing, and the rise of the American teenager. In P. E. Jamieson & D. Romer (Eds.), *The changing portrayal of adolescents in the media since 1950* (pp. 27–58). Oxford: Oxford University Press.

Park, R. E. (1940). News as a form of knowledge: A chapter in the sociology of knowledge. *The American Journal of Sociology, 45*(5), 669–686.

Parker, A. (2012, January 28). Twitter is a critical tool in Republican campaigns. Retrieved from http://www.nytimes.com/2012/01/29/us/politics/twitter-is-a-critical-tool-in-republican-campaigns.html?_r=1

Parks and Demonstration (2011, October 5). [Cable TV], Jon Stewart's *The Daily Show*.

Pew Research Center, The. (2006, July 30). Online papers modestly boost newspaper readership. Retrieved from http://people-press.org/files/legacy-pdf/282.pdf

Pew Research Center, The. (2008, August 17). Key news audiences now blend online and traditional sources. Retrieved from http://people-press.org/http://people-press.org/files/legacy-pdf/444.pdf

Pew Research Center, The. (2010, September 12). Americans spending more time following the news. Retrieved from http://people-press.org/files/legacy-pdf/652.pdf

Pew Research Center, The. (2010) Millennials: A portrait of generation next. Retrieved from http://pewsocialtrends.org/files/2010/10/millennials-confident-connected-open-to-change.pdf

Pew Research Center, The. (2011). The generation gap and the 2012 election. Retrieved from http://www.people-press.org/files/legacy-pdf/11-3-11%20 Generations%20Release.pdf

Phillips, K. (2007, June 13). 2008: Obama girl and more. Retrieved from http://the caucus.blogs.nytimes.com/2007/06/13/2008-obama-girl-and-more/

Plouffe, D. (2009). *The audacity to win: The inside story and lessons of Barack Obama's historic victory.* New York, NY: Viking.

Pogue, D. (2012, February 15). A scrapbook on the Web catches fire. Retrieved from http://www.nytimes.com/2012/02/16/technology/personaltech/reviewing-pinter-est-the-newest-social-media-site.html?_r=1

Poindexter, P. (2008, February 6). When gender counts against you. *Austin American-Statesman*, p. A15.

Poindexter, P. (2008a). Factors contributing to the sex divide in newspapers and television news. In P. Poindexter, S. Meraz, & A. S. Weiss (Eds.), *Women, men, and news: Divided and disconnected in the news media landscape* (pp. 17–34). New York, NY: Routledge.

Poindexter, P. (2008b). Finding women in the newsroom and in the news. In P. Poindexter, S. Meraz, & A. S. Weiss (Eds.), *Women, men, and news: Divided and disconnected in the news media landscape* (pp. 65–84). New York, NY: Routledge.

Poindexter, P. (2008c). IM, downloading, Facebook, and teen magazines. In P. Poindexter, S. Meraz, & A. S. Weiss (Eds.), *Women, men, and news: Divided and disconnected in the news media landscape* (pp. 48–62). New York, NY: Routledge.

Poindexter, P. (2008d). Strengthening the news connection with women and cultivating the next generation. In P. Poindexter, S. Meraz, & A. S. Weiss (Eds.), *Women, men, and news: Divided and disconnected in the news media landscape* (pp. 317–333). New York, NY: Routledge.

Poindexter, P. (2008e). Trouble in the news media landscape. In P. Poindexter, S. Meraz, & A. S. Weiss (Eds.), *Women, men, and news: Divided and disconnected in the news media landscape* (pp. 3–6). New York, NY: Routledge.

Poindexter, P. (2008f). When women ignore the news. In P. Poindexter, S. Meraz,& A. S. Weiss (Eds.), *Women, men, and news: Divided and disconnected in the news media landscape* (pp. 35–47). New York, NY: Routledge.

Poindexter, P. (2010a). Millennials and News Summit Opening Remarks.

Poindexter, P. (2010b, October 19). Why young voters' participation matters at midterm. Retrieved from http://www.utexas.edu/know/2010/10/19/poindexter3/

Poindexter, P. M. (2011). African-American images in the news: Understanding the past to improve future portrayals. In S. D. Ross & P. M. Lester (Eds.), *Images that injure: Pictorial stereotypes in the media* (pp.107–120. Santa Barbara, CA, Praeger.

Poindexter, P., Heider, D., & McCombs, M. (Winter 2006). Watchdog or good neighbor? The public's expectations of local news. *The Harvard International Journal of Press/Politics, 11*(1), 77–88.

Poindexter, P. M., & McCombs, M. E. (Spring 2001). Revisiting the civic duty to keep informed in the new media environment. *Journalism & Mass Communication Quarterly, 78*(1), 113–126.

Poindexter, P., Meraz, S., & Weiss, A. S. (Eds.). (2008). *Women, men, and news: Divided and disconnected in the news media landscape.* New York, NY: Routledge.

Poindexter, P. M., Smith, L., & Heider, D. (2003). Race and ethnicity in local television news: Framing, story assignments, and source selections. *Journal of Broadcasting & Electronic Media, 47*(4), 524–536.

Press favors Obama. (2008, July 24). Retrieved from http://www.thedailyshow.com/watch/thu-july-24–2008/press-favors-obama

Press widely criticized, but trusted more than other information sources. (2011, September 22). Retrieved from http://people-press.org/2011/09/22/press-widely-criticized-but-trusted-more-than-other-institutions/

Rampell, C. (2011, March 1). More college graduates take public service jobs. Retrieved from http://www.nytimes.com/2011/03/02/business/02graduates.html?pagewanted=all

Report of the National Advisory Commission on Civil Disorders. (1968). New York, NY: Bantam.

Roberts, C. (1975). The presentation of blacks in television network newscasts. *Journalism Quarterly, 52*(1), 50–55.

Rock the Vote. (n.d.). Retrieved from http://www.rockthevote.com/about/history-rock-the-vote/#1992

Rosenthal, P. (2011, December 2). Chicago Tribune's RedEye to increase distribution. (2009). Retrieved from http://newsblogs.chicagotribune.com/towerticker/2009/12/chicago-tribunes-redeye-to-increase-distribution.html

Rothfield, A. (2012, February 22). Addressing the political gender gap with Citizen Jane. Retrieved from http://www.usatodayeducate.com/staging/index.php/election2012/addressing-the-political-gender-gap-with-citizen-jane

Safer, M. (2007). The Millennials are coming. Retrieved from http://www.cbsnews.com/video/watch/?id=3486473n

Scenes from the storm. (n.d.). Retrieved from http://submit.nytimes.com/hurricaneirene

Schmitz Weiss, A. (2008). Online news: Factors influencing the divide between women and men. In P. Poindexter, S. Meraz, & A. S. Weiss (Eds.), *Women, men, and news: Divided and disconnected in the news media landscape* (pp. 117–128). New York, NY: Routledge.

Schramm, W., Lyle, J., & Parker, E. B. (1960). Patterns in children's reading of newspapers. *Journalism Quarterly, 37*, 35–40.

Seligson, H. (2011, June 25). Job jugglers, on the tightrope. Retrieved from http://www.nytimes.com/2011/06/26/business/26work.html?pagewanted=all

Seventeen: A large, diverse & affluent audience. (n.d.). Retrieved from http://www.seventeenmediakit.com/hotdata/publishers/seventeen/advertiser/8224701/2756893/Teen_Demo.pdf

Shoemaker, P. J., & Reese, S. D. (1996). *Mediating the message: Theories of influences on mass media content.* White Plains, NY: Longman.

St. John, O. (2011, June 24). Americans doing more work on weekends. Retrieved from http://www.usatoday.com/money/workplace/2011–06–22-time-use_n.htm

Standard definitions: Final dispositions of case codes and outcome rates for surveys. (2011). Retrieved from http://www.aapor.org/AM/Template.cfm?Section=Standard_Definitions2&Template=/CM/ContentDisplay.cfm&ContentID=3156

Stantis, S. (2010, March 7). The newspaper says. *The New York Times Week in Review,* p. 2.

Stephens, M. (1997). *A History of news.* Fort Worth, TX: Harcourt Brace College.

Survey: New U.S. Smartphone growth by age and income. (February 20, 2012). Retrieved from http://blog.nielsen.com/nielsenwire/online_mobile/survey-new-u-s-smartphone-growth-by-age-and-income/

Sutter, J. D. (2011, July 6). The changing face of America's youth. Retrievedfrom http://articles.cnn.com/2011–07–06/us/hispanic.youth.majority_1_hispanic-growth-census-data-ethnic-groups?_s=PM:US

Tapper, J. (2007). Music video has a "crush on Obama." Retrieved from http://abcnews.go.com/Politics/story?id=3275802&page=1

Teen Vogue. (n.d.). Retrieved from http://www.condenast.com/brands/teen-vogue/media-kit/print

Teens know what they want from online news: Do you? (n.d.). Retrieved from http://www.naafoundation.org/docs/Foundation/Research/teensknow_full.pdf

Tuchman, G. (1978). *Making news: A study in the construction of reality.* New York, NY: The Free Press.

Valian, V. (1999). *Why so slow? The advancement of women.* Cambridge, MA: The MIT Press.

Voting and registration in the election of November 2008. (2010, May). Retrieved from http://www.census.gov/prod/2010pubs/p20–562.pdf

Waldman, S. (2011). *The information needs of communities: The changing media landscape in a broadband age.* Durham, NC: Carolina Academic Press.

"We are the world" tune brings out the best of America's 46 stars (1985, February 18). *Jet,* 60–64.

Weaver, D. H., Beam, R. A., Brownlee, B. J., Voakes, P. S., & Wilhoit, G. C. (2007). *The American journalist in the 21st century: U.S. news people at the dawn of a new millennium.* Mahwah, NJ: Lawrence Erlbaum Associates.

Weaver, D. H., Beam, R., Brownlee, B. J., Voakes, P. S., & Wilhoit, G. C. (2003). *The American journalist in the 21st century: Key findings.* Paper presented at the AEJMC.

Weaver, D. H., Wilhoit, G. C., & Reide, P. (1979, July 20). *ANPA News Research Reports, 21.*

Weeks, L., & Sanders, S. (2012, February 9). Over bowls of soup, donors find recipe for change. Retrieved from http://www.npr.org/2012/02/09/146138924/over-bowls-of-soup-donors-find-recipe-for-change?sc=17&f=1001

Westley, B. H., & Severin, W. J. (1964, Winter). A profile of the daily newspaper non-reader. *Journalism Quarterly, 41,* 45–50, 156.

White, D. M. (1950). The "gate-keeper": A case study in the selection of news. *Journalism Quarterly, 27,* 383–390.

Wilson, A. (2012a, March 24). This story rings true. Retrieved from http://www.facebook.com/#!/pages/Millennials-and-News/181390031899756

Wilson, A. (2012b, February 21). High gas prices. Retrieved from http://www.facebook.com/#!/pages/Millennials-and-News/181390031899756

Wilson, A. (2012c, January 28). Click like. Retrieved from http://www.facebook.com/#!/pages/Millennials-and-News/181390031899756

Wilson, A. (2012d, February 9). A feel good story. Retrieved from http://www.facebook.com/#!/pages/Millennials-and-News/181390031899756

Wilson, A. (2012e, February 22). What do you think? Retrieved from http://www.facebook.com/#!/pages/Millennials-and-News/181390031899756

Wilson, B. (2008). *Encouraging a newspaper reading habit in college students: Prior experiences with newspapers and the development of civic interest.* Saarbucken, Germany: VDM Verlag Dr. Muller.

Woodward, B. (2011). Comments on Oprah.

Wright, C. R. (1986). *Mass communication: A sociological perspective* (3rd ed.). Boston, MA: McGraw-Hill College.

Zerba, A. (2008). Reaching young adults begins with change. In P. Poindexter, S. Meraz, & A. S. Weiss (Eds.), *Women, men, and news: Divided and disconnected in the news media landscape* (pp. 155–174). New York, NY: Routledge.

Zerba, A. (2009). *Re-thinking journalism: How young adults want their news* (Unpublished dissertation). The University of Texas at Austin.

Zerba, A. (2011, Autumn). Young adults' reasons behind avoidances of daily print newspapers and their ideas for change. *Journalism & Mass Communication Quarterly, 88*(3), 597–614.

Zmuda, N. (2011, March 3). Coca-Cola launches global music effort to connect with teens. *Advertising Age.* Retrieved from http://adage.com/article/global-news/coca-cola-launches-global-music-effort-connect-teens/149204/

INDEX